Multilateralism and Regionalism in Global Economic Governance

Reconciling regionalism and multilateralism is a challenge common to all branches of global economic governance. While the Bretton Woods/GATT (WTO) institutions, a decades-old multilateral framework for global economic governance, are facing serious challenges to their effectiveness, regional frameworks are emerging as complementary or alternative means of global economic governance. The real challenge is how to reconcile multilateralism and regionalism in global economic governance. This book tackles this problem by analysing issues of multilateral/regional conciliation and coordination in global economic governance, focusing on Asia.

Chapters of the book deal with challenges of multilateralism and regionalism in three fields of global economic governance: global monetary/financial governance, global investment governance and global trade governance. The major regional focus is on Asia, though some chapters deal with regionalism in Europe and North America. Topics include the Asian Monetary Fund and Asian financial architecture, open accession provisions of regional trade agreements and APEC's role in multilateral investment rules.

As a whole, the book elucidates the contemporary reach of Asian regionalism in global economic governance and shows the neat balance between regionalism and multilateralism in global economic governance. It is of particular relevance to students and practitioners of international economic law, international political economy, international finance and international economics, both with and without an Asian focus.

Junji Nakagawa is Professor of International Economic Law at the Institute of Social Science, University of Tokyo, Japan. His publications include *International Harmonization of Economic Regulation* (Oxford University Press, forthcoming), *Anti-Dumping Laws and Practices of the New Users* (Cameron May 2007) and *Managing Development: Globalization, Economic Restructuring and Social Policy* (Routledge 2006).

Routledge Studies in the Modern World Economy

1 **Interest Rates and Budget Deficits**
A study of the advanced economies
Kanhaya L. Gupta and Bakhtiar Moazzami

2 **World Trade after the Uruguay Round**
Prospects and policy options for the twenty-first century
Edited by Harald Sander and András Inotai

3 **The Flow Analysis of Labour Markets**
Edited by Ronald Schettkat

4 **Inflation and Unemployment**
Contributions to a new macroeconomic approach
Edited by Alvaro Cencini and Mauro Baranzini

5 **Macroeconomic Dimensions of Public Finance**
Essays in honour of Vito Tanzi
Edited by Mario I. Blejer and Teresa M. Ter-Minassian

6 **Fiscal Policy and Economic Reforms**
Essays in honour of Vito Tanzi
Edited by Mario I. Blejer and Teresa M. Ter-Minassian

7 **Competition Policy in the Global Economy**
Modalities for co-operation
Edited by Leonard Waverman, William S. Comanor and Akira Goto

8 **Working in the Macro Economy**
A study of the US labor market
Martin F. J. Prachowny

9 **How Does Privatization Work?**
Edited by Anthony Bennett

10 **The Economics and Politics of International Trade**
Freedom and trade: Volume II
Edited by Gary Cook

11 **The Legal and Moral Aspects of International Trade**
Freedom and trade: Volume III
Edited by Asif Qureshi, Hillel Steiner and Geraint Parry

12 **Capital Markets and Corporate Governance in Japan, Germany and the United States**
Organizational response to market inefficiencies
Helmut M. Dietl

13 **Competition and Trade Policies**
Coherence or conflict
Edited by Einar Hope

14 **Rice**
The primary commodity
A. J. H. Latham

15 **Trade, Theory and Econometrics**
Essays in honour of John S. Chipman
Edited by James C. Moore, Raymond Riezman and James R. Melvin

16 **Who Benefits from Privatisation?**
Edited by Moazzem Hossain and Justin Malbon

17 **Towards a Fair Global Labour Market**
Avoiding the new slave trade
Ozay Mehmet, Errol Mendes and Robert Sinding

18 **Models of Futures Markets**
Edited by Barry Goss

19 **Venture Capital Investment**
An agency analysis of UK practice
Gavin C. Reid

20 **Macroeconomic Forecasting**
A sociological appraisal
Robert Evans

21 **Multimedia and Regional Economic Restructuring**
Edited by Hans-Joachim Braczyk, Gerhard Fuchs and Hans-Georg Wolf

22 **The New Industrial Geography**
Regions, regulation and Institutions
Edited by Trevor J. Barnes and Meric S. Gertler

23 **The Employment Impact of Innovation**
Evidence and policy
Edited by Marco Vivarelli and Mario Pianta

24 **International Health Care Reform**
A legal, economic and political analysis
Colleen Flood

25 **Competition Policy Analysis**
Edited by Einar Hope

26 **Culture and Enterprise**
The development, representation and morality of business
Don Lavoie and Emily Chamlee-Wright

27 **Global Financial Crises and Reforms**
Cases and caveats
B. N. Ghosh

28 **Geography of Production and Economic Integration**
Miroslav N. Jovanović

29 **Technology, Trade and Growth in OECD Countries**
Does specialisation matter?
Valentina Meliciani

30 **Post-Industrial Labour Markets**
Profiles of North America and Scandinavia
Edited by Thomas P. Boje and Bengt Furaker

31 **Capital Flows without Crisis**
Reconciling capital mobility and economic stability
Edited by Dipak Dasgupta, Marc Uzan and Dominic Wilson

32 **International Trade and National Welfare**
Murray C. Kemp

33 **Global Trading Systems at Crossroads**
A post-Seattle perspective
Dilip K. Das

34 **The Economics and Management of Technological Diversification**
Edited by John Cantwell, Alfonso Gambardella and Ove Granstrand

35 **Before and beyond EMU**
Historical lessons and future prospects
Edited by Patrick Crowley

36 **Fiscal Decentralization**
Ehtisham Ahmad and Vito Tanzi

37 **Regionalisation of Globalised Innovation**
Locations for advanced industrial development and disparities in participation
Edited by Ulrich Hilpert

38 **Gold and the Modern World Economy**
Edited by MoonJoong Tcha

39 **Global Economic Institutions**
Willem Molle

40 **Global Governance and Financial Crises**
Edited by Meghnad Desai and Yahia Said

41 **Linking Local and Global Economies**
The ties that bind
Edited by Carlo Pietrobelli and Arni Sverrisson

42 **Tax Systems and Tax Reforms in Europe**
Edited by Luigi Bernardi and Paola Profeta

43 **Trade Liberalization and APEC**
Edited by Jiro Okamoto

44 **Fiscal Deficits in the Pacific Region**
Edited by Akira Kohsaka

45 **Financial Globalization and the Emerging Market Economies**
Dilip K. Das

46 **International Labor Mobility**
Unemployment and increasing returns to scale
Bharati Basu

47 **Good Governance in the Era of Global Neoliberalism**
Conflict and depolitization in Latin America, Eastern Europe, Asia and Africa
Edited by Jolle Demmers, Alex E. Fernández Jilberto and Barbara Hogenboom

48 **The International Trade System**
Alice Landau

49 **International Perspectives on Temporary Work and Workers**
Edited by John Burgess and Julia Connell

50 **Working Time and Workers' Preferences in Industrialized Countries**
Finding the balance
Edited by Jon C. Messenger

51 **Tax Systems and Tax Reforms in New EU Members**
Edited by Luigi Bernardi, Mark Chandler and Luca Gandullia

52 **Globalization and the Nation State**
The impact of the IMF and the World Bank
Edited by Gustav Ranis, James Vreeland and Stephen Kosak

53 **Macroeconomic Policies and Poverty Reduction**
Edited by Ashoka Mody and Catherine Pattillo

54 **Regional Monetary Policy**
Carlos J. Rodríguez-Fuentez

55 **Trade and Migration in the Modern World**
Carl Mosk

56 **Globalisation and the Labour Market**
Trade, technology and less-skilled workers in Europe and the United States
Edited by Robert Anderton, Paul Brenton and John Whalley

57 **Financial Crises**
Socio-economic causes and institutional context
Brenda Spotton Visano

58 **Globalization and Self Determination**
Is the nation-state under siege?
Edited by David R. Cameron, Gustav Ranis and Annalisa Zinn

59 **Developing Countries and the Doha Development Round of the WTO**
Edited by Pitou van Dijck and Gerrit Faber

60 **Immigrant Enterprise in Europe and the USA**
Prodromos Panayiotopoulos

61 **Solving the Riddle of Globalization and Development**
Edited by Manuel Agosín, David Bloom, George Chapelier and Jagdish Saigal

62 **Foreign Direct Investment and the World Economy**
Ashoka Mody

63 **The World Economy**
A global analysis
Horst Siebert

64 **Production Organizations in Japanese Economic Development**
Edited by Tetsuji Okazaki

65 **The Economics of Language**
International analyses
Edited by Barry R. Chiswick and Paul W. Miller

66 **Street Entrepreneurs**
People, place and politics in local and global perspective
Edited by John Cross and Alfonso Morales

83 **The Political Economy of Integration**
Jeffrey Cason

84 **Critical Issues in Air Transport Economics and Business**
Rosario Macario and Eddy Van de Voorde

85 **Financial Liberalisation and Economic Performance**
Luiz Fernando de Paula

86 **A General Theory of Institutional Change**
Shiping Tang

87 **The Dynamics of Asian Financial Integration**
Edited by Michael Devereux, Philip Lane, Park Cyn-young and Wei Shang-jin

88 **Innovative Fiscal Policy and Economic Development in Transition Economies**
Aleksandr Gevorkyan

89 **Foreign Direct Investments in Asia**
Edited by Chalongphob Sussangkarn, Yung Chul Park and Sung Jin Kang

90 **Time Zones, Communications Networks, and International Trade**
Toru Kikuchi

91 **Miraculous Growth and Stagnation in Post-War Japan**
Edited by Koichi Hamada, Keijiro Otsuka, Gustav Ranis, and Ken Togo

92 **Multilateralism and Regionalism in Global Economic Governance**
Trade, investment and finance
Edited by Junji Nakagawa

Multilateralism and Regionalism in Global Economic Governance

Finance, trade and investment

Edited by Junji Nakagawa

Routledge
Taylor & Francis Group
LONDON AND NEW YORK

First published 2011
by Routledge
2 Park Square, Milton Park, Abingdon, Oxon, OX14 4RN

Simultaneously published in the USA and Canada
by Routledge
605 Third Avenue, New York, NY 10017

Routledge is an imprint of the Taylor & Francis Group, an informa business

British Library Cataloguing in Publication Data
A catalogue record for this book is available from the British Library

Library of Congress Cataloging in Publication Data
Multilateralism and regionalism in global economic governance : trade, investment and finance / [edited by] Junji Nakagawa.
p. cm. -- (Routledge studies in modern world economy ; 92)
Includes bibliographical references and index.
ISBN 978-0-415-59569-8 (hb) -- ISBN 978-0-203-81394-2 (eb)
1. International economic relations. 2. Regional economics.
3. Regionalism. 4. Globalization--Economic aspects. I. Nakagawa, Junji, 1955–
HF1359.M847 2011 337--dc22
2010050805

ISBN 13: 978-0-415-59569-8 (hbk)
ISBN 13: 978-0-203-81394-2 (ebk)

Typeset in Times New Roman
by Bookcraft Ltd, Stroud, Gloucestershire

Contents

Illustrations

Figures

Tables

Contributors

Douglas W. Arner is Director of the Asian Institute of International Financial Law and Professor in the Faculty of Law, University of Hong Kong.

Ross P. Buckley is a Professor of Law in the Faculty of Law, University of New South Wales, Australia.

Markus Burgstaller is a Senior Associate at Hogan Lovells, London, UK.

Seung Pil Choi is an Associate Professor in the Law School, Hankuk University of Foreign Studies, Seoul, Korea.

Seraina N. Gruenewald is a PhD candidate at the University of Zurich, Switzerland, and a Visiting Researcher at the Yale Law School, USA.

Daniel R. Kalderimis is a Principal at Chapman Tripp, Wellington, New Zealand.

Tomohiko Kobayashi is an Associate Professor at Otaru University of Commerce, Japan.

Meredith Kolsky Lewis is a Senior Lecturer and Co-Director at the New Zealand Centre of International Economic Law, Victoria University of Wellington Faculty of Law, and a Visiting Professor of Law at Georgetown University Law Center (2010–11), USA.

Chunbao Liu is a doctoral candidate at McGill University Faculty of Law, Canada.

Junji Nakagawa is a Professor of International Economic Law at the Institute of Social Science, University of Tokyo, Japan.

Lotte Schou-Zibell is a Senior Economist in the Central West Regional Department, Asian Development Bank.

J. Anthony VanDuzer is a Professor in the Common Law Section of the Faculty of Law, University of Ottawa, Canada.

Rolf H. Weber is a Professor of Private, International Economic and European Law at the University of Zurich, Switzerland, and a Visiting Professor at the University of Hong Kong.

Acknowledgements

The essays in this volume arose out of the inaugural conference of the Asian International Economic Law Network (AIELN(I)), held at the University of Tokyo on 3 August 2009. AIELN is a regional grouping of the Society of International Economic Law (SIEL). It was established by the Asia-based members of SIEL with the goal, among others, of promoting research, education and practice of international economic law in Asia. AIELN(I) featured the same topic as the title of this volume, presented more than 25 speakers and was attended by more than a hundred delegates. All of the contributors to this volume attended AIELN(I) and read his/her paper. The chapters are revised and updated versions of those papers.

I wish to acknowledge first the contribution of all the speakers at AIELN(I) for their role in ensuring the success of the conference. Thanks also go to the following members of the AIELN steering committee for their collaborative work in the organization and preparation of AIELN(I): Ichiro Araki, Douglas Arner, Ross Buckley, Won Mog Choi, Henry Gao, Jürgen Kurtz, Meredith Kolsky Lewis, Chin Leng Lim, Bryan Mercurio, Saadia Pekkalen, Shin-yi Peng and Heng Wang. I must also acknowledge SIEL for its support in logistics and public relations for AIELN(I). A particular debt is owed to Professor Colin Picker, Executive Vice-President of SIEL, for his attendance at AIELN(I). Thanks to financial support from the Egusa Foundation and Murata Science Foundation, partial support to some of the speakers for international travel was possible. Special thanks also go to Yuri Usami for her role as general manager of AIELN(I).

Versions of chapters or parts of chapters in the present book have been published as follows:

Chapter 4: Seung Pil Choi, 'Legal and Institutional Approach to the Needs and Possibilities of Financial Cooperation System in East Asia', *Journal of International and Area Studies*, 14(2).

Chapter 6: Meredith Kolsky Lewis, 'The Prisoners' Dilemma Posed by Free Trade Agreements: Can Open Accession Provisions Provide an Escape?', *Chicago Journal of International Law*, 11(2).

Chapter 9: Markus Burgstaller, 'European Law Challenges to Investment Arbitration', in Waibel, M., Kaushal, A., Chung, L. and Balchin, C. (eds), *The Backlash against Investment Arbitration*, Kluwer Law International; Markus

Burgstaller, 'The Future of Bilateral Investment Treaties of EU Member States', in Bungeberg, M. (ed.), *International Investment Law and EU Law* (*European Yearbook of International Economic Law*, special issue), Springer Verlag.

I am very grateful to the publishers in question for permission to publish here.

Last but not least, our special thanks go to our editor, Ms Yong Ling Lam, for her patience and encouragement; to Bookcraft, our proof editor, Nick Morgan and Christopher Feeney for their efficient and imaginative proof editing.

March, 2011 in Tokyo
Junji Nakagawa

1 Multilateralism and regionalism in global economic governance

An introduction

Junji Nakagawa

Introduction

The legal and institutional framework for governing the world economy for the past 65 years, the Bretton Woods/GATT (WTO) system,[1] is suffering from decreasing effectiveness. The financial crisis triggered by the bankruptcy of Lehman Brothers in September 2008 rapidly spilt over globally, aggravating not only the global financial system but also the real economy. However, the three pillars of the Bretton Woods/GATT (WTO) system have played a limited role in dealing with the crisis.

The IMF has been monitoring member countries' monetary and financial policy, but it could not prevent the outbreak of the current crisis. Nor could it prevent its global contagion. The IMF provided emergency lending to Iceland and Central and Eastern European countries totalling US$50 billion, but that was far smaller than the amount provided by major developed countries and emerging market countries in rescuing their own domestic financial markets, based on the policy coordination achieved through the relatively newly born G20.[2]

The World Bank provided a record US$89 billion in support to developing and middle-income countries between July 2008 and January 2010,[3] but its role as principal provider of long-term development finance seems to have substantively declined, considering the far larger amount of finance provided by emerging economies, notably China, Brazil and India, and those provided through private firms in developed countries investing in developing countries during the same period.

In the wake of the financial crisis, in February 2009, the director-general of the WTO reported to the Trade Policy Review Body on trade developments associated with the financial crisis, enumerating a number of measures taken by WTO member countries to protect their domestic industries at the expense of imports.[4] In addition, following a request by G20 leaders, the WTO secretariat, together with the secretariats of the OECD and UNCTAD, has regularly been reporting on G20 countries' protectionist measures in trade and investment.[5] Though these had the effect of informing the world about WTO member countries', and notably G20 countries', trade/investment restrictive measures associated with the crisis, their effect as deterrents to such measures was limited, as is shown by the fact that many G20 countries still maintain such measures or have introduced new ones.[6]

On the other hand, while the Doha Round of the WTO, which was launched in November 2001, has been virtually stalled for the past several years with a limited chance of an early conclusion, a number of bilateral and regional free trade agreements (FTAs) have been concluded since the late 1990s, and are expected to be concluded among the members of the WTO, which further reduces the status of the WTO as a main forum for trade liberalization.

The Bretton Woods/GATT system was established as a quintessential multilateral framework for the management of the post-war world economy at the initiative of the USA. It reflected the view that the Great Depression and the subsequent block economy had contributed to the outbreak of World War II. After 65 years, the current financial crisis demonstrates the weakness in the Bretton Woods/GATT (WTO) system in preventing crisis and in dealing with it. Does this mean the end of the Bretton Woods/GATT (WTO) system? Is the world heading towards regional economic blocks and protectionism?

This book will try to answer these questions by analysing the relationship between multilateralism and regionalism in global economic governance, with a regional focus on Asia. It argues that the relationship between multilateralism and regionalism substantially differs sector by sector, and that efforts have been made in each sector to achieve a delicate balance between multilateralism and regionalism, though there are instances of conflict between these two methods of global economic governance.

This chapter comprises five sections. The first elucidates the concept of global governance and the two main methods in global governance, namely multilateralism and regionalism. The following three sections describe the relationship between multilateralism and regionalism in three sectors of the world economy – monetary/financial affairs, international trade and international investment – and briefly introduce the chapters brought together in the book. The final section offers some conclusions.

Changing structure of global economic governance

The concept of global governance

The concept of governance came to be used in academic literature in the 1990s to refer to a group of new phenomena where, as a result either of the malfunctioning of the existing government or of the emergence of new issues, a new governing system was introduced. It refers to new governing systems at various levels and/or in various issue areas, including corporate governance, local governance, welfare governance, regional governance (notably the EU) and global governance.

The meaning of 'governance' differs slightly for each level or issue area. For instance, local governance and welfare governance refer to a situation where the existing government, local or national, does not function well in achieving its policy goals. Corporate governance refers to a situation where the existing management structure of a corporation, which differs country by country or company by company, needs to be reorganized for better corporate performance or better management accountability to its stakeholders, including board members, shareholders and employees. On the other hand, global governance refers to a situation where global issues[7] may not be solved effectively by the existing inter-state system, such as international law and international organizations.

There has been no central government in the world, and global issues have been solved mainly through inter-state systems such as international law, international organizations or international regimes.[8] Global governance refers to a situation where such existing inter-state system of governing global issues has come to be malfunctioning, and new actors including NGOs, individuals and firms, new methods including informal regimes[9] and organizations and new norms are needed to supplant or even replace the existing inter-state system for solving global issues.

There is no authentic definition of the term 'global governance', but the most comprehensive and representative is that of the Commission on Global Governance, who define it as:

> the sum of many ways individuals and institutions, public and private, manage their common affairs. It is a continuing process through which conflicting or diverse interests may be accommodated and cooperative action taken. It includes formal institutions and regimes empowered to enforce compliance, as well as arrangements that people and institutions either have agreed to or perceive to be in their interest.[10]

This definition comprises the four fundamental factor of global governance, namely:

1 the purpose (management of the matters of common interest, which cover a wide range of issues from military/security to economic, environmental, public health and human rights);
2 the actors (both public and private actors including national governments, international organizations, NGOs, individuals and firms);
3 the methods (both formal and informal regimes and organizations, multilateral, regional, bilateral and unilateral methods); and
4 the norms (for accommodating interests and for coordinating actions).

As Yoshinobu Yamamoto aptly points out,[11] 'global governance' and 'international regime' have a lot of factors in common. Both have a common function of managing and/or solving global issues through cooperation among relevant actors (governance as 'function'[12]). But, as Yamamoto points out, they differ in the structure or mechanism for achieving such function. Notably, they differ in actors, methods and issue areas (governance as 'structure'). An international regime is constituted by sovereign states as sole actor, uses rules as sole method for solving issues and ordinarily aims at solving issues in a single issue area. On the other hand, global governance comprises not only sovereign states and international organizations but NGOs, individuals and firms. It employs not only rules but also many other methods, including programmes and concerted actions, and cooperative methods at multilateral, regional, bilateral and unilateral levels.

Finally, it aims at solving issues in a broad range of areas where a solution at the global level is needed. This comes from the acknowledgement among scholars and practitioners that a number of global issues emerged in the 1990s which need the involvement of multiple actors and the employment of multiple methods for their solution.[13]

Global economic governance – issue areas and methods

Global governance covers a wide range of issue areas, but the focus of this book is limited to global economic governance, that is, governance for solving issues in the global economy. As this limited focus is still broad, covering all kinds of global economic issues including movement of goods, capital, humans, information and any combination thereof, this book covers the three major sectors of the global economy, namely global monetary/financial affairs, international trade and international investment. This selection of issue areas is primarily based on the traditional classification of international economic law, namely international monetary/financial law, international trade law and international investment law.[14]

One striking characteristic of global economic governance in these three sectors is the difference in the method of governance – the difference in the extent to which a multilateral system provides rules and principles for governing the sector and the difference in the extent to which formal legal rules provide guidance. Governance of global monetary/financial affairs is characterized by the weak but constant involvement of multilateral system (the Bretton Woods system *sensu stricto*[15]) and the prevalence of informal policy coordination through the club-model mechanism (G7, G8 and G20). Governance of international trade, on the other hand, is characterized as rule-based governance provided by a multilateral institution (the GATT and the WTO). Governance of international investment is different from either, as it is increasingly governed by rules but they come from bilateral agreements (bilateral investment treaties (BITs) and investment chapters of FTAs), not from multilateral agreements. The difference comes from the different historical paths that these governance mechanisms have taken in each sector (path dependency).

On the other hand, there is a common characteristic in the contemporary governance mechanisms in these sectors, that is, the surge of regionalism. A regional governance mechanism has come to play a greater role in monetary/financial affairs, notably in Europe and, to a lesser extent, in Asia as well. In international trade, an increasing number of bilateral and regional FTAs are being concluded, while the Doha negotiation has been almost stalled for quite some time. In international investment, BITs, investment chapters of FTAs and investor-state arbitration based on them have constantly been the major governance mechanism, but their number has been rapidly increasing during the past two decades.[16]

The recent surge of regionalism has made the task of governing the global economy more complicated and burdensome than before, since it has added to the methods of governance and the resulting burden of coordination among the different methods of governance. In the following sections, we will briefly discuss this issue in each field of global economic governance.

Global monetary/financial governance

The post-war system for global monetary/financial governance

The Bretton Woods system *sensu stricto*, notably the IMF, was envisioned as the quintessential framework for post-World War II monetary/financial governance. Reflecting the global monetary/financial environment at the time of its crafting, the envisioned role of the Bretton Woods system in global monetary/financial governance was limited to introducing and maintaining an adjustable dollar-pegged currency system with a marginal provision of short-term liquidity by the IMF, combined with the prospective liberalization of current account transactions which would enable trade liberalization among the member countries. Liberalization of capital account transactions was deemed to be a far-reaching goal.[17]

As is well known, the international monetary system that began after World War II was very different from the system that the architects of Bretton Woods had envisioned. The transition period from war to peace was much longer than was anticipated. Full convertibility of the major developed countries was not achieved until the end of 1958, although the IMF had started its operation in 1947.

With the establishment of current account convertibility by the European members in 1958, the Bretton Woods system was in operation. Each member intervened in the foreign exchange market, either buying or selling dollars, to maintain its parity within the 1 per cent margins. The USA in turn pegged the price of the dollar at $35 per ounce by buying and selling gold. Thus, each currency was anchored to the dollar and indirectly to gold. This system was different from what its architects had envisioned in two aspects. First, instead of a system of equal currencies, it evolved into the gold dollar system. Initially, it was a gold standard with two key currencies, the dollar and the pound. But the role of the pound as a key currency declined steadily until, by the sterling devaluation of November 1967, its official use was limited to the sterling area. Parallel to the decline of sterling was the rise in the dollar as a key currency. Use of the dollar as both a private and an official international currency increased dramatically in the 1950s and continued into the 1960s. With full convertibility, the dollar's role as an intervention currency led to its use as international reserve.[18]

The second important difference between the actual Bretton Woods system and the intentions of the Articles was the evolution of the adjustable peg system into a virtual fixed exchange rate system. Between 1947 and 1967, there were few changes in parities of the G10 countries, with the exception of the Canadian float in 1950, devaluations by France in 1957 and 1958 and minor revaluations by Germany and the Netherlands in 1961, because the monetary authorities were unwilling to accept the risk associated with discrete changes in parities – loss of prestige, the likelihood that others would follow and the pressure of speculative capital flows.[19]

As the system evolved into a fixed exchange rate gold dollar standard, three interconnected problems emerged: adjustment, liquidity and confidence. Under the Bretton Woods system, concern over unemployment delayed the deflationary adjustment required by a deficit country and, together with the use of short-term capital controls, considerably muted the automatic mechanism of balance of payments adjustment.[20] The liquidity problem in the Bretton Woods system was that the various sources of liquidity were not enough to finance the growth of output and trade. The world's monetary gold stock was insufficient by the late 1950s, IMF unconditional drawing rights were meagre and the supply of US dollars depended on the US balance of payments, which in turn was related to the vagaries of government policy and the confidence problem. The confidence problem involved a portfolio shift between dollars and gold. As outstanding dollar liabilities held by the rest of the world's monetary authorities increased relative to the US monetary gold stock, confidence in the dollar decreased, because the probability of all dollar holders being able to convert their dollars into gold at the fixed price decreased.

During the period from 1958 to 1967, the US balance of payments deficits steadily increased and a number of solutions to the US adjustment problem were proposed, including expansion of the IMF's resources,[21] securing resources outside the IMF[22] and the creation of an alternative international reserve media, the last of which led to the creation of the special drawing right (SDR) in 1968, which began operation on 1 January 1970.[23]

The shift to a floating exchange system

The Bretton Woods system became unstable until it collapsed with the termination of the convertibility of the dollar in August 1971. In order to retain the central role of the dollar in the international monetary system, developed countries and the IMF agreed in December 1971 on a realignment of par values.[24] However, in spite of the realignment of par values, the US deficit increased and the dollar fell in the foreign exchange market. In February 1973, the dollar was devalued again, but the pressure on the dollar continued. In March 1973 the dollar par value was abandoned and the dollar became a floating currency, convertible into other currencies through the foreign exchange market.[25] Major currencies followed suit and became floating currencies.

The surveillance function of the IMF (Article IV.3 of the Articles of Agreement) was substantively transformed as a result of this. It no longer had to survey member countries' exchange rate policy for the purpose of maintaining a fixed exchange rate system. Instead, its surveillance came to be conducted for the purpose of overseeing general monetary/financial and macroeconomic policy of member countries. The clients of IMF's short-term lending changed as well. It no longer had to provide short-term lending to cover the current account deficits of its developed country members. Instead, IMF's lending came to cover short- to mid-term deficits of developing countries, notably emerging market countries and former socialist countries that were hit by currency/financial crisis.

A similar shift of purposes and clients of lending occurred with the World Bank. In spite of its drafters' original intension to provide mid- to long-term lending for reconstruction following wartime damage, the vast majority of such lending was provided outside the World Bank through the Marshall Plan. The major clients of the World Bank were developing country members from its inception, and more and more emerging market countries and former socialist countries became its clients.

One important result of this change of purposes and clients was that developed countries were no longer the clients of the Bretton Woods institutions. This does not mean that developed countries no longer had to coordinate their monetary/financial system and macroeconomic policies. On the contrary, the need for such coordination substantively increased as a result of the shift to floating exchange rate systems in the 1970s and accelerated financial liberalization in the 1980s.

Financial liberalization promoted the growth of global financial markets, but it also accompanied an increasing volatility in all prices and its spread (contagion) across markets and national borders. A local crisis came to have a larger and swifter contagious effect, as was exemplified by a global spread of debt crises in the 1980s and the 1990s.[26] In order to tackle these problems brought about by financial liberalization and the resulting financial globalization, developed countries invented a number of new mechanisms for global monetary/financial governance. They can be classified into three groups according to their areas of operation: coordination of macroeconomic policy, crisis management and regulation of private financial institutions.

Coordination of national macroeconomic policy

With floating exchange rates, the supply and demand for a currency are equated in the foreign exchange market. This does not assure an appropriate balance of payments. Also, with floating rates, capital flows may be greatly distorted because of inappropriate differences in interest rates and speculation in foreign exchange markets. This led to the need to coordinate national monetary policies among national monetary authorities, notably central banks, which was beyond the mandate of the IMF. Instead, developed countries devised an informal forum for such monetary policy coordination, or club-model monetary governance.

The first attempt at club-model macroeconomic policy coordination was the G7[27] summit meeting held in Paris in 1975. The G7 summit meeting has since been held regularly to discuss macroeconomic policy coordination and occasional issues of common political interest.[28]

A similar club-model scheme was launched for monetary policy coordination by the Plaza Accord in 1985, whereby the finance ministers and central bank governors of France, West Germany, Japan, the UK and the US (G5) agreed to depreciate the dollar in relation to the yen and the Deutschmark by jointly intervening in foreign exchange markets.[29] On 22 February 1987, the finance ministers and central bank governors of Canada, France, West Germany, Japan, the UK and the US (G6)[30] agreed to halt the continued decline of the dollar caused by the Plaza Accord (Louvre Accord).[31] Following the Louvre Accord, the G7 became a quintessential forum for monetary policy coordination among national monetary authorities of major developed countries.

On the other hand, since the Mexican debt crisis of 1982, the IMF has expanded its role of surveying its member countries' monetary and macroeconomic policy through a conditionality attached to its contingency lending to those countries that suffer from debt crises and/or currency/financial crises. Major targets were newly industrialized countries (NICs) and least developed countries in the 1980s, and former socialist countries since the late 1980s.[32] The World Bank presumed additional surveillance functions through its Structural Adjustment Lendings (SALs).[33]

Thus, there was a division of labour between the G7 and the IMF/World Bank in the surveillance of national monetary and macroeconomic policy. While the surveillance targets of the former were the monetary and macroeconomic policy of developed countries, the latter was targeting those of developing and transition countries.

Institutional framework for crisis management

The Mexican debt crisis of 1982 reinvigorated an existing institutional framework for crisis management, the Paris Club. The Paris Club was established in 1956 by sovereign creditors to prevent a default of their lending to Argentina. It had since been held sporadically to deal with sovereign debt default problems (in 1966 (Indonesia), 1976 (Zaire) and 1981 (Poland)).

As the majority of creditors in the Mexican debt crisis were private banks, it was settled outside the Paris Club. However, the Mexican crisis was so serious in the amount of debt and in its contagious effect and prolonged solution, that it stimulated the Paris Club to adopt partial debt forgiveness in place of debt rescheduling in 1988 (the Toronto terms).[34] The Paris Club has since been the principal forum for dealing with sovereign debts with sovereign creditors.[35]

Financial liberalization since the 1980s and notably in the 1990s increasingly enabled many developing countries and former socialist countries to finance their development/transition from private creditors in addition to multilateral (IMF, World Bank and regional development banks) and sovereign creditors. This required enhanced coordination of bailout processes among the different categories of sovereign debts. Early cases of such multi-level bailout coordination were conducted informally until the Asian financial crisis of 1997, which led to the creation of a new institutional framework for multi-level bailout coordination, namely the G20, in 1999.

The G20 was established to bring together systematically important industrialized and developing countries to discuss key issues in global economy.[36] It was created as a response both to the Asian financial crisis and to a growing recognition that key emerging market countries were not adequately involved in global monetary/financial governance.[37] It started as an informal consultative forum among the major economic powers for dealing with financial crisis of an unprecedented size. However, events since the Lehman shock of 2008 added a couple of new elements to the structure and function of this club-model mechanism.

First, the G20 has been expanding its issue coverage, leading to a virtual overlapping of issue coverage among the G20 and existing mechanisms, both multilateral institutions and informal club-model forums. Currently, the G20 covers monetary and macroeconomic policy coordination, crisis management, global financial regulation, combating transnational money laundering and terrorist financing and transparency and information exchange on tax matters.[38]

Second, to effectively deal with this overlapping issue coverage problem, the G20 has introduced a number of coordinating mechanisms, including the establishment of the Financial Stability Board (FSB) in April 2009 at the second G20 members' summit held in London. The FSB is the successor to the Financial Stability Forum (FSF). The FSF was established by the G7 finance ministers and central bank governors at their meeting in Bonn in February 1999, for the purpose of enhancing cooperation among national and international supervisory authorities and international financial institutions. It would bring together (i) national monetary/financial authorities; (ii) sector-specific international groupings of national financial regulatory authorities (Basel Committee, etc.); (iii) international financial institutions charged with surveillance of domestic and international financial systems and monitoring/fostering implementation of standards created by (ii) above (IMF, World Bank and regional development banks); and (iv) committees of central bank experts concerned with the financial market infrastructure and its functioning.[39]

Compared with its predecessor, the FSB, which held its inaugural meeting in Basle in June 2009, is equipped with an enlarged membership to cover G20 members and an enhanced institutional structure. It has an FSB Plenary, a steering committee and three standing committees – for vulnerability assessment, supervisory and regulatory cooperation and standards implementation. Also, in order to take over earlier FSF work on cross-border crisis management, the FSB established a Cross-Border Crisis Management Working Group under the Standing Committee for Supervisory and Regulatory Cooperation.[40]

Global financial regulation and its monitoring

While the global financial market achieved record growth in the 1980s and 1990s, it witnessed an increasing number of failures of financial institutions, which seriously damaged financial markets across borders. This stimulated national financial supervisory authorities to strengthen their domestic financial regulations and international harmonization.[41]

Focusing on banking regulation, international harmonization got off the mark with the Basel Accord made by the Committee on Banking Regulation and Supervisory Practice (the Basel Committee) in 1988.[42] The Basel Accord consists of (i) the constituents of capital; (ii) the risk weights for calculation of assets; (iii) a target standard ratio (8 per cent); and (iv) a transitional period (until the end of 1992).[43] After several revisions, the Basel Accord was replaced by Basel II in 2004.[44] The basic principle of Basel II was that banks take primary responsibility in risk management under the supervision of domestic banking authorities. Basel II also expanded the risk coverage by adding operational risks to the calculation of risk weights.[45]

Although the Basel Accord was not legally binding, it was practically implemented by more than 100 countries, including non-member countries of the Basel Committee, as an important regulatory benchmark for the soundness of international banking activities.[46]

The rise of regional monetary system in Asia

It is against these backgrounds that this book tries to deal with the recent challenges to global monetary/financial governance, focusing on the surge of regionalism in Asia. Four chapters deal with these challenges. In Chapter 2, 'How to avoid anticompetitive effects of state interventions in times of financial crisis', Rolf Weber and Seraina Gruenewald take up the issue of state intervention in its financial sector to avert greater damage to the financial system and the economy at large. They discuss the competition implications of such governmental support measures, including the immediate market distortions among individual financial institutions and the longer-term repercussions as a result of the promotion of the moral hazard problem. By identifying international eligibility criteria for state interventions in times of financial crisis, based on the EU state aid regime, they depict regulatory perspectives on state intervention and argue for further regulatory steps at international level. Specifically, they argue that state intervention should be (i) non-discriminatory and objectively granted; (ii) proportionate with a view to their scope and time limitation; and (iii) designed in a way that minimizes negative spill-over effects.

As we saw in the preceding paragraphs, there exist no international laws that regulate steps taken by individual states in dealing with a financial crisis, and state intervention is justified as emergency measures taken by a state in the exercise of its sovereignty. The arguments of Weber and Gruenewald are, therefore, forward looking, and they deserve serious consideration by multilateral governance institutions, notably the G20.

The remaining three chapters deal with the regional initiatives which have been taken in Asia for the improvement of monetary/financial governance in the region. Douglas Arner and Lotte Schou-Zibell provide a broad overview of the international financial architecture and the recent reforms thereto resulting from the global financial crisis since the Lehman Shock of September 2008 in Chapter 3, 'Designing an Asian financial architecture'. They note that these recent reforms enhance the role of empowered Asian economies (China, India, Indonesia, South Korea and Japan) in global fora and institutions, such as the IMF, G20 and the FSB. At the same time, they argue that weaknesses in the international financial architecture suggest scope for continued development of Asian regional alternatives, to address issues including liquidity, liberalization, regulation and exchange rate volatility.

Arner and Schou-Zibell then argue for the development of an effective and complementary regional financial architecture in Asia, which has a limited albeit expanding history, notably since the outbreak of the Asian financial crisis in 1997. Most promising areas include regional arrangements for the provision of liquidity, which is being developed through the Chiang Mai Initiative Multilateralization (CMIM). However, they argue, even under the CMIM, crisis resolution at the sovereign level remains within the IMF, with support from the Asian Development Bank (ADB) and the World Bank.

In contrast to the modest argument of Arner and Schou-Zibell for the regional financial architecture in Asia, Seung Pil Choi, in Chapter 4, 'Institutional approach to the needs and possibilities of a financial cooperation system in East Asia', strongly argues for the enhancement of regional financial architecture in Asia. After tracing the history of financial cooperation in East Asia since the Asian financial crisis of 1997, Choi draws a comprehensive framework of regional financial cooperation and integration, consisting of four stages: the first stage includes currency swap arrangements; the second includes multilateral currency swap arrangements; the third stage includes a regional monetary fund; and the last stage is the regional common currency system. He observes that the current stage of financial cooperation in Asia seems to have passed the first stage and transferred to the second stage. Looking into the further stages in financial cooperation, he argues, enhanced institutionalization will be needed, where harmonization of standards and so forth will be carried out. He expects that there will be a fierce debate on this. He points out another obstacle to the enhancement of financial cooperation in Asia, that is, the historical and political conflict among Korea, China and Japan. He concludes that various exchanges and close cooperation should be conducted among the three countries to settle the conflict before they achieve enhanced financial cooperation in East Asia.

Finally, in Chapter 5, 'East Asian financial integration: a road ahead', Ross Buckley examines the substantive objectives for the fully fledged Asian Monetary Fund (AMF). He argues that closer financial integration is much needed in East Asia because the Washington Consensus policies promulgated by the IMF and the World Bank have been a conspicuous failure in promoting development. He bases his argument on the assertion that East Asian countries achieved economic growth through a very different set of policies, policies that allow a larger role for government, that prioritize inbound equity investments over debt and focus on investments that bring with them high technology and management expertise and policies that emphasizes nation building through investment in education and public health rather than the repayment of foreign debt. He calls this set of policies the Asian Consensus, and argues that an AMF could develop and promulgate this Asian Consensus and thereby pioneer new approaches to the development challenge.

Buckley further argues that closer financial integration is much needed in East Asia because it could benefit from its massive foreign exchange reserves. An AMF could work to more fully develop regional bond markets and take other initiatives to keep the region's savings in the region. Greater regional financial self-sufficiency, he argues, would serve to insulate the region from the volatility that comes with a dependence on foreign capital.

Global trade governance

The success of the WTO and its ironic results

Global trade governance experienced substantive transformation of both structure and functions during the past couple of decades. The GATT, which had started with 23 contracting parties, mostly developed countries, kept its club-model character throughout its history, even though it increasingly attracted developing countries and, after the late 1980s, former socialist countries. Trade liberalization was promoted through several rounds of multilateral trade negotiation, and the decisions used to be taken by consensus, with the adoption of the results agreed on among the four major members (the USA, the EC, Canada and Japan) in the Green Room. Disputes among members were settled through a dispute settlement mechanism, which was gradually elaborated to secure prompt and reliable solutions. However, even at its most advanced stage, the GATT dispute settlement mechanism left room for its breakup, because a party to the dispute could block the establishment of a panel, or the adoption of the report of the panel, by blocking the consensus needed.

The WTO took over the GATT, but introduced several new elements to the governance of global trade. First of all, the WTO became a virtually universal organization for trade liberalization. It originally started with 128 members and it had 153 members as of November 2010, with 30 countries on the list of observers who are conducting accession negotiation. Second, the WTO is equipped with a highly judicialized dispute settlement mechanism. Establishment of a panel and the adoption of the reports of the panel and the Appellate Body were practically automated with the introduction of the negative consensus formula. The establishment of the Appellate Body enhanced confidence in the quality of reports provided through the dispute settlement procedure. These contributed to the success of the WTO dispute settlement mechanism. By the end of October 2010, as many as 418 complaints were filed, and many were settled either through panel and Appellate Body procedure or through bilateral negotiation.

Ironically, the universalization of the WTO and the success of the judicialized dispute settlement mechanism seem to have contributed to the undermining of the WTO as a forum for trade liberalization. The four major members of the GATT can no longer take the decisive role in the conclusion of negotiation. Instead, consensus building takes much more time and many more steps by which a small group of countries, which represents the different views of the wider membership, tries to iron out differences before bringing the product of their efforts to progressively larger groups of countries so that more and more views can converge. Eventually, the document is brought before the entire membership for approval.[47] This 'concentric circles' approach is adopted for each item of the negotiating agenda, and the grouping of membership differs item by item. This has made the negotiating process much more time-consuming. This has in turn made it more difficult for WTO members to reach a package deal in the whole negotiation, because they find it more difficult to form coalitions in a wide range of items under negotiation.

The success of the WTO dispute settlement mechanism has also increased the difficulty of reaching consensus in the Doha negotiation, because members of the WTO, whether they are developed countries or developing countries, know well that the results of the negotiation will be enforced through the dispute settlement mechanism, and, therefore, they are almost invariably reluctant to assume any legal obligation that they might incur in the future.[48]

The surge of bilateral and regional FTAs in East Asia

Figure 1.1 shows that the number of bilateral and regional FTAs[49] has been steadily increasing since the mid-1990s, and the cumulative number of their WTO notification exceeded 450 by the end of 2009. Considering the number of FTAs currently under negotiation, this trend will continue in the foreseeable future.

Although various attempts have been made to explain the recent surge of FTAs, which took place almost concurrently with the establishment of the WTO, it is certain that the success of the WTO and the resulting ironic undermining, which we saw in the preceding section, contributed to the surge in FTAs. In light of the difficulty in reaching agreement in trade negotiation under the WTO, it is fairly reasonable for many countries to seek further trade liberalization through bilateral or regional channels.

Competitive dynamics have added momentum to this trend in East Asia. Until the mid-1990s, most countries in the region had given priority to multilateral trade liberalization (GATT and APEC) and had rarely concluded bilateral or regional FTAs. However, they then realized that earlier FTAs by their trading partners outside the region had put them at competitive disadvantage, and so they joined the global FTA frenzy.[50]

The prolonged Doha negotiation has also contributed to the competitive dynamics of FTAs in East Asia, at least to a certain extent, because some countries in the region, most notably Singapore and South Korea, have been actively

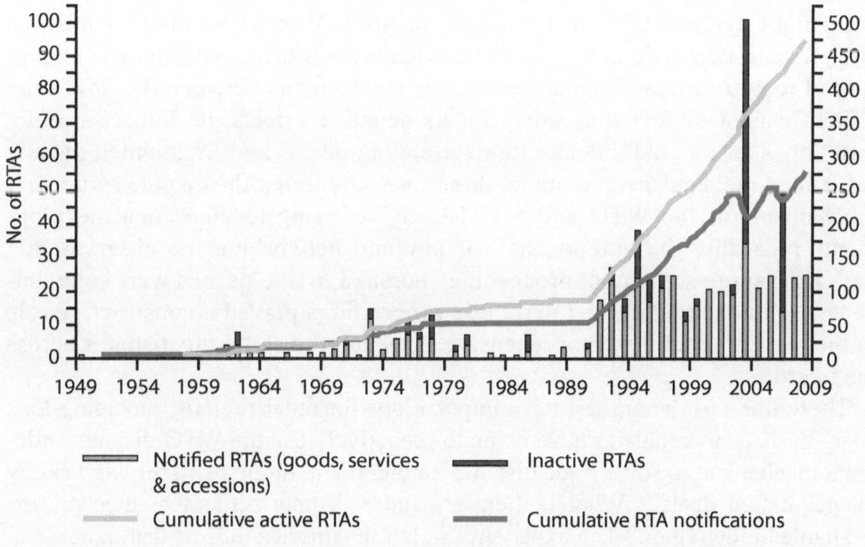

Source: WTO online at <http://www.wto.org/english/tratop_e/region_e/regfac_e.htm>

Figure 1.1 Evolution of regional trade agreements in the world, 1948–2009

accumulating specific trade remedy provisions in their bilateral FTAs, which reflect their negotiating stance in the Doha negotiation on rules (standard setting strategy).[51]

The proliferation of FTAs brings adverse effects as well. The noodle bowl effect of complicated and conflicting rules of origin among FTAs is among the most frequently discussed.[52] Fragmentation of trade rules and dispute settlement mechanisms between the FTAs and the WTO is another. A classic issue of the compatibility of FTAs with the rules of the GATT/WTO, namely Article XXIV of the GATT 1994, should also be addressed. Two chapters will deal with some of these issues and challenges of FTA proliferation in the context of East Asia.

Meredith Lewis, in Chapter 6, 'Open accession provisions in FTAs: a bridge between regionalism and multilateralism?', suggests adopting a pragmatic approach to the Article XXIV problem that would entail (i) clarifying the meaning of 'substantially all the trade' in Article XXIV; (ii) holding new FTAs to the agreed-to definition; and (iii) permitting existing FTAs to either conform to the new definition or to amend their agreements to include an open accession provision, if one is not already in place. Although open accession provision may be perceived as too soft, she argues, it would at least provide the potential for further liberalization and for a degree of multilateralization of existing regionalism, as is currently being seen with the open accession P-4 Agreement (the Trans-Pacific Economic Partnership Agreement between New Zealand, Singapore, Brunei and Chile) serving as the starting point for a broader Trans-Pacific Strategic Econmic Partnership Agreement (TPP) that will include the US, Australia and even Japan.

In Chapter 7, 'Dynamic process of transnational dispute settlement as an autopoietic system? Lessons from cases in North America involving the WTO, NAFTA and domestic laws', Tomohiko Kobayashi deals with the fragmentation of legal rules and dispute settlement mechanisms between the WTO and FTAs. Instead of focusing solely on its negative effects, he looks carefully into how states actually deal with overlapping norms and fragmented dispute settlement mechanisms, taking up three cases involving the dispute settlement mechanisms of the WTO and NAFTA. By referring to theoretical developments regarding the autopoiesis[53] of law and networking, he observes that parallel dispute settlement proceedings pursued by the parties were interconnected with each other, and that these proceedings played a constructive role in the parties' reaching comprehensive agreement to settle the disputes across the board.

These findings, he argues, have implications for other regions, including East Asia. East Asian countries have come to proactively use the WTO dispute settlement mechanism to solve trade disputes among them, though still relying heavily on negotiated deals.[54] What if there are more dispute settlement mechanisms available in the region? The experience in North America tells us that increase in the dispute settlement mechanisms will not necessarily lead to the legalization of dispute settlement, though it might enhance final settlement of disputes that may not conform to the rules of either the WTO or of the FTAs.

Global investment governance

Proliferation of international investment agreements

Global investment governance is characterized by the lack of a multilateral framework for the promotion and protection of foreign investment. Although several attempts were made at establishing multilateral rules on investment in the past, most recently the Multilateral Agreement on Investment (MAI) sponsored by the OECD,[55] none has been successful, mainly because of the resistance of developing countries to agreeing on general rules for the protection of foreign investment.

This does not mean that developing countries have always resisted agreeing on rules for the protection of foreign investment *at any level*. On the contrary, they have been parties to a number of bilateral investment treaties (BITs) and FTAs which contain chapters on investment, expecting that such agreements may attract foreign investment. The total number of such international investment agreements (IIAs) exceeded 3,000 by the end of 2009.[56]

In parallel to the expanding IIAs, the number of investor-state arbitration cases has been continuing to increase, totalling 357 by the end of 2009.[57] It is worth noting that the overwhelming majority of the claims were initiated by investors from developed countries,[58] since this shows a unique characteristic of global investment governance, namely, it has been developed as a regime for the protection of investors' interests against the exercise of host states' sovereignty, where investors are from developed countries and host states are developing countries. This one-way traffic characteristic of global investment governance can be explained by its historical origin. It originated in the case law and diplomatic practice of Europe and the USA in the late nineteenth and early twentieth century to protect their investors' interests in Latin America.[59]

Changing landscape of global investment governance

The recent proliferation of IIAs and investor-state arbitration cases points to the systemic evolution of global investment governance from a rapid expansion of IIAs at a bilateral level to a more integrated and elaborate approach. There are indications that the landscape of IIAs is consolidating in several respects, including (i) efforts to create regional – notably South–South – investment areas; (ii) the competence shift within the EU, which is likely to lead to an increasing number of IIAs by the EU;[60] and (iii) efforts by numerous countries to reassess their international investment policies (Russian Federation in 2001, France in 2006 and Colombia, Mexico, Austria and Germany in 2008) to better align them with development considerations.[61]

It is against these backgrounds that four chapters address contemporary challenges to global investment governance, three of them focusing on Asia.

Anthony VanDuzer, in Chapter 8, 'APEC's role in rationalizing international investment obligations', takes up the coherence challenge created by the proliferation of IIAs. Increasing number of IIAs concluded in an uncoordinated manner have resulted in a universe of IIAs which is becoming more diverse and complex, presenting a serious challenge to policy coherence on at least two levels for each country: coherence between domestic policy and international obligations and coherence among different international obligations. Another challenge to coherence is that the dispute settlement procedures are not the same in all treaties. Varying procedures make it harder for states to effectively manage their participation in dispute settlement and their exposure to liability.

He explores the possibility of APEC (Asia-Pacific Economic Cooperation) responding to these challenges by developing a more coherent international investment regime. As a broad grouping of developed and developing countries whose overall goal is to facilitate sustainable economic growth through trade and investment liberalization in the Asia-Pacific region, he argues, APEC is well placed to work towards coherent investment rules among its member countries. However, the failure of APEC to adopt a model investment chapter for FTAs at its summit meeting in November 2008 suggests that the diversity in its membership may be a substantial impediment to real progress in achieving coherence in the IIAs they negotiate.

In Chapter 9, 'Vertical allocation of competences for investment treaties in the European Union', Markus Burgstaller deals with the possibility of securing coherence among IIAs by vertically allocating competences for IIAs within the framework of European regional integration. Under the original EC Treaty, the common commercial policy (CCP) did not extend to foreign direct investment. However, recent developments cast doubt on EU member states' competence to conclude, amend and uphold their BITs. First, following the judgment of the European Court of Justice (ECJ) in infringement proceedings against some member states, Austria and Sweden may be obliged to denounce some of their BITs. Second, the European Commission's Minimum Platform on Investment of 27 November 2006 extends the Community's competence and may render member states' current BIT practice in violation of EC law.

As the Treaty of Lisbon came into force in late 2009, the EU will be exclusively competent to conclude comprehensive investment treaties with third states. This would strengthen the Commission's negotiating power in the promotion and protection of foreign direct investment. It would also lead to efficiency gains, since a BIT between the EU and a third state would protect the investments of 27 member states at the same time. However, even after the coming into force the Treaty of Lisbon, the continued fragmentation of competences between the union and its member states as a result of the limitation of the EU's competence in relation to foreign direct investment, excluding portfolio investment, is likely to cause confusion both within the EU and with the third states.

An important difference between international trade law and international investment law is the presence in the former, but not usually in the latter, of general exception provision to preserve the regulatory autonomy of the state for the sake of public goods. Daniel Kalderimis, in Chapter 10, 'Investment treaties and public goods', asserts that this reflects the different philosophical basis of the GATT/WTO regime of 'embedded liberalism' as opposed to the 'laissez-faire liberalism' of most BITs.

He then examines how investor-state arbitrations have dealt with conflicts between investor rights and regulatory autonomy in the absence of general exception. He suggests that the absence has contributed to inconsistent and unpersuasive reasoning. As arbitral tribunals should not be forced to create a new law in this area, he suggests that BITs should expressly refer to public goods so that host states may pursue their legitimate policy objectives such as sustainable development and protection of internationally recognized human rights.

In Chapter 11, 'China's evolving international investment treaty policy towards liberalism', Chunbao Liu analyses and compares the role of BITs and FTAs in China's investment policy. Some recent empirical studies based on sample FTAs have identified dramatic changes in the international investment framework. However, there is no comparative study between BITs and RTAs that focuses on one country. This chapter studies China's practice not only because China has remained as the largest FDI recipient among developing countries, but also because it has been the second-largest contracting party to BITs as well as an active RTA negotiator.

Through comparative analysis, he asserts that, although the number of FTAs is still dwarfed by that of BITs, older generations of China's BITs tend to be replaced by investment rules in FTAs instead of revised BITs. He also asserts that international investment rules have been evolving towards becoming more investor-friendly in both China's BITs and FTAs, which can be explained by domestic regulatory reform and the protection of China's outward investment.

Conclusion: revitalizing multilateralism in global economic governance

We have outlined the major trends and challenges in global economic governance in three major sectors: monetary/financial affairs, international trade and international investment. Although the governance structure and functions are different in these sectors, reflecting the different historical paths that these governance mechanisms have taken in each sector, there is a common characteristic in the contemporary governance mechanisms in these sectors, that is, the surge of regionalism.

Asia is not an exception. Asia is actively taking regional initiatives in all three sectors. In monetary/financial affairs, East Asia has been an active promoter of regional financial cooperation since the Asian financial crisis. Asia has also been among the most aggressive promoters of bilateral and regional FTAs, BITs and investment chapters in FTAs since the mid-1990s. In consequence, it was the common goal of the contributors to this book to elucidate the extent to which the recent surge of regionalism in Asia has changed the whole landscape of global economic governance. Contributors' answers to this question vary, reflecting the difference in the historical paths of the governance mechanisms of each sector and the difference in the contributors' research interests. Overall, though, this book shows the reader a delicate balance between multilateralism and regionalism in global economic governance as a result of recent developments in the three sectors, focusing on Asia.

Notes

1 The Bretton Woods system *sensu stricto* refers to the international monetary system established by the Bretton Woods Conference, or the United Nations Monetary and Financial Conference, held in Bretton Woods, NH, USA, in July 1944, which established the International Monetary Fund (IMF) and the International Bank for Reconstruction and Development (IBRD), which today is part of the World Bank Group. The Bretton Woods system *sensu lato*, or the Bretton Woods/GATT (WTO) system, refers to the post-World War II international monetary/financial and trade system which comprises the IMF, IBRD and the General Agreement on Tariffs and Trade (GATT), which was succeeded by the World Trade Organization (WTO) in 1995.

2 G20, or the Group of Twenty Finance Ministers and Central Bank Governors, was established in 1999, with the mission of 'contributing to the strengthening of the international financial architecture and providing for opportunities for dialogue on national policies, international co-operation, and international financial institutions'. See G20, Mandate. Online. Available HTTP: <http://www.g20.org/about_what_is_g20.aspx>. The members of the G20 are Argentina, Australia, Brazil, Canada, China, France, Germany, India, Indonesia, Italy, Japan, Korea, Mexico, Russia, Saudi Arabia, South Africa, Turkey, UK and USA. The EU, represented by the rotating Council presidency and the European Central Bank (ECB), is the twentieth member of the G20.

3 The World Bank, 'The Financial Crisis: What the Bank Is Doing'. Online: Available HTTP: <http://www.worldbank.org/financialcrisis/thebankinitiatives.htm>.

4 See WTO News, 'Lamy "We Must Remain Extremely Vigilant"', 9 February 2009. Online. Available HTTP: <http://www.wto.org/english/news_e/news09_e/tpr_09feb09_e.htm>.

5 See WTO, 'Reports on Recent Trade Developments'. Online. Available HTTP: <http://www.wto.org/english/news_e/archive_e/trdv_arc_e.htm>.

6 The joint summary of the OECD/WTO/UNCTAD report on G20 trade and investment measures of 14 June 2010 noted that 'there has been a decline in the number of new measures and in their coverage of trade … there is a growing risk of an accumulation of trade restricting measures implemented since the outbreak of the crisis'. See OECD/WTO/UNCTAD, *Report on G20 Trade and Investment Measures (November 2009 to Mid-May 2010), Joint Summary on G20 Trade and Investment Measures*, 14 June 2010, p.4. Online. Available HTTP: <http://www.wto.org/english/news_e/news10_e/summary_oecd_unctad_june10_e.pdf>.

7 There is no precise definition of 'global issues'. It ordinarily refers to those issues in the world whose solution requires the cooperative efforts of a wide range of actors including international organizations, national governments, private firms and NGOs. See, for instance, Yamamoto (2008: 23).

8 'International regimes' are defined as 'principles, norms, rules, and decision-making procedures around which actor expectations converge in a given issue-area'. See Krasner (1982: 185).

9 See, for instance, Cutler (2003).

10 Commission on Global Governance (1995: 2–3).

11 Yamamoto (2008: 171–3).

12 Yamamoto (2008: 171).

13 From the viewpoint of international regime theory, the emergence of the concept of global governance can be described as 'governancization of international regimes'. See Yamamoto (2008: 172–3).

14 See, for instance, Qureshi (2007).

15 See n.1, above.

16 The number of BITs reached 2,750 at the end of 2009. This does not include the number of investment chapters in bilateral and regional free trade agreements which contain similar provisions for investment promotion and investment protection. See UNCTAD (2010a: 81–2). The number of investor-state arbitrations initiated in 2009

was 32, bringing the total number of known cases to 357 by the end of the year. See UNCTAD (2010a: 83).

17 See Nakagawa (forthcoming a).

18 The ratio of the dollar in world international reserves increased from 6 per cent in 1948 to 41 per cent in 1971, while that of sterling declined from 22 per cent to 6 per cent during the same period. See Bordo (1993: 48, Fig.1.15).

19 Bordo (1993: 50).

20 Bordo (1993: 50–1).

21 The IMF's resources were expanded by a 50 per cent increase in members' quotas in 1960 and a 25 per cent increase in 1966.

22 Members of G10 developed an extensive network of swaps and standby arrangements to help members in the event of a payment crisis, such as the Basle arrangements and the General Arrangements to Borrow (GAB) of 1961. See Bordo (1993: 54).

23 Articles of Agreement of the IMF, amended by the modifications approved by the Board of Governors in Resolution 23-5, adopted 31 May 1968, effective 28 June 1969.

24 See Bernstein (1995: 93–4).

25 Bernstein (1995: 94).

26 See Nakagawa (forthcoming a).

27 Canada, France, West Germany, Italy, Japan, the UK and the USA. Since 1998, Russia has been an official member of G7 (G8).

28 See Hajnal (1999).

29 Announcement of the Ministers of Finance and Central Bank Governors of France, Germany, Japan, the United Kingdom and the United States (Plaza Accord), signed 22 September 1985. Online. Available HTTP: <http://www.g8.utoronto.ca/finance/fm850922.htm>.

30 Italy attended the meeting but did not sign the accord.

31 Statement of the G6 Finance Ministers and Central Bank Governors (Louvre Accord), signed 22 February 1987. Online. Available HTTP: <http://www.g7.utoronto.ca/finance/fm870222.htm>.

32 See Lastra (2002).

33 See Mosley, Harrigan and Toye (1991).

34 See Easterly (2002).

35 The Paris Club, 'Historical Development'. Online. Available HTTP: <http://www.clubdeparis.org/sections/composition/historique-50-ans>.

36 G20, 'What Is the G20?' Online. Available HTTP: <http://www.g20.org/about_what_is_g20.aspx>.

37 See Kirton (2010).

38 G20, 'What Is the G20?'

39 FSB, 'History'. Online. Available HTTP: <http://www.financialstabilityboard.org/about/history/htm>.

40 FSB, press release, 'Financial Stability Board Holds Inaugural Meeting in Basel', ref. no. 28/2009, 27 June 2009, pp.1–2. Online. Available HTTP: <http://www.financialstabilityboard.org/press/pr_090627.pdf>.

41 See Nakagawa (forthcoming b: Chapter 8).

42 Basel Committee on Banking Supervision, *International Convergence of Capital Measurement and Capital Standards*, July 1988. Online. Available HTTP: <http://www.bis.org/publ/bcbs04A.pdf>.

43 See Nakagawa (forthcoming b: Chapter 8.1b).

44 Basel Committee on Banking Supervision, *International Convergence of Capital Measurement and Capital Standards: A Revised Framework*, June 2004. Online. Available HTTP: <http://www.bis.org/publ/bcbs107.pdf>.

45 See Nakagawa (forthcoming b: Chapter 8.1c).

46 Nakagawa (forthcoming b: Chapter 8.1b).

47 WTO, Doha Development Agenda: July 2008 Package, 'How the Meeting Was Organized'. Online. Available HTTP: <http://www.wto.org/english/tratop_e/meet08_org_e.htm>.

48 See, for instance, the remarks of the participants of a roundtable on Japanese trade policy, conducted March 2005, in Nakagawa *et al.* (2005).
49 FTAs (free trade agreements) consist of customs unions and free trade areas. In GATT/WTO terms, they are described as regional trade agreements (RTAs).
50 See, for instance, Solís, Stallings and Katada (2009).
51 See Nakagawa (2009).
52 See Baldwin (2006).
53 Autopoiesis is the process whereby an organization produces itself.
54 Nakagawa (2007).
55 See, for instance, Muchlinski (2000).
56 See UNCTAD (2010: 81–2).
57 UNCTAD (2010: 83).
58 UNCTAD (2010: 83).
59 See Borchard (1915).
60 The Treaty of Lisbon came into force on 1 December 2009. Article 207(1) of the Treaty stipulates that foreign direct investment falls within the bounds of common commercial policy. This shifts responsibilities in the field of foreign direct investments from member states to the EU, though uncertainties remain as to the exact extent of the EU's new role in this area. See UNCTAD (2010: 84n.16).
61 UNCTAD (2010: 85).

2 How to avoid anticompetitive effects of state interventions in times of financial crisis

Rolf H. Weber and Seraina N. Gruenewald

Introduction

The financial crisis of 2007–9 was unprecedented in its global impact. The heavy disruptions in the global financial markets prompted governments all over the world to launch extensive support measures for distressed financial institutions – along with monetary and fiscal policy initiatives – in order to avert greater damage to their domestic financial markets and economies. With the US$700 billion Troubled Asset Relief Program (TARP), the US government implemented the greatest public support package in the history of the United States, although – according to recent estimates – the effective cost to the taxpayer is much lower than originally expected. Support measures by the member states of the European Union, as approved by the European Commission from October 2008 until October 2010, amounted to almost €4.6 trillion (European Commission 2010b: 9).[1]

Whether the measures taken by governments target specific financial institutions or constitute across-the-board rescue packages or guarantee schemes, they generally encompass some sort of state aid or subsidy to the financial sector. This has raised fears of anticompetitive effects of governments' crisis management policies. Public support allows beneficiary financial institutions to gather deposits at the expense of other, 'independent' institutions, leading to a situation which clearly interferes with the competitive level playing field. At a more general level, bank bailouts promote the moral hazard problem, thus stimulating the risk-taking of large, interconnected banks to the detriment of smaller financial institutions and the economy at large.

Albeit not yet entirely determinable, the support measures also had more subtle distortive implications (see Weber 2009: 432). Under the impression of the severity and permanence of the financial crisis and as a result of pressure from voters, governments felt constrained to protect domestic businesses and jobs from the effects of the global financial and economic decline. Emergency support measures in the financial sector were thus often accompanied by more or less explicit political requests to primarily lend to domestic banks on the interbank market, to favour credits to local businesses and to support domestic jobs in turn. Although a joint report of the World Trade Organization (WTO), the Organisation for Economic Co-operation and Development (OECD) and the United Nations

Conference on Trade and Development (UNCTAD) stated that protectionist policy responses have been limited (OECD, WTO and UNCTAD 2010), many financial institutions have – in answer to the crisis – refocused their activities on their domestic markets.

Several pieces have been written on potential anticompetitive effects of state interventions (e.g. Koenig 2008; Weber 2009; Beck *et al.* 2010) and on how bank support measures during the recent financial crisis may have affected trade in international services (e.g. OECD 2009; Weber and Grosz 2009; van Aaken and Kurtz 2010; de Meester 2010). Others have focused on the legality of state support measures under the EU state aid regime (e.g. Weber and Gruenewald 2009; Zimmer and Blaschczok 2010; Wielpütz 2010; Marsden and Kokkoris 2010). As regulators and politicians – after a considerable period of emergency policy – are shifting their attention to developing longer-term responses to the crisis, it seems to be the appropriate time to take a step forward and to identify approaches to mitigate future competition distortions in times of financial distress. Against this background, this chapter argues that state interventions – as far as they become necessary in the future – must be internationally coordinated and put on a multilateral basis, especially with regard to major cross-border financial institutions. Recent turmoil in financial markets is a clear reminder of the extent to which financial markets are integrated and international in scope. To avoid distortions to competition in international financial services because of state interventions by individual nation states, common eligibility criteria need to be defined, which could form the foundation of governments' support measures in the future.

Establishing a framework for state interventions in times of financial crisis should not be considered in isolation but understood as a part of a set of broader initiatives which are currently being launched internationally to strengthen the financial system. The reforms to the financial framework for crisis prevention and supervisors' prompt corrective actions can be expected to mitigate the probability and severity of bank failure, thus also reducing the need for public support measures and bailouts. Nevertheless, the endeavors to prevent financial crises do not provide a guarantee that financial institutions and markets will escape financial turmoil in the future. Crisis prevention and management are thus interacting functions which should both obey the principle of competitive level playing fields.

Competition in financial markets

Analysing the degree and characteristics of competition in the financial sector is a complex issue. Since the liberalization process, financial institutions compete with each other in terms of cost minimization and allocative efficiency. However, competition in the financial sector is inherently imperfect, especially as a result of asymmetric information and low customer mobility (OECD 2009: 8–10).

This section sets the stage as it looks at the interaction of banking and competition by outlining why financial institutions – in their role as financial intermediators – are considered a special case compared to other, non-financial firms. It then explores the relationship between competition in financial markets and financial stability, on which the recent financial crisis has cast a new light.

Special nature of financial institutions

Financial institutions have several characteristics which make them special compared to non-financial firms. These specifics of banking should be reflected in the handling of distressed financial institutions both from a resolution (e.g. Hüpkes 2009: 277–8; Lastra 2006: 129–32) and a state aid perspective. This chapter concentrates on the latter perspective, elaborating on potential anticompetitive effects of state aids in times of financial crisis and on how they could be avoided.

Inherent riskiness and dependence on confidence

It is widely acknowledged that the financial sector is particularly vulnerable to instability as a result of banks' maturity transformation function. Financial institutions 'transform assets to match the short-term supply of funds in small amounts (from their depositors) and the long-term demand in large amounts from their borrowers (Beck *et al.* 2010: 9). The maturity transformation role depends heavily on the existence of a sound financial system that allows banks to cope with liquidity risk.

This inherent riskiness of financial institutions is reinforced by the fact that the banking business to a great extent rests upon confidence, while the traditional competition parameters – in particular, price – seem to be less important than in the commercial and industrial sectors. If confidence in the viability of a bank diminishes, panic may result and depositors may start withdrawing their funds regardless of their consumption needs (OECD 2009: 4). Their reliance on customer and market confidence makes financial institutions prone to runs and may lead to a sudden drying-up of the interbank market, as was observable at the outset of the recent financial crisis. While the danger of bank runs may have become less acute in the past years thanks to the implementation of deposit insurance schemes, potential disruptions in banks' refinancing markets remain a challenge to financial stability and demand the availability of alternative short-term liquidity support, provided in particular through lender of last resort lending by central banks.

Interconnectedness and contagion

The risk of contagion is another particularity of the banking sector. The direct and indirect linkages (e.g. parallel investments and common behavior) between financial institutions and markets, which have increased substantially in the recent past, mean that the failure of a major bank (or even just rumours about its potential insolvency) can have an adverse impact on numerous other financial institutions within and across borders (OECD 2009: 5). In contrast to other sectors, where the removal of one company would normally be in its competitors' interests, the failure of one bank may thus lead to a run on other, interconnected banks.

The contagion effects can be purely reputational, and thus be based on the expectations of banks' customers, or relate to banks' connectivity. In the former case, depositors may, as a result of a bank failure, conclude that their own bank is at risk and may choose to immediately withdraw their deposits. Reputational contagion may affect banks with similar organizational characteristics, banks which invest in the same types of assets or it may simply be the effect of a panic leading to indiscriminate deposit withdrawals (Beck *et al.* 2009: 11). In the latter case, contagion may occur because banks hold claims on other banks. The existing complex network of mutual bank obligations stems in particular from the growing interbank market and increasingly sophisticated payment systems. More indirectly, banks' balance sheets are interconnected because of the interdependency of their portfolios. If a bank in distress is forced to sell some of its assets, changes in asset prices may be induced affecting the portfolios of all other financial institutions and potentially leading to a downward spiral of asset prices (OECD 2009: 6).

Social costs of failure

Through these various channels, financial distress in an individual financial institution can affect the whole financial system and eventually also the real economy. The social costs of a bank failure may thus extend far beyond the costs it produces for its owners (Beck *et al.* 2009: 10). However, financial institutions are unlikely to internalize the systemic externalities they cause for other financial institutions and the economy as a whole, which is why the state has to step into the breach and regulate banks' risk-taking (see Schwarcz 2008: 206).

The main role of deposit-taking banks is to provide payment services to their customers and to give access to credit to the economy. If a systemically relevant bank fails, disruptions in the payment system have an impact on countless households, companies and other financial institutions. Simultaneously, such failure also negatively affects the bank's borrowers while their relationship, in which both the bank and their corporate customers have invested, is resolved (Beck *et al.* 2009: 10).

Financial stability and competition policy

The recent financial crisis has provoked diverging reactions with regard to the role of competition policy in the financial sector (see Beck *et al.* 2010: 1–2; OECD 2009: 13). Some have argued that financial stability should be given priority over all other public concerns, including those of traditional competition policy; according to this argument, competition regulators should be put on hold and competition rules suspended for the duration of the crisis. Others have feared that state interventions would lead to massive distortions of competition in the financial sector and have thus proposed to apply competition rules even more forcefully than during 'normal times'.

The literature has not (yet) achieved a consensus on the relationship between competition and financial stability. Indeed, much remains unknown as to what drives competition and what are the benefits and costs of greater competition, in part because the empirical literature has faced the challenge of measuring competition in an accurate way (Beck *et al.* 2010: 17; Claessens 2009: 7). On the one hand, financial intermediation may benefit from new technologies promoted by competition as it provides possibilities for greater risk sharing and diversification. On the other hand, it has been argued that more concentrated and less competitive financial systems are more stable as banks have better profit opportunities, bigger capital buffers and thus fewer incentives to take excessive risks (see Beck *et al.* 2010: 18–19 for an overview).

The balance between competition and stability in the banking sector is delicate but not necessarily conflicting. Given the benefits which may result from competition in the financial industry, policymakers should not seek to reduce instability by restricting competition; competition and stability are not *per se* incompatible (Beck *et al.* 2010: 3). Competition policy should be applied to financial institutions with sensitivity to the circumstances that distinguish the financial industry from other economic sectors. To mitigate the danger of fragility stemming from excessive risk-taking, prudential regulation and supervision should be used instead (Claessens 2009: 8).

Competition implications of state interventions

Before the chapter turns to the regulatory perspectives with regard to state interventions in times of financial crisis, this section elaborates on the potentially distortive effects of such interventions. It begins by outlining the types of support measures adopted during the recent financial crisis (and its predecessors) and then discusses their immediate and longer-term competition implications.

Types of state interventions

The financial turmoil which started infesting the global financial system in mid-2007 prompted a number of economically developed countries to intervene in their financial markets. While the extent and scope of the support granted to financial institutions and markets differed substantially among these countries, clear patterns with respect to the type of interventions can be observed.

At the outset of the crisis, governments and supervisors stressed their willingness to make use of the existing safety-net arrangements. Most developed countries, including the EU member states and the USA, announced that they would increase the amount of deposits protected under their deposit insurance regimes. The main form of intervention during this time was the provision of liquidity through collateralized lending and other schemes. In providing liquidity to individual banks in distress, central banks appear to have deviated somewhat from the 'classic view' of the lender of last resort function, according to which – at least during 'normal times' – central banks should lend freely at a penalty rate and against good collateral (see Bagehot 1873). This understanding aims to ensure that lender of last resort lending is not used to deal with individual bank insolvencies and is strictly confined to emergency situations. During the recent financial crisis (as during other crises before), however, it was difficult for central banks to distinguish between illiquid and insolvent financial institutions.

As asset prices plunged after the failure of the US investment bank Lehman Brothers in September 2008, the general concern transformed from liquidity to solvency problems (Claessens 2009: 4). It was feared that market turmoil would lead to a cascade of bank failures within and across national borders. While central banks maintained their discount window facilities and liquidity provision for short-term wholesale funding markets, governments introduced further-reaching forms of support to counteract financial institutions' solvency problems and sustain confidence in their viability. These included public guarantees of certain, or all, bank liabilities, capital injections to financial institutions and purchases of illiquid or non-performing assets. In some countries, several banks were effectively nationalized; others have become subject to (assisted) mega-mergers with large competitors.

Immediate implications

The support measures taken during the crisis have generally had the intended effects and have helped stabilize financial systems and impede loss of confidence. However, these measures are by nature distortive, both directly as they support financial institutions in non-market ways and indirectly as they potentially distort resource allocation (Claessens 2009: 4). State support obviously privileges the beneficiary financial institutions to the detriment of institutions which operate without public funding. Economic studies have, for instance, documented that banks which do not receive public support are induced to adjust their risk-taking in reaction to shrinking profitability because of the public support of competing banks (e.g. Hakenes and Schnabel 2004).

From a competition perspective, it was important to ensure an appropriate degree of differentiation among financial institutions in granting state support to forestall an undue advantage for distressed or poorly performing banks compared to banks which were fundamentally sound and better performing. The financial crisis had implications for all financial institutions in the affected markets, albeit to a very different extent. With regard to some banks, the crisis revealed and exacerbated weaknesses in their strategic and organizational structure which had already existed before turmoil started. Distress in other, principally sound and thriving financial institutions, in contrast, originated from the general and exceptional market conditions. Governments were thus confronted with the difficulty of distinguishing between financial institutions with solely exogenous difficulties and those with endogenous problems stemming, for example, from inefficient strategies and structures or excessive risk-taking (see Weber 2009: 432).

Immediate distortions could also be observed with regard to financial institutions from different segments of the market and between small and large financial institutions. If state support is granted to a particular segment of financial institutions, other segments of the financial industry may find their deposit base eroded. In the USA, for example, the guarantee scheme for money market funds, which was implemented at the outset of the crisis, led to large deposit outflows at commercial banks (see Claessens 2009: 5). Furthermore, state support was often limited to a country's largest banks, with serious competitive disadvantages for smaller ones.

The immediate implications of state interventions were, however, not limited to the national level. In most countries, actions initially focused on providing domestic support, thus favouring domestic over foreign institutions. If domestic banks have access to liquidity and/or capital (at considerably lower costs), their competitive position may be enhanced significantly compared to their competitors abroad. The implementation of support measures thus forced other countries to follow with similar measures (the 'beggar thy neighbour' effect) (see Weber 2009: 432–3). Furthermore, state interventions seeking to encourage lending to the real economy often had a (more or less explicit) bias toward local lending, putting international operations at a disadvantage (Claessens 2009: 6).

Longer-term implications: moral hazard and 'too big to fail'

Even more worrying than the immediate anticompetitive effects of state interventions in times of financial crisis is their interference with the competitive level playing field in the longer run. The failure of Lehman Brothers demonstrated that several financial institutions have grown so large, complex and/or interconnected that their failure may threaten the stability of the financial system. During the crisis, governments did not have a viable alternative to bailing out these 'too big to fail' ('too complex to fail', 'too interconnected to fail') institutions given the potentially exorbitant social costs their failure would have caused.

Up to the financial meltdown of 2007–9, most governments and central banks had pursued a policy of 'constructive ambiguity', seeking to keep it a secret to the market whether and to what extent they would be willing to intervene in financial institutions and markets in case of financial distress. Given that governments worldwide – in unprecedented efforts – have spent an extraordinary amount of money to stabilize financial markets, this policy has lost its credibility. As a consequence, systemically important institutions obtained virtually overnight a factual government guarantee (see Weber 2009: 434–5), which incentivizes them to grow even further and to engage in unduly risky business activities (the moral hazard problem).

Financial institutions with 'too big to fail' status are one of the biggest economic problems which developed countries are currently facing. It seems that the series of bailouts during the financial crisis may have encouraged moral hazard on the part of all large and interconnected banks which assume they are 'too big to fail' (and not simply those that were bailed out). Dealing with moral hazard will need a thorough and systematic regulatory response. At the core of the problem is the fact that current national (bank) insolvency regimes do not provide for an orderly liquidation of systemically relevant financial institutions. Even though some countries have introduced or are in the process of introducing a special resolution regime for large, interconnected banks (see, e.g., Weber and Gruenewald 2010: 234–5), these remain solely national initiatives which do not suffice in the case of cross-border financial activity.

While an international bank insolvency regime appears to be wishful thinking in the short-term future (Weber and Gruenewald 2010: 236), scholars, politicians and policymakers are discussing various strategies which would at least mitigate the 'too big to fail' problem.

1 A first set of proposals aims to enhance the resilience of large financial institutions. A majority of financial markets experts advocate the implementation of progressive capital adequacy requirements, making it increasingly expensive for financial institutions to grow 'too big to fail'. Other prudential measures that are being proposed include the implementation of a leverage ratio, contingent capital requirements and higher liquidity standards for large banks.
2 A more radical set of proposals seeks to *a priori* limit financial institutions' size and activities. A regulatory size limit would trigger, as soon as the limit is reached, a splitting-up or asset stripping of the bank. Similar is the so-called 'Volcker rule', named after the former chairman of the US Federal Reserve, Paul Volcker, which aims to restrict banks from making certain types of speculative investments if they are not executed on behalf of their customers.[2]
3 A last set of proposed measures attempts to compensate the competitive advantages of systemically relevant banks by imposing on them a levy or tax. These measures include the implementation of resolution funds (funded by a bank levy) to facilitate the resolution of failing banks in ways which avoid contagion.[3] However, while compensatory measures mitigate the problem of 'too big to fail' financially, they do not eliminate the *ex ante* expectations of creditors that large financial institutions will be bailed out and thus fail to combat the inherently anticompetitive market situation we are currently facing. If implemented inappropriately, compensatory measures may even reinforce the moral hazard problem, resulting in an increased dependence of the financial sector on public funds in crisis situations in the future.

Regulatory perspectives

Turning to the potential solutions to the problem of distortive state interventions in times of financial crisis, this section looks into the perspectives for future regulatory reform. It begins by outlining why a multilateral approach is needed and then proceeds to identify common eligibility criteria for state interventions which could be applied on an international scale.

A global approach

The recent financial crisis demonstrated that financial stability is an issue which is not confined to national jurisdictions but inherently global in scope. Instability within large, interconnected financial institutions may entail negative externalities for the entire financial system through both potential direct contagion effects and effects on collateral and capital markets. Simultaneously, the bailout of such financial institutions could have substantial spill-over effects on competitors, other sectors and other states – both in a positive and a negative sense. On the one hand, public aid for financial institutions may distort the efficient allocation of funds in the banking sector. On the other hand, state interventions may also have positive repercussions for competitors as they counteract adverse price trends in refinancing markets and increase confidence in the viability of financial institutions in general (Beck *et al.* 2010: 51). This implies that not only financial institutions but also states are highly interconnected when it comes to combating and managing systemic financial crises.

Nevertheless, states will most likely not agree to impose stringent *ex ante* restrictions upon themselves with regard to their crisis management efforts if other states do not follow suit and consider similar criteria for financial support to their domestic markets. As a result of the increasing integration of the global financial system, it is not enough to take measures in order to address anticompetitive effects of state interventions at the national level, although this is a step in the right direction; there obviously is a need for multilateral mechanisms (see also Claessens 2009: 11–15). For a global problem, global solutions have to be found (Weber 2009: 436).

The G20, which is more representative and inclusive than the smaller G8, emerged as the key economic group in the wake of the global financial crisis. The G20 finance ministers met every few months to coordinate the crisis response and to promote economic stabilization and growth. From the beginning, the leaders emphasized that the actions taken to combat the implications of the crisis should be 'grounded in a commitment to free market principles' (G20 2008a: 4). They upheld their commitment to an open economy in the course of their close collaboration to combat financial instability throughout the crisis (G20 2009a: 6–7, 2009b: 18–19, 2010: 13). Given that an international framework for state interventions in times of financial distress does not exist, the G20 leaders' 'informal' cooperation was surprisingly successful – at least at the peak of the crisis. Nevertheless, more explicit legal foundations would aid the aim of avoiding anticompetitive effects of state interventions. This chapter thus suggests determining and applying basic eligibility criteria for state support measures to the financial sector in financial crisis situations at the international level.

Identifying international eligibility criteria

It is no mean feat to identify eligibility criteria for emergency state interventions on a global scale. International regulatory guidelines unavoidably impair nation states' sovereignty, and with regard to their crisis management, which is traditionally seen as a purely national concern, states can be expected to be particularly sensitive to international restrictions (see Weber 2009: 436). Furthermore, given their large scope of application, such eligibility criteria should not be overly restrictive in order to leave enough room for adaption to national or regional particularities. Nor should they be circumscribed so openly that they can be circumvented or ignored or have no effect at all.

In striking this balance, the state aid regime of the EU could provide a starting point. While its application was heavily influenced by political considerations of the member states which were numerous in providing support to the financial sector (Weber and Gruenewald 2009: 67), the EU state aid system managed to adapt to the circumstances of the financial crisis. It provided comprehensive and generally accepted standards for member states' emergency interventions (European Commission 2008, 2009a, 2009b; see also Koenig 2008: 627) and thus established legal certainty at a fairly early stage in the financial turmoil. Broadly speaking, the state aid regime applied in the EU was based on three main principles: non-discrimination, proportionality and the minimization of negative spillover effects. In what follows, these principles are discussed in turn and adapted to fit an international context (see also Weber 2009: 237–8).

NON-DISCRIMINATION

As a basic premise, governments should be obliged to make their decision on whether and how to intervene in financial markets during a crisis on the basis of non-discriminatory and objective criteria. Therefore, the importance of a financial institution in the particular financial and economic system should be the determining aspect, while the bank's nationality and home country, respectively, must not influence governments' decision-making (see also OECD 2009: 14).

The strict prohibition of discriminatory criteria in providing state support will ensure that public resources are allocated in an economically efficient way. According to public sentiment, the support of foreign financial institutions with domestic taxpayers' money is often considered even more grotesque than is the case with domestic institutions and is thus not easy to get accepted politically. The existence of multilateral rules would, however, ensure reciprocity of non-discrimination, making compliance – at least theoretically – mutually beneficial for the involved nation states.

The principle of non-discrimination – having been established and tested in international trade law – should not only apply to the decision whether to support a particular financial institution but also to the timing and collateral conditions of the support. Multilateral rules should ensure that a foreign institution receives the same amount of support, at the same time and in return for the same business restrictions as a comparable domestic institution. Otherwise nation states may be incentivized to undermine non-discrimination by distinguishing between domestic and foreign financial institutions in more subtle ways.

PROPORTIONALITY

Governments should also adhere to the principle that they provide only the minimum support required to ensure financial stability. While state interventions aim to avert inefficient bank failures and to maintain intermediation during times of financial crisis, financial distress can also act as a mask for economically undesirable subsidization. Both the extent and the duration of state interventions should thus be proportionate to the relative importance of the beneficiary institutions and the magnitude of financial instability.

Albeit not always feasible, it should be the general goal that government support is provided on the basis of at-arm's-length conditions (see Weber 2009: 437). This may imply a substantial surcharge on credit lines provided by the government for those risks private creditors are not willing to take. The price of shares acquired by the state to recapitalize a distressed financial institution should be as close to market prices as possible, thus coming at a discount (compared to the situation before market freezing) which reflects the risks related to the investment.

At the height of a crisis, the proper pricing of state support is not an easy task as markets freeze and governments often lack sufficient information (and know-how) to valuate the support granted under the given time constraints. Corrective measures after the crisis are thus an essential aspect of complying with the principle of proportionality. Market corrections which were postponed by the support measures must take place in an orderly restructuring procedure as soon as market conditions ease.

The principle of proportionality also implies that state interventions should be limited in time. While a general maximum duration for support measures would be inappropriate, governments should commit to end financial support as soon as the beneficiary banks start recovering from market turmoil. To determine the right timing for an exit is a balancing act. A premature withdrawal of state support can jeopardize the sustainable recovery of financial activity and stability. If the exit comes too late, state support will distort competition and promote inefficient market structures. To incentivize financial institutions to withdraw from state support as soon as it is no longer needed, it may be reasonable to link public funding with substantial competitive disadvantages, including restrictions on executive compensation and dividend distribution. Such restrictions led to an early repayment of public funds by several beneficiary financial institutions in the USA during the recent crisis.

MINIMIZATION OF NEGATIVE SPILL-OVER EFFECTS

As far as the design of state interventions is concerned, it is important that governments attempt to minimize negative spill-over effects on competitors of beneficiary financial institutions. To maintain a level playing field beneficiary banks must be prevented from abusing their preferential position by extensively depressing prices or canvassing customers and investors. While they should be able to develop and recover, publicly supported financial institutions should be restrained from expanding aggressively to the detriment of non-beneficiary competitors. Safeguards to control beneficiary banks' competitive behaviour may include limitations to the size of their balance sheets, obligations to use profits primarily for the establishment of adequate equity capital and market share ceilings.

Simultaneously, there may be a need for clear rules concerning the usage of public funds by beneficiary financial institutions. State support is (or should be) provided for the sole purpose of stabilizing the financial system and ensuring the provision of credit to the economy. Business conduct which is inconsistent with this purpose, namely the provision of excessive compensation to executives having contributed to the banks' financial distress and marketing or advertising which explicitly relates to the state support, should be impeded (see European Commission 2008: 11–12). While governments should desist from making day-to-day decisions in place of the bank's management, they should make it plain to financial institutions that unfair competition rules are applied rigorously if state support is exploited and that disregard of these rules will be punished.

Conclusions

Financial crises, including the most recent financial meltdown of 2007–9, have repeatedly prompted governments to intervene in their financial sector to avert greater damage to the financial system and the economy at large. By granting lender of last resort lending, issuing public guarantees for certain or all liabilities of failing banks, providing capital injections and purchasing illiquid or non-performing assets, governments have sought to keep financial turmoil under control.

This chapter has looked into both the immediate and longer-term competition implications of these state interventions. During the recent crisis, immediate distortions could be observed with regard to distressed and poorly performing banks compared to banks which were fundamentally sound and better performing, with respect to financial institutions from different segments of the market and between small and large financial institutions. Furthermore, since most countries – at least initially – focused on providing domestic support and thus favoured domestic over foreign institutions, others (if at all possible) were forced to follow with similar measures to avoid competitive advantages for their domestic markets. More dramatic than the immediate anticompetitive effects of state interventions is their interference with the competitive level playing field in the longer run. As financial institutions which are considered to be 'too big to fail' obtained virtually overnight general government guarantee, large banks are incentivized to grow even further and engage in unduly risky business activities in order to obtain or preserve this beneficiary status (moral hazard). The chapter has outlined several strategies which are being discussed in various countries to mitigate the moral hazard problem.

While government support in times of financial crisis is to some extent inherently anticompetitive, most of its negative distortive effects depend on its design and accompanying conditions. Given the increasing integration of financial markets, this chapter has argued that state interventions in response to a financial crisis are an issue of global importance. Although regional approaches, such as the state aid system within the EU, are a step in the right direction, eventually global solutions have to be found.

Using the EU state aid regime as a starting point, this chapter has sought to identify international eligibility criteria for state interventions in times of financial crisis. It has argued that governments should adhere to the principles of non-discrimination and proportionality and that they should take safeguards to minimize negative spill-over effects. While the non-discriminatory distribution of government support would ensure an economically efficient allocation of public resources, the principle of proportionality would help prevent undesirable subsidizations in that it limits the support's scope and duration. Furthermore, by restraining beneficiary financial institutions from expanding aggressively to the detriment of non-beneficiary competitors, governments would be able to maintain a level playing field while providing the support necessary to contain financial instability.

Notes

1 See Petrovic and Tutsch (2009) for a comprehensive overview of EU member states' rescue measures during the peak of the recent crisis.
2 A modified version of the 'Volker rule' was recently introduced in the USA through the Dodd-Frank Wall Street Reform and Consumer Protection Act of 2010 (H.R.4173).
3 The creation of harmonized resolution funds by the member states was proposed by the European Commission (European Commission 2010a).

3 Designing an Asian financial architecture

Douglas W. Arner and Lotte Schou-Zibell

Introduction

During the post-war period, from the 1950s to the 1980s, individual economies in Asia adopted a range of models to support economic growth and development. These ranged from Soviet-derived models of state ownership and control to liberal laissez-faire, with approaches to finance varying from model to model.[1] During this period, economic regionalism generally and financial regionalism especially were very limited, with Asian economies focusing primarily on their relations with developed Western markets and financial systems.

During the 1990s, Asian economies focused on increasing integration with the global economy and financial system, adopting Washington Consensus policies supporting financial liberalization. In addition, economic interactions within the region (especially trade and investment) began to increase. At the same time, the role of finance in the Asian growth model set the stage for the Asian financial crisis of 1997–8.

The Asian financial crisis marked an important turning point in the role of finance in most Asian economies and the beginning of significant economic and financial regionalism in East Asia,[2] as economies looked to common interests not appropriately addressed through the existing international financial architecture, rejecting especially involvement with the International Monetary Fund (IMF). During the following decade, Asian economies continued to focus on export-led growth, but now combined with gradual financial liberalization, regional cooperation on issues of common concern and accumulation of defensive foreign exchange reserves.

The global financial and economic crisis which commenced in 2007 marks another important turning point in Asia's development. In the wake of the crisis (with its main impact in the region to date resulting from collapse in trade to developed markets in 2008–9) regional consensus has shifted to support economic rebalancing away from strategies dominated by exports to Europe and the United States and towards more balanced domestic economies and economic relationships regionally and internationally. In addition, consensus now exists to enhance domestic and regional financial development to maximize benefits of savings resources generated in the region.

In Asia, the global financial crisis highlights the necessity of addressing a range of issues relating to finance. In addition to domestic and regional considerations, the crisis provides an opportunity to enhance the international financial architecture, not only to improve its efficacy but also to enhance the role of empowered Asian economies in global fora and institutions, such as the IMF, Group of 20 (G20) and Financial Stability Board (FSB). At the same time, weaknesses in the international financial architecture suggest scope for continued development of Asian regional alternatives, to address issues including liquidity, liberalization, regulation and exchange rate volatility. At the same time, recent experiences in the European Union and especially the euro area highlight the importance of carefully considering potential weaknesses and risks in regional financial arrangements.

In what follows, the first section provides an overview of the global financial crisis and G20 and regional responses. From this basis, the next section discusses reforms to the international financial architecture, followed by a section that argues for the development of effective and complementary regional financial architecture. The final section looks forward to challenges and policy options for the region.

The global financial and economic crisis: implications for finance in Asia

In essence, the global financial crisis resulted from an unprecedented period of excessive borrowing, lending and investment incentivized by a series of significant economic and regulatory factors.[3] Investment excesses were largely the result of two economic factors: first, the period of low interest rates in Japan in the wake of the onset of its banking crisis at the beginning of the 1990s and in the United States following the bursting of the dotcom bubble in 2001; and second, the imbalances in saving and investment between the Anglo-American economies, especially the United States and United Kingdom, and the rest of the world, particularly Japan, the People's Republic of China (PRC) and major oil-producing economies such as Russia and Saudi Arabia, largely resulting from accumulation of foreign exchange reserves in the wake of experiences during the Asian financial crisis of 1997–8. The combination of low interest rates and large volumes of investment funds from outside the United States and the United Kingdom supported massive investment in debt securities in New York and London designed to produce an appealing combination of perceived safety and attractive yields.

As a result of lack of transparency resulting from complexity and risk distribution, a process of adverse selection, loss of confidence, changes in market psychology and investor preferences amongst wholesale market participants combined to produce a closure of the primary interbank funding mechanisms in the global financial markets, eventually leading to the failure of significant international financial institutions around the world. Complexity and lack of transparency in relation to financial markets, institutions and products, moral hazard and improperly designed financial infrastructure and regulatory systems hindered appropriate responses. Following coordinated international action across late 2008 and 2009 to address systemic financial issues, in 2010, questions arose with respect to both future growth prospects in the United States and European Union as well as structural weaknesses in euro area monetary and fiscal systems, resulting in a new phase of the crisis, currently expressed in continuing concerns regarding growth prospects and fiscal and financial sustainability in developed economies.

International responses

At the international level, the G20 has assumed the leading role in coordinating responses and reforms. In addressing the causes and necessary responses to the global financial crisis, in November 2008, the leaders of the G20 established five main principles to guide reforms: (1) strengthening transparency and accountability; (2) enhancing sound regulation; (3) promoting integrity in financial markets; (4) reinforcing international cooperation; and (5) reforming the financial architecture. For each of these five principles, the G20 established a detailed action plan, incorporating both immediate and medium-term actions. The detailed action plan established the core content of the refinements to international financial regulatory standards now taking place through fora such as the FSB and the Basel Committee on Banking Supervision (BCBS). In the context of actions, G20 leaders tasked finance ministers to give highest priority to six areas: (1) mitigating against pro-cyclicality in regulatory policy; (2) reviewing and aligning global accounting standards, particularly for complex securities; (3) strengthening the resilience and transparency of credit derivatives markets and reducing their systemic risks, including by improving the infrastructure of the OTC markets; (4) reviewing compensation practices as they relate to incentives for risk-taking and innovation; (5) reviewing the international financial architecture; and (6) defining the scope of systemically important financial institutions and determining their appropriate regulation and oversight.

In April 2009, G20 leaders pledged to do whatever is necessary to: (1) restore confidence and growth; (2) repair the financial system; (3) strengthen financial regulation; (4) fund and reform the international financial institutions; (5) reject protectionism and promote global trade and investment; and (6) build an inclusive, green, and sustainable recovery. In relation to financial regulation and supervision, the leaders committed to build a stronger, more globally consistent supervisory and regulatory framework for the future financial sector, to support sustainable growth and serve the needs of business and citizens. In September 2009, the G20 reiterated its support for existing initiatives and committed to continuing implementation of agreed actions

In June 2010, G20 leaders refocused attention on financial sector reform under a four-pillar structure as well as further developing principles relating to balanced growth going forward, with the next leaders' meeting in South Korea in November 2010 set to review progress not only in relation to regulatory issues but also in respect to reform of the international financial architecture.

For Asia, the key lessons of the crisis are the needs to enhance mechanisms to address economic and financial stability and to rebalance economies towards greater domestic consumption, regional trade and investment and more effective domestic and regional financial systems. In looking to financial regulation, G20 responses provide the initial framework of analysis not only across the Asian G20 members but more broadly as well.

In addressing financial regulation objectives, the leaders initially focussed on five major areas. First, in relation to international cooperation and international financial standards, the Financial Stability Forum (FSF) was renamed and reconstituted as the FSB (Financial Stability Board), including all G20 countries, FSF members, Spain and the European Commission.[4] This is the foundation of reform of the system of international financial standards.[5] In relation to surveillance, the FSB and IMF were directed to develop appropriate macroeconomic and financial early warning systems. In addition, the G20 committed to take action against non-cooperative jurisdictions, including tax havens.[6] Second, in relation to the scope of regulation, leaders committed to reshaping regulatory systems to address macroprudential risks and that regulation should be extended to all systemically important financial institutions (SIFIs), instruments and markets, including systemically important hedge funds and regulation and supervision of credit rating agencies. Third, in relation to corporate governance, the leaders endorsed new principles on pay and compensation[7] and committed to supporting sustainable compensation schemes and the corporate social responsibility of all firms. Fourth, in relation to prudential regulation, in the context of eventual recovery (now taking hold in Asia), the leaders agreed to improve the quality, quantity and international consistency of capital, including regulation to prevent excessive leverage and require buffers of resources to be built up in good times. Fifth, in relation to transparency, the G20 called on accounting standard setters to improve standards on valuation and provisioning and achieve a single set of high-quality global accounting standards.

In June 2010, the G20 reformulated its financial sector reform agenda under four pillars: (1) a strong regulatory framework; (2) effective supervision; (3) resolution and addressing systemic institutions; and (4) transparent international assessment and peer review.[8] Despite the range of coverage, it remains open to debate whether the G20 response to date, if implemented prior to the global financial crisis, would have in fact been sufficient to prevent its occurrence – arguably the central policy objective at this point in time.

Regional responses

Given that it was not at the epicentre of the crisis, the region's response to the global financial crisis has been more limited than that of the United States and Europe. First, the Asian Development Bank (ADB) has received support for a capital increase from its shareholders, intended to finance additional resources to weakened economies in the region. Second, ADB has extended additional financing and developed a range of new facilities. Third, in February 2009 ASEAN+3 committed itself to the Chiang Mai Initiative Multilateralization (CMIM), although work is ongoing in relation to administrative and implementation arrangements. As an interim arrangement, this function is being undertaken by ADB in coordination with the ASEAN Secretariat.

In looking forward, the crisis provides an important opportunity to strengthen both the international and regional financial architecture.

Developing regional financial standards

Asian regionalism in the development of financial norms and standards has a limited, albeit expanding history. In the initial post-war period, focus was very much on domestic development, with a range of competing models adopted, from central planning and financial allocation to economic laissez-faire, with a range of developmental state models (including administrative direction of financial allocation) gradually emerging as the most successful. In this period, and in the context of the Bretton Woods system's restrictions on capital movements and domestically oriented financial systems, in fact very limited attention was paid to financial standards at the international level or even in the context of Europe. We do see, however, initial developments in Asia, first with the development of the SEANZA (South East Asia, New Zealand, Australia) forum from the late 1950s, focusing on central bank communication and cooperation in shared training needs. In addition, with the success of post-war Japanese development, Japan begins to increase its profile in international economic and financial organizations, joining the OECD in 1964. At the same time, from the late 1960s, initial movements take form towards increasing Asian voice in international institutions, with SEACEN (South East Asian Central Banks) and the development of the South East Asia voting group in the IMF and World Bank, and the creation of ADB (1966).

Following these initial steps, focus across the 1970s continued to be domestic financial development in the region, increasingly modelled on the Japanese experience and developmental model (including administrative direction of financial allocation). International cooperation in development of financial norms and standards also remained limited, albeit expanding across the 1970s on a largely informal basis. As a result, there was little need or demand for Asian regionalism in this respect. In the wake of the collapse of the Bretton Woods international monetary system and the return of cross-border finance and currency instability, the 1970s witnessed the initial beginnings of a range of transnational regulatory networks, such as the BCBS based at the BIS in the early 1970s, and the establishment of the Library Group (1974), Group of 6 (G6, 1975) and G7 (1976), all including Japan.

Across the 1980s and 1990s, as capital movements were increasingly liberalized and finance globalized, international cooperation in development of financial norms and standards increased, largely on the basis of transnational networks. During this period, Asian countries increased participation in related international institutions, largely taking on the consensus supporting financial liberalization and seeking to learn from the Western experience, without any desire or move towards leadership but also increasingly recognizing the value of communication in relation to regional issues with the establishment of EMEAP (Executives' Meeting of East Asia Pacific Central Banks) in 1991. With the Asian financial crisis in 1997–8 came the first major impetus for Asian regionalism in supporting regional financial stability and regionalizing international cooperation and coordination.

Following the Asian financial crisis, in the area of finance, East Asian countries felt the need for alternatives to international mechanisms such as the IMF. In the wake of the Asian financial crisis, cooperation in relation to financial norms and standards through EMEAP, ASEAN/ASEAN+3 and ADB has increased dramatically. At the same time, the regional consensus shifted away from financial liberalization and towards export-led growth and reserve accumulation in the context of monetary and financial stability domestically, regionally and internationally. Efforts during this period focused on bond market development through the Asian Bond Market Initiative (ABMI), alternative liquidity arrangements through CMI and initial steps towards regionalization of international financial norms and standards.

At the international level, following the Asian financial crisis, transnational networks addressing international financial norms and standards were institutionalized through the FSF, G20 (operating at finance minister and central bank governor level until 2008) and the IMF/World Bank FSAP (Financial Sector Assessment Program). It is during this period as well that international institutions such as the BIS and IOSCO began to court Asian participation, in some cases in direct competition with regional institutions such as EMEAP, with the BIS establishing its first regional office (in Hong Kong, China) in 1998. At the same time, East Asia's participation in the FSAP has been more limited than that of other regions, reflecting to some extent a continuing distrust of the IMF and also increasing support for more regionally tailored approaches. Finally, it is during this period that Asia's first international financial norm and standard setting organization is established, the Islamic Financial Services Board (IFSB) in 2002 (in Kuala Lumpur), and that ASEAN agrees to regional limited liberalization of financial services (with the development of the financial provisions of the AFAS (ASEAN Framework Agreement on Services)) and develops the first regional versions of international financial standards (with the ASEAN and Plus Standards Scheme in 2008).

In the wake of the global financial crisis of 2007–9, new impetus has emerged for Asian regionalism in the development of financial norms and standards. At the international level, Asian participation is being courted with the expansion of the G20 to heads of government meetings (with South Korea hosting in 2010) and the restructuring of the FSF into the FSB, including expansion of membership and governance to parallel the G20 not only in the FSB but also across the major international financial regulatory organizations (BCBS, IOSCO, IAIS (International Association of Insurance Supervisors), IASB (International Accounting Standards Board)). Within the region, countries are working to establish an AFSD (Asian Financial Stability Dialogue) and also looking toward regional arrangements to support monetary and financial stability, such as an Asian currency and/or Asian Monetary Fund, building upon CMIM.

Today, international financial norm and standard development takes place mainly through the G20 (agreeing overall policy) and the FSB/BIS (coordinating international standard-setting organizations such as the BCBS, etc.), with domestic implementation (supported by the World Bank and ADB, among others) and regional implementation in the European Union (and increasingly ASEAN) and monitoring through the FSB and IMF. At the same time, trade in financial services operates in parallel through the WTO as well regionally in the European Union and to a more limited extent in ASEAN/+3/+6.

In Asia, the ASEAN/+3/+6 finance ministers process to some extent plays a policy-setting role, with CMIM (ASEAN+3) and most recently with ASEAN's adoption of a capital market integration plan in 2009. Regional financial and monetary policy cooperation also takes place through EMEAP and the BIS ACC, with support from BIS. Standards have largely been taken from the international process, but with increasing moves to develop regionally tailored equivalents both through regional groups of international organizations such as IOSCO and increasingly through ASEAN. At the same time, there are initial steps to develop an Asian Financial Stability Dialogue to coordinate regional cooperation, coordination and standard development. Implementation of international standards is widespread in the region but willingness to participate in international monitoring through the IMF is limited (though likely to increase as a result of G20 commitments to FSAP participation). Likewise, regional trade in financial services liberalization is limited but with the potential to increase. As a result of the global financial crisis, there is the potential for regionalism at all levels of financial norm and standard development to increase, not only in the context of ASEAN/+3/+6 but also more widely, in order to support financial stability and development.

In looking forward, regional financial cooperation and integration in Asia has reached a point where further development can best be obtained through deepening institutionalization towards more formal, rules-based regional arrangements. In this context, the overriding objectives across the region continue to be, first, economic growth and development and, second, social, economic, financial and political stability – twin objectives which sometimes conflict but which also indicate potential avenues for formalizing regional arrangements relating to finance.

Reforming the international financial architecture

Beyond questions of financial regulation, the global financial crisis raises the question of whether there is a need to reform or redesign the international financial architecture. On balance, the arrangements put in place following the Asian financial crisis were neither effective in preventing a global systemic financial crisis nor (with the possible exception of the G20) effective in dealing with such a global systemic crisis when it actually occurred. At the very least, the fundamental features underlying the original post-war design (open trade, fixed exchange rates, domestically oriented finance and coordinated development assistance) no longer exist, with the exception of liberal trade. Today, the nature of the global economy is that of a largely open trading system, generally floating exchange rates, globalized finance and decentralized support for development. As demonstrated by the global financial crisis, the global financial system remains prone to periodic instability and crises.

The G20 and the international financial architecture

While most of the focus of the November 2008 G20 meeting was on economic coordination and regulatory responses, under the fifth principle, the G20 committed 'to advancing the reform of the Bretton Woods institutions so that they can more adequately reflect changing economic weights in the world economy'.[9] In this respect, the G20 Action Plan mandated six immediate actions and three medium-term actions.[10]

The first immediate action directed the FSF to broaden its emerging economy membership, resulting in the inclusion of members of the G20 which were not FSF members, i.e. China, Brazil, India, Russia and Turkey.[11] Other major standard-setting bodies, including the BCBS and IOSCO, have now modified their membership and/or governance structures to varying extents. The second immediate action item delineated responsibilities, with the IMF focusing on surveillance and the FSF focusing on standard setting, and mandates increased cooperation between the IMF and FSF, especially in integrating regulatory and supervisory processes into the macroprudential framework and conducting early warning exercises. The third directed the IMF to take a leading role in drawing lessons from the crisis, in close coordination with the FSF and others. The fourth committed to a review of the adequacy of resources of the IMF, the World Bank Group and other multilateral development banks, with increases as necessary. At the same time, these institutions were directed to review and adapt their lending instruments to meet members' needs and to revise their lending roles in light of the crisis. The fifth was an agreement to explore ways to restore emerging market and developing country access to finance in the context of the crisis, including private capital flows. Finally, MDBs were directed to put in place arrangements to support countries with good records and sound policies.

The medium-term actions are more ambitious. First, the G20 committed to comprehensive reform of the Bretton Woods institutions so that they can more adequately reflect changing economic weights in the world economy and be more responsive to future challenges, with emerging and developing economies to be given greater voice and representation. Second, the IMF was directed to conduct vigorous and even-handed surveillance reviews of all countries as well as giving greater attention to their financial sectors, including improving integration of the FSAP, all in support of providing improved macrofinancial policy advice. Third, the advanced economies and the IMF committed to providing necessary capacity-building programmes for emerging market and developing economies to support implementation of international regulatory standards.

In their April 2009 statement, G20 leaders built significantly on these initial commitments. In relation to strengthening global financial institutions, the G20 provided detail of their headline US$850 billion funding commitments, with additional details provided in a second annexe, the IFI Declaration.[12] In addition, the IMF was directed to implement a new Flexible Credit Line (FCL), and to reform lending and conditionality 'to ensure that its facilities address effectively the underlying causes of countries' balance of payments financing needs, particularly the withdrawal of external capital flows'.[13]

As a second element, the April 2009 G20 statement addressed issues relating to the relevance, effectiveness and legitimacy of the IMF and MDBs. Specifically, the mandates, scope and governance of these entities are to be reviewed and reformed 'to reflect changes in the world economy and the new challenges of globalization'.[14] Better strategic oversight and decision making are mandated to enhance credibility and accountability.[15]

At Pittsburgh, G20 leaders reaffirmed their earlier commitments, but extended them in one significant respect: the G20 designated itself as the 'premier forum' for international economic cooperation but did not extensively address reform of the international financial architecture beyond reaffirming previous commitments. In June 2010, the G20 committed once more 'to strengthening the legitimacy, credibility and effectiveness of the IFIs' and outlined progress on capital increases and other previous commitments.[16] Importantly, the G20 tasked finance ministers and central bank governors 'to prepare policy options to strengthen global financial safety nets' with the goal of building a more stable and resilient international monetary system, addressing in particular capital flow volatility, financial fragility, crisis contagion and the role of the IMF.[17]

As a result, discussions relating to reform of the international financial architecture were a key theme of the Seoul summit in November 2010. Specifically, in relation to MDB reforms to enhance effectiveness, efficiency and accountability, the G20 outlined a number of reform commitments – already on-going – to build 'not just bigger MDBs, but better MDBs, with more strategic focus on lifting the lives of the poor, underwriting growth, promoting security, and addressing the global challenges of climate change and food security'.[18] These include: (1) commitments to further support the poorest countries in a financially prudent way; (2) specific actions for greater transparency, stronger accountability, improved institutional governance, deeper country ownership, more decentralization and use of country systems; (3) deeper support for private sector development as a vital component of sustainable and inclusive development; and (4) recommitting to their core development mandates and taking up a greater role in the provision of global solutions to transnational problems, such as climate change and food security.

In addressing related issues, this chapter first considers the international financial architecture, before turning to the regional financial architecture.

Enhancing the international financial architecture

If the objective of the international financial architecture is a framework to support sustainable global development based upon liberal trade and global finance, the current framework, while largely effective in supporting trade liberalization (through the WTO and an ever-increasing range of regional arrangements, including across Asia and especially throughout ASEAN+3/+6), has not been effective in supporting financial stability. At the international level, a range of proposals have been made to address related issues.

In achieving these objectives, attention should be given to the aspects which have proved necessary in the context of the global economy. First, there is a clear need for some sort of mechanism to support economic cooperation and coordination, the role now being filled by the G20. Second, trade arrangements are at the heart of the design, with special needs for financial liberalization and cross-border provision of services. Third, there is a need for some system of macroeconomic policy standard setting and monitoring, to some extent the role that the IMF plays through its surveillance activities. This would include monetary arrangements. Fourth, if finance is to remain globalized, there is a clear necessity for appropriate financial stability and development arrangements to both prevent financial crises and to resolve those crises which do occur, at the sovereign level and at the level of global financial institutions and markets. Fifth, sustainable development is now no longer just a domestic issue but one with global implications – positive and negative.

In looking at these issues, from the overall objective and specific needs, one can turn to questions of organization and allocation of responsibilities, mandates and powers and only then to questions of the design of individual organizations, including membership, governance, funding, independence and accountability.

Coordination

The need for international economic cooperation and coordination has been clearly demonstrated by the variety of arrangements which have been attempted – the League of Nations, the BIS, the UN, OECD, Comecon, the European Economic Community, the various 'G's and most recently the G20. At the most basic level, it is clearly significant for heads of government and senior economic officials to meet periodically at the multilateral level in order to discuss common issues and concerns which are probably an unavoidable element of a global economy. However, immediately issues of inclusiveness and exclusiveness arise: who should be there and who should not in order to have the most effective discussion? These are issues that have been at the centre of recent discussions in Asia, with ASEAN+3 emerging as the most developed mechanism to date.

On balance, though perhaps a bit unwieldy, the G20 has during the current crisis emerged as a relatively effective forum for cooperation and coordination. A similar group (of 16) has also been active in climate and trade negotiations. The general view amongst members is that the G20 is both useful and appropriate and probably does not require any greater level of formality than has previously been the case, albeit with the probable exception of the need for some sort of formal secretariat to provide support.

For Asia, the question is how to achieve a common voice in the G20, in order to balance the United States and European Union. In this context, ASEAN+3 and ASEAN+6 could provide such a mechanism, with the AFSD playing a similar role in the context of the FSB.

Trade

Overall, the WTO has not been overly significant during the global financial crisis. However, it has arguably played an important role in providing an outlet for disputes arising from crisis-inspired protectionist inclinations of a range of countries around the world. In addition, in the wake of the global crisis, the WTO has been the focus of increasing attention in relation not only to traditional trade-related disputes but also other issues such as currency valuations. At the same time, the April G20 directive to the WTO to engage in third-party monitoring of protectionist measures is a potentially significant development for the organization and its role in the global economy. At the least, it is indicative of general support for continued global trade. Nonetheless, the Doha Round remains largely stalled, not only as a result of the crisis but also as a result of attention being directed to other issues such as food, energy and climate change.

In addition, while support continues for liberalization of trade in goods, issues respecting investment, competition and financial services have largely been abandoned, with interest in these issues in all likelihood suffering as a result of the crisis. In respect of financial services, the crisis likely means that there will be very limited support for further liberalization in the near future. This provides the possibility of advancing related issues in the regional context, especially relating to investment and financial services liberalization.

Macroeconomic and monetary policy

In a global economy, and especially one with a global financial system, problems in one economy can quickly spread to another, whether or not similarly situated. This was a clear lesson of crises in the 1980s, 1990s and today, most recently in the context of Greece. As a result, self-protection indicates the need for some sort of mechanism for monitoring the macroeconomic stability of countries. While this could be done at the bilateral level (and is in some cases), efficiency arguments would suggest the use of the centralization of this sort of function – perhaps in some cases at the regional level as well as at the global level. Such monitoring includes transparency at the sovereign level (one area in which changes following the Asian financial crisis have been largely effective) as well as issues relating to fiscal policy and monetary policy.

In the context of macroeconomic policy, the IMF has arguably been rather effective in terms of both enhancing transparency and in providing external monitoring (through its data, research and surveillance functions). As such, there is a strong argument for building upon its effectiveness in these areas. At the same time, it has been much less effective in the context of financial stability (which has not been part of its central mandate) and development (where its structural adjustment policies and approaches have been subject to much criticism). In this context, discussions are underway on reforming the IMF's mandate – an important opportunity to clarify and focus its role and resources to more closely match the needs of today's global economy and financial system.

This crisis has brought back to light questions regarding international currency arrangements which have largely been dormant since the 1970s and the end of the Bretton Woods system of fixed exchange rates. In this context, the highest-profile proposals have been put forward by the Stiglitz Commission and the PRC. These begin with the premise that, as demonstrated by the current global financial crisis, the risks of the current system of floating exchange rates exceed its benefits and fail in the overall objective of supporting trade and enhancing economic growth and financial stability. In place of the current system, both propose a new system based on an international reserve currency disconnected from individual nations and able to remain stable. While this is not a new idea, harking back to ideas of Keynes and discussions from the 1970s, it is the first major proposal along these lines from a major economy in decades.

Given the clear problems with developing any sort of international currency arrangement – such as financial services and investment – this is an area on which regional attention could focus. This in fact has been the approach taken in the EU since the 1970s, resulting in the single currency, and is currently under early discussions in Asia. At the same time, while currency arrangements can be regionalized, global macroeconomic surveillance remains essential – a fact highlighted by the global financial crisis. In addition, regional macroeconomic and financial surveillance mechanisms also have clear value, as demonstrated both by the Asian financial crisis and the more recent global financial crisis, especially in the context of the eurozone.

Financial stability and development

As highlighted by the November 2008 and April 2009 G20 meetings, financial regulation has been the central focus at the domestic, regional and international levels in the context of the current crisis. In looking forward, three elements need to be addressed: first, crisis prevention (largely focusing on regulation); second, crisis management (largely focusing on liquidity arrangements); and third, crisis resolution (focusing on mechanisms to address both sovereign and global financial institution crises).

CRISIS PREVENTION: REGULATION

As a result of the global financial crisis, the pre-existing system based on the FSF, while not fundamentally a cause of the crisis, has been exposed as insufficient to meet the realities of global finance and its attendant risks. In looking at this issue, there are a variety of potential approaches.

At the most fundamental level is the question which was addressed at Bretton Woods: whether on balance finance should be global. While the decision taken at Bretton Woods was in the negative, in the context of the global financial crisis, despite some misgivings, the consensus appears to be settling in favour of continued globalization of finance, albeit with enhanced mechanisms for prevention and resolution of the problems arising.

In this context, the discussion have in many ways followed the forms of global administrative law, with a range of approaches ranging from a traditional hard-law treaty-based approach centred on a formal international organization down to uncoordinated domestic responses. While the latter have been found to be ineffective in the context of global finance (albeit not domestic finance under the Bretton Woods design), despite periodic proposals for a global financial regulator, a traditional international law/institution approach does not seem feasible at this time, even in the context of the European Union: issues of domestic sovereignty continue to make a global regulator for global finance unlikely for the foreseeable future. In looking forward, on balance, it appears to make little sense to incorporate financial regulation into the WTO framework, both because the WTO system is already overburdened and also as a result of its focus on negotiated liberalization combined with dispute resolution, which is not overly useful in the context of financial regulation. At the same time, however, if amendments are to be undertaken to the IMF Articles of Agreement, then this would also present an opportunity to provide the Fund with a specific mandate and related tools with respect to financial stability.

At the other end of the spectrum, purely soft-law cooperative arrangements (such as the BCBS and the 1988 Basel Capital Accord) as existed until 1999 have proved ineffective in preventing and resolving international crises such as the Asian financial crisis. Following financial crises in the 1990s, to some extent, the cooperative mechanisms were given a greater level of coordination through the FSF and a higher level of formality through the FSAP monitoring mechanisms. Once again, however, a hardened soft-law approach of coordinated networks with limited external monitoring of compliance proved insufficient to address either prevention or resolution of a truly global financial crisis.

Discussion has thus turned towards intermediate arrangements. At the next level down from a formal international law/international organization approach are discussions of creating a formal legal underpinning for the existing network model. While this is the approach which is largely being pursued in the European Union following the Larosière Report, with European authorities composed of domestic agencies responsible for setting regional regulation but with domestic enforcement, this approach has to date not been followed at the international level and may still prove impossible even in the EU context.

Instead, the approach which has been adopted at the international level by the G20 is a further strengthening of the pre-crisis system, through the transformation of the FSF into the FSB, with a wider range of member commitments and strengthened peer review and external monitoring mechanisms. Overall, the FSB might work reasonably well when it comes to coordination and prevention functions without it being a formal, legally based international institution, but the issue which remains is how to handle cross-border financial institution failures. Although the FSB will play a role in facilitating discussion among its members, what is lacking from the system is the ability to put its members under binding obligations that will lead to a greater willingness to burden-share the costs of cross-border bank failures. Some form of binding arbitration mechanism might be the best way to achieve this (and this in fact is the approach being pursued in the European Union), but without a more formal and binding arrangement for burden sharing and dispute resolution arrangement, probably through a formal treaty and/or international organization, the problems raised by the failure of global financial institutions will not be adequately addressed by the current approach to international financial regulation. As in many ways these were among the major causes of the systemic phase of the global financial crisis, failing to properly address these issues must be seen as either indicating that significant risks will continue to exist in the context of global finance or a tacit conclusion that finance and financial institutions will no longer in fact be global. Unfortunately, based on the unsuccessful experience of the IMF's proposals for a sovereign debt restructuring mechanism,[19] the outlook in the context of the perhaps even more complicated arena of failure resolution mechanisms for cross-border financial institutions is not overly bright.

CRISIS MANAGEMENT: LIQUIDITY

Assuming that crises will happen in future – both at the economy level and in individual global financial institutions and markets – there is a clear need to put in place appropriate liquidity arrangements in advance. One lesson of the current crisis has been the essential need for appropriately structured mechanisms for liquidity provision in times of stress: a lender of last resort ready to provide liquidity to solvent borrowers on the basis of any reasonable collateral. Those central banks (such as the ECB) which planned in advance for such circumstances and built the appropriate systems were those which were best placed to manage liquidity provision during the acute phases of the current crisis.

At the international level, there are two sides to this: economies which experience temporary liquidity problems (including a range of major emerging market economies during 2008–9) and private financial institutions. In relation to economies, the initial response largely came from the major central banks (especially the Federal Reserve and to a more limited extent the ECB) through swap and credit lines. This, however, is a function which could reasonably be centralized with the IMF and MDBs – a process which appears to be now underway, through the IMF FCL (Flexible Credit Line) and a range of MDB initiatives. The weakness – already identified by the G20 – is that any such arrangement in today's global financial system must be backed by the availability of very large amounts of money, certainly beyond the Fund's current capacity. As such, the mechanism – essentially an emergency liquidity mechanism – requires major extension of the IMF's access to funding, including SDR (special drawing right) allocations and multilateral borrowing arrangements, potentially from not only public sector lenders but also private sector lenders. In addition, regional arrangements – such as those being developed through CMIM and currently being considered in the EU – can provide a useful addition to international arrangements.

At the level of private financial institutions, the Fund is probably not well suited as a potential lender of last resort. As a result, it seems that individual private financial institutions are likely to remain quite closely associated with their home jurisdiction and the major central banks of jurisdictions in which they operate. This highlights the usefulness not only of swap lines from major reserve currency central banks but also regional arrangements.

CRISIS RESOLUTION

Unfortunately, not all crises are liquidity crises, and it is certain that in future both economies and individual financial institutions will periodically face insolvency.

In the context of resolving international insolvencies, the IMF has emerged as the default option: if problems are not severe, bilateral central bank, sovereign or regional assistance may be available. However, in circumstances involving severe financial problems where financial system stability is at stake, the politically acceptable solution has been to turn to the IMF. This was certainly the reaction in Asia in the wake of the Asian financial crisis but even in the context of Asia's discussions relating to IMF alternatives, in the context of severe sovereign fiscal problems, the IMF would in all likelihood be involved, much as has been the case in the EU with Greece.

Unlike sovereign crises, it is certain that the Fund is not the appropriate entity to address crises in individual financial institutions. At the moment, the solution is largely domestic, suggesting that individual economies must require separately capitalized and regulated subsidiaries rather than cross-border branching in financial services and highlighting one of the greatest conflicts between financial services liberalization (negotiated through the WTO) and the requirements of domestic financial stability. As noted above, any other solution probably requires an international treaty, perhaps administered by the FSB. To the extent that international arrangements cannot be put in place, there is a clear role for regional arrangements, especially regional economic arrangements (such as ASEAN/ASEAN+3/ASEAN+6) which include provisions supporting cross-border provision of financial services.

The Asian regional financial architecture

Overall, many of the G20 commitments relating to the international financial architecture are now in progress, with significant steps agreed by the November G20 meeting in Seoul. At the same time, while international arrangements are highly significant, it is likely that certain aspects which are not realizable at the global level may instead be dealt with at the regional level. In this context, the European Union provides the leading example but also highlights the very real difficulties involved for other regions, including across Asia.

The extent of financial integration among East Asia's emerging and developing economies and Japan matches neither the rhetoric expended in its support after the region's 1997–8 financial crisis nor the degree of regional economic integration.[20] Asian financial integration has been subject to considerable but equivocal attention. Initiatives to encourage financial integration have in particular addressed trade in financial services, cooperation in external monetary operations and capital market reform.[21]

Trade in financial services

Limited growth has occurred in regional trade in financial services, and any improvement is likely to occur only slowly. To date, cooperation in financial services liberalization has made limited progress. At the same time, the various ASEAN+3/+6 trade agreements in force or under negotiation all address trade in financial services, in addition to goods trade and investment. As these agreements are implemented and their use develops, it is likely that aspects relating to financial services trade will receive increasing attention as financial institutions seek to maximize opportunities in the region. At the same time, as clearly demonstrated by the EU's experience in the global financial crisis, liberalization of trade in financial services brings with it much greater potential complications than is the case with trade in goods or even investment. As financial institutions expand regionally, the region will need to pay particularly close attention to addressing risks raised by cross-border financial institutions, including especially their regulation and resolution.

Monetary affairs

Regional monetary cooperation is mainly evidenced by ASEAN+3 short-term credit lines. An Asian Monetary Fund was mooted during the 1997–8 crisis, when several Asian states required sudden infusions of credit, but was abandoned after intense US opposition.[22] The 2000 ASEAN+3 Chiang Mai Initiative (CMI) was intended to promote regional cooperation by means of bilateral currency swap agreements among central banks.[23] More recently in 2008 and 2009, ASEAN+3 finance ministers agreed the outline of a new accord to pool additional international reserves on a more considerable scale (CMIM), totaling US$120 billion in commitments, with the PRC, Japan and South Korea together providing 80 percent of the total and ASEAN members the remainder.[24]

The functions allotted to CMIM will include an independent surveillance process that would precede drawings or advances, either as an ongoing monitoring exercise or specific to requests for credit, and for the scheme to be credible – regardless of its scale of commitments – those resources will need to be both separated from existing national resources and beyond the collaborative arrangements to which ASEAN+3 states are accustomed.

Capital market development

Post-crisis attention to regional capital market development initially focused on the debt and money markets but has recently begun to consider wider securities market reform.[25] Work on debt market development has comprised three collaborative efforts: the ASEAN+3 Asian Bond Market Initiative (ABMI), APEC's efforts in developing securitization and work by members of the Asia Cooperation Dialogue (ACD). It also includes EMEAP central banks' pooling of international reserves in two Asian Bond Funds in 2004 and 2005, with additional funds under discussion. As in similar matters, success has been limited thanks to the reluctance of state actors to cede national governance to create regional policy capital. This has been most evident in the supremacy of national currency policies, to the detriment of collaborative market reform and constraining initiatives on regional trade in financial services or monetary cooperation. Little effort has been made to sanction non-bank financial intermediaries holding foreign regional assets, although they typically enjoy far greater freedom to acquire higher-rated OECD investments.

The role of ADB?

ADB combines regional interests and elements of regional governance. While its operations focus on regional development, 19 of the Bank's 67 shareholders are non-Asian OECD members that together account for 34.96 per cent of votes in the bank's supervisory board of governors. Members of the G7 hold 39.56 per cent of votes in the board of governors, the latter electing a 12-person board of directors, four of whom represent non-Asian members. The PRC, Japan, the United States and India each nominates a director to serve their sole interests. As with other Asian organizations, the regional interests of ADB policy may not coincide with the aims of all shareholders. Asian policymakers have been supportive of ADB efforts because of the weak institutional basis of other bodies, including ASEAN and APEC.

At the same time, ADB has given material support to financial sector cooperation, and policymakers may welcome its efforts because of a lack of resources and institutional weaknesses in ASEAN and APEC. ADB, for example, became involved in a coordinating function with the CMI in 2005 and established six groups in 2002 to support market development with funding and technical assistance at the same time as the launch of the ABMI by ASEAN+3. The bank also engages in local currency funding transactions to support market development and supports dissemination of a range of local debt capital market data.[26]

More significantly, an Office of Regional Economic Integration (OREI) was established in 2005 to seek to promote economic cooperation and integration among the bank's developing member countries. As a reflection of the potential of this role, a 2007 study by an ADB Eminent Persons Group[27] supported this initiative, with its consequent emergence as a central strategy in the long-term strategic framework of ADB – Strategy 2020.[28]

Designing an Asian financial architecture

Could the current global financial crisis provide an incentive to financial sector development and integration in the region? Asia's financial systems have so far been less systemically affected than certain developed economies in Europe or North America, although Asian banks and other intermediaries have suffered losses in capitalization and confidence in a similar, though less dramatic, fashion to their Western competitors.

The global financial crisis has hastened changes to the setting for international economic and financial cooperation, chiefly a migration from the G7 and G10 mechanisms to the G20, which includes the PRC, India, Indonesia and Japan from Asia and the enlargement of the FSB. As a result of the crisis and the view that the participation of major developing economies especially from Asia is central to its resolution and also to necessary reforms to the international financial architecture, Asian states are being asked to assume a new prominence at the international level, with the PRC's role becoming increasingly prominent.

As discussed above, any redesign of the international architecture should have a number of central elements: (1) economic policy cooperation, coordination and surveillance; (2) trade in goods and services liberalization; (3) financial stability and development arrangements (including prevention, management and resolution); and (4) sustainable development coordination and assistance.[29] Assuming that these issues will not entirely be addressed at the international level, it is important for discussions in Asia to look to address necessary elements on a regional basis.

At present, economic policy cooperation and coordination in Asia takes place through ASEAN/+3/+6 finance ministers' meetings and EMEAP, and surveillance is largely limited to the IMF and ADB. Looking forward, these arrangements may be sufficient for coordinative purposes; however, surveillance arguably requires a higher level of attention, with the CMIM having the potential to provide an appropriate framework, if effectively designed and implemented.

Trade in goods is being addressed to date through ASEAN/+3/+6 treaty-based arrangements. However, based on the WTO experience, as these develop, it is likely that a more effective dispute resolution framework may become necessary, although at the moment the international arrangements through the WTO seem to be fulfilling this function. In financial services, because of the interaction between liberalization and stability, these issues are likely to become more problematic, as has been the case in the EU during the current global financial crisis. While liberalization may proceed, especially as regional and global financial institutions seek greater market access, it would appear best for economies for the foreseeable future to adopt arrangements for cross-border provision on the basis of separately capitalized and regulated subsidiaries rather than following the passport system which has been adopted in the EU.

In relation to financial stability, initial discussions have now taken place regarding the possibility of establishing an AFSD, with a standard-setting and surveillance mandate similar to that of the FSB but operating in the regional context – in this context, EU experiences are likely to be highly relevant. Such an arrangement could have significant benefits not only in enhancing financial stability but also in providing guidance and direction for financial sector development in the region.

The CMIM provides the outline of a potential crisis management structure and a likewise potentially important liquidity mechanism in the region, though its eventual effectiveness will largely depend upon the design of its implementation arrangements. However, even under the CMIM, crisis resolution at the sovereign level – as in the Asian financial crisis – remains with the IMF, with support from ADB and the World Bank. As is the case generally, there are no arrangements to deal with resolution of individual financial intermediaries other than at the domestic level, nor with the contagion impact of systemic losses of confidence that affect several or all states in a region.

If CMIM were to evolve into an AMF, it would seem logical to combine liquidity provision and macroeconomic standard setting and monitoring with more formalized arrangements for developing and monitoring regional financial regulatory standards, based on the experiences of the FSB and the EU, with arrangements of a firmer nature than those of the FSB currently but not at the same level as those in Europe. One model is IOSCO's Multilateral Memorandum of Understanding (MMOU, with a self-regulatory structure applying to standard setting and monitoring, with support for implementation from the ADB.

This highlights the important link between the macroeconomic and financial stability standard-setting and monitoring arrangements in the operations of the liquidity mechanisms of any AMF. The division between liquidity issues and sovereign financial crises is not always clear; and both this issue and the supporting mechanisms merit the greatest design attention. CMIM will itself require dedicated resources to be effective and give confidence, even if the preparatory development work can be accommodated by a collaborative arrangement to which the member states are most accustomed. Institutional developments of this kind also provide an opportunity to consider the proper organization of the functions outlined here, whether or not formalized in a new AMF, including purposes, extent of non-Asian involvement if any, conditions for usage and whether any single state will lead the initiative.

Conclusion: challenges ahead and policy options

In looking forward in the context of the international and regional financial architecture, issues include mechanisms to address currency and financial stability and reduce the need for domestic reserve accumulation, with the potential to formalize the CMIM into an AMF. In addition to reserve cross-sharing and macroeconomic monitoring, an AMF should also address related issues, including regionalized financial regulatory norms and standards and their monitoring, along with coordinating financial liberalization. In other words, an AMF could provide the formal mechanism to underlie the AFSD. An appropriately structured AMF could also serve both an accreditation function and an incentive function for countries which are not currently involved in CMIM. In other words, AMF membership could be predicated on achieving certain minimum requirements necessary to participation. Such membership requirements could provide guidance and incentives for developing Asian countries to move in these directions in terms of macroeconomic and financial stability.

Beyond stability, there is a clear need for financial sector development across the region, first to support regional allocation of financial resources and second to support economic growth. In this context, Asian financial norms and standards should focus not only on stability but also development – quite different from existing international or EU norms. While an AMF is most useful for centralizing and formalizing stability related functions, the ADB is probably the best locus for supporting continued financial development in the region – a role it is already playing effectively and which it has prioritized going forward. In looking forward, the ADB can play an increasing role in both supporting financial stability in the region and supporting economic growth through appropriate financial sector development, especially as the region restructures its economy and financial sector towards more balanced growth and development.

Notes

1 The opinions expressed in this chapter are those of the authors and do not reflect those of their respective institutions. For discussion, see Liu, Arner and Lejot (forthcoming).
2 See Arner, Lejot and Wang (2010: 1).
3 For detailed discussion, see Group of 30 (2009); de Larosière *et al.* (2009); Financial Services Authority (UK) (2009); Arner (2009).
4 See Arner and Taylor (2009).
5 For discussion of the development of the system of international financial standards prior to the global financial crisis, see Weber and Arner (2007).
6 See OECD Global Forum on Taxation (2009).

7 Financial Stability Forum (2009b).
8 G20 (2010).
9 G20 (2008a: 3).
10 See G20 (2008b: 5).
11 Financial Stability Forum (2009a).
12 G20 (2009b) ('G20 IFI Declaration').
13 G20 (2009a: para. 18).
14 G20 (2009a: para. 20).
15 G20 (2009a: para. 20).
16 G20 (2010: 5-6 and 22–7).
17 G20 (2010: 6).
18 G20 (2010: 23–4).
19 See IMF, 'Report of the Managing Director to the International Monetary and Financial Committee on a Statutory Sovereign Debt Restructuring Mechanism', 8 April 2003. Online. Available HTTP: <http://www.imf.org/external/np/omd/2003/040803.htm>.
20 See Arner, Lejot and Wang (2010).
21 Financial cooperation through tax treaties are beyond the scope of this analysis.
22 A regional monetary fund was discussed again within ASEAN+3 in April 2006 in terms of benefits associated with a long-term currency alliance and monetary union.
23 See ASEAN+3 (2000).
24 ASEAN+3 (2008) (2009).
25 ASEAN+3 is studying cooperation among exchanges and regulators to encouraging cross-border trading.
26 See http://asianbondsonline.adb.org.
27 Eminent Persons Group (2007). The group comprised Supachai Panitchpakdi, Isher Judge Ahluwala, Nobuyuki Idei, Caio Koch-Weser, Justin Yifu Lin and Lawrence Summers.
28 ADB (2007).
29 See, generally, Arner and Buckley (2010).

4 An institutional approach to the needs and possibilities of a financial cooperation system in East Asia

Seung Pil Choi

Introduction

Since the 1997 Asian financial crisis, international cooperation among East Asian countries has intensified, including currency swap deals under the Chiang Mai Initiative. It has come about through the limitation of financial cooperation under the existing IMF system and the increase in foreign trade and capital market transactions in the East Asian region. Before the crisis, East Asian financial cooperation was based on intensifying relationships with the United States or European countries rather than regional integration, and the IMF was at the centre (B. H. Cho 2006: 124). Under such a system, however, East Asian countries had limited success coping with the financial market instability caused by a temporary lack of liquidity or an increase of rapid capital movement, despite the steadiness of the fundamentals. Accordingly, East Asian countries began a discussion on the construction of a financial cooperation system in the region. Looking for concrete steps, they are making progress in the establishment of an Asian Monetary Fund (AMF), which is the financial cooperation system among nations in the region, as well as currency swap, and they are also discussing the establishment of an Asian common currency.

Overview of the current international finance system

Today, in the event of a crisis caused by the free movement of capital and the shortening of the investment period, the international finance market does not react on a regional basis, and the crisis shows a rapid diffusion as a result of mutual investments and contagion effects. However, the countermeasures by international finance institutions to cope with the crisis appear to be very limited in terms of speed and effectiveness. Accordingly some researchers suggest that the structure of international finance needs to be reorganized in order to deal with the crisis more swiftly and effectively, and they suggest intensifying regional financial cooperation.

Critical assessment of the decision-making structure of the IMF and its operation

The decision-making structure of the IMF

There is a wide gap between the decision-making structure of the IMF and the economic strength of member countries. Despite the continuous increase of quota-based voting rights, in which a single vote is allotted per one hundred thousand SDR, it is indicated that the balance of voting rights between advanced and developing countries has been upset, as the 250 basic voting rights symbolizing the right to equality among member nations have not changed. It is also perceived as a problem that the quota, which defines a voting right, is not in proportion to the GDP of many member countries (Sohn 2007; Lee 2004: 902). The reason the weighted voting system has been incorporated into Article 12, Clause 5, item (a) of the IMF Agreement was a rational consideration that decision-making on international monetary and financial affairs should correspond to the actual economic strength of the member countries. Today, on the contrary, the quota system is facing the criticism that it cannot reflect the actual economic strength of developing countries (W.-H. Kim 2002: 91). In any case, as the change of quotas requires over 85 per cent of total votes, it appears that quota change will be difficult in reality when the United States and Europe are against the change. Reflecting such a situation, the shares of Korea, Turkey, Mexico and China were increased at the September 2006 Annual Meeting of the IMF, and the Fund is expected to write a report on coordination on quotas for each country by 2013.

This change does not necessarily indicate increase in the influence of these countries. The highest decision-making body of the IMF is the Board of Governors, but the actual power and authority belong to the Executive Board. The Executive Board consists of the US, Japan, Germany, the UK, France, and 19 member countries representing 19 groups into which the remaining member countries are split. Of these 19 seats, China, Russia and Saudi Arabia have a permanent seat, which means that the rest of the 187 members, excluding these 8 countries, find it difficult to exert any influence on the decision-making process of the Executive Board. The IMF is tackling these problems through continual quota increase according to economic power, but aptly reflecting the opinions of developing countries remains a difficult goal to achieve.

Supply policy and 'conditionality'

Much criticism of the conditions for receiving IMF funds has been voiced by the nations receiving funds. In particular, in cases of a temporary international payments imbalance conditions include liberalization of foreign exchange, exchange rate devaluation, higher interest rate, financial deficit management and facilitating foreign investment. Various questions have been raised about whether policies like liberalization of foreign exchange, high interest rate and liberalization of foreign investment should be compulsory.

The term 'conditionality' is often used and refers to conditions that are annexed to IMF lending in order to carry out the economic stabilization programme provided by the IMF. In the case of a country which tries to borrow IMF funds in excess of the reserve tranche, it must comply with the economic stabilization programme of the IMF annexed to such funding when it receives the funds. The mechanism of such programmes is what is called a Stand-by Agreement, and the borrowing country must implement a broad range of monetary and financial policies listed in the Agreement. Such economic stabilization programmes are annexed to the Fund support service because of Fund suspicions about the chances of the borrowers solving their balance-of-payment problems without them (Dell 1981: 11; Kim 1991: 501).

In the case of the Asian financial crisis, however, a positive side may be acknowledged, as the country's economy recovered in a relatively short time through IMF support, the moral hazard question (banks 'too big to fail') was addressed and inefficiencies were eliminated in many sectors through the Fund's economic stabilization programme. At the same time, the country has experienced social problems, such as social imbalance, the collapse of big companies and social polarization. These problems were caused by the secondary effects of the programme and continued for about eight years after the completion of IMF support.

The fact that the conditionality attached to the IMF lending to crisis-hit Korea was similar to that applied to Latin America in the 1980s, despite of different economic circumstances, has raised the question whether the measures adopted were appropriate (Stiglitz 2002: 125–52). Partly in response to this question, when the IMF issued guidelines for financial support after the Asian financial crisis it made an effort to address such tasks as securing the voluntary actions of supported countries, simplifying the support conditions and considering the basic economic condition of supported countries, but there still seems to be no big difference in the IMF's current conditionality package (Lee 2008: 11)

The failure of the IMF's efforts to raise transparency and liability as part of the imposition of conditionality and the limited success of improving transparency in the governance structure of the IMF have provided the incentive to establish a new-style monetary fund in the region.

Intensifying the role of G20 and its limit

During the progress of the recent financial crisis stemming from the United States, the greatest help, which eased the anxiety in the international finance market and restored its normal function, came from the G20 Summit, not the IMF. The G20 was established in 1999 as a forum for information exchange and discussion among finance ministers and central bank governors of the developed countries and emerging economies. The G20 Summit was launched in November 2008 based on the proposal of Sarkozy, the French president, in August of that year. Its purpose was to provide international mutual assistance to prevent the global expansion of the financial crisis and discuss how to set up a new international finance and monetary order (Bretton Woods II). At the April

2009 London Summit held to cooperatively overcome the international finance crisis, various approaches were proposed, including the G20's taking over the function of the IMF and reform of IMF governance. It may be considered remarkable progress that the G20 presented a concrete action plan that includes intensification of cooperation in macro-economic policies, intensification of the financial supervisory function centred on FSB (Financial Stabilization Board), intensification of risk control over hedge funds and sharing information on tax avoidance. The action plan is classified as soft law, which is the basis of the major principles of international financial law. The tendency to use soft-law instruments comes from the fact that each country's legal norms are differently applied according to the development of the financial market in each country and from the fact that that all countries are taking a broad view of introducing international financial norms as the influence of the financial sector on the actual economy has increased.

The greatest weakness of the G20 is that it has not taken the form of traditional international organizations, so it cannot maintain continuous activities and has no power to make legally binding norms. Besides, the fact that the G20 has a relatively wide range of subject matter hinders the forum from playing a core role in international financial cooperation, compared to the IMF, which focuses

Table 4.1 Main points of financial cooperation action plan, G20 London Summit

Detailed fields	*Main points*
Intensification of mutual assistance in macro-economy	• agreeing on expansion of financial expenditure and extensional monetary policy • expanding loan support for emerging economies and poor countries • declaring avoidance of policies related to financial protectionism
Reform of international financial institutions	• establishing a financial stabilization committee • making efforts to improve the IMF quota and voting system • making efforts to implement the innovation plan for World Bank • securing financial resources and expansion of access limit related to intensification of support for developing countries and emerging economies
Intensification/ improvement of financial supervision and regulations	• checking the recommendations of the G20 according to the FSB and IMF • expanding BCBS member countries • intensifying hedge-fund risk control through registration and information dissemination • executing periodic supervision on credit rating agencies • intensifying supervision on risk taking of financial institutions' employees and compensation system • readjusting of accounting standards for financial instruments • operating the FSAP in order to raise the level of transparency in financial regulation

Source: www.G-20.org.

on economic and financial problems caused by the international payments imbalances. For the matters presented as an action plan by the G20 Summit to be complied with, they should be imposed through a multilateral international agreement. However, in reality, the recently announced action plan does not impose compulsory obligations on the participants.

The G20 recently addressed this, and it became a new global economic organization with norm-creating capacity. The G20 Pittsburg Summit in September 2009 gave birth to such capacity. At this Summit G20 member countries clarified the cooperative relationship of the G20 with the existing organizations, including IMF and FSB, and characterized itself as a premier forum for international economic cooperation that establishes norms in the world's financial markets, as it does now by holding regular summits.

The FSB has come into the spotlight in connection with the new role of the G20 in financial stability. The FSB is not an affiliated organization of the G20 as it was formed in the process whereby the FSF (Financial Stabilization Forum), established by the G7 in 1999, became a Board. But its prestige has been raised as it plays the reporting role on financial stability at the G20 Summit. Twenty-three countries and 12 related institutions, including IMF, BIS, OECD, the World Bank and IOSCO are members of the FSB.

The function of the FSB includes assessing vulnerabilities affecting the global financial system, promoting co-ordination and information exchange for financial stability, monitoring and advising for regulatory policy, setting guidelines for supervision, supporting contingency planning for cross-border crisis management, collaborating with the IMF to conduct early warning exercises and reporting to the International Monetary and Financial Committee (IMFC) and the G20 finance ministers and central bank governors on financial stability. Currently its prime function would be establishing guidelines for international financial supervision. While the G20 is mainly strengthening supervision on the world's financial markets after the financial crisis, FSB has been the actual executive office of the G20, and it has already been constituted as a new creator of financial norms by setting new guidelines. This does not mean that the FSB actually creates or proposes new norms, rather that it coordinates measures based on standards set by the IMF or BIS.

Despite the expanding role of the G20 and the FSB, these institutions mostly focus on removing unstable elements in global financial markets and the international mutual assistance system so that there is still a need for a financial cooperation system among East Asian countries in order to strengthen regional economic cooperation and regional currency order, as well as to prevent financial crisis in the region. There has been no flexible system in the region to support timely and flexible crisis management, as was witnessed in the Asian financial crisis in 1998, and the G20 would find it difficult to support in time as a result of the possibility of objection from members outside the region and/or delay in decision-making.

Establishment of an East Asian financial cooperation system and possibility of its intensification

East Asian financial cooperation: a brief history

Discussion of East Asian financial cooperation has a short history, with its roots in the Asian financial crisis of 1997 (B.-H. Cho 2006: 125; Cho 2008: 281). Discussions on the common interests of the countries in the region began in earnest with the outbreak of that crisis (Y.-S. Kim 2002: 353). The early discussion concerned the AMF, which was suggested by Miyazawa-Initiative from Japan at a conference held by the IMF in Hong Kong in 1998. However, discussions failed to progress because of objections by the advanced countries (mainly the USA) and the IMF on the grounds that it would not be helpful in stabilizing the international financial system (Choi 2006: 19; Fukushima 2004: 11–12).

However, the necessity of a new financial cooperation system in the East Asian region had already been widely recognized, so the effort to develop a financial cooperation plan kept going even after the failure of the AMF initiative.

At the summit meeting of ASEAN+3 countries, held in Manila in 1999, the head of each country agreed on the need to prevent a currency crisis in the region through mutual assistance. In order to give shape to this plan, the finance ministers of ASEAN countries and the three major countries in East Asia, namely Korea, Japan and China, got together in Chiang Mai in 2000. A Chiang Mai Initiative was announced, which aimed at the conclusion of currency swap agreements among the countries in the region, so that foreign exchange liquidity could be supplied quickly in the event of a financial crisis in the region in the future. In July 2001, Korea and Japan concluded a bilateral currency swap agreement, and similar agreements between Korea and China and China and Japan were concluded in June 2002 and March 2002, respectively.

Besides such fund-raising effort to supply liquidity in an emergency, a joint supervision system for financial stability, namely the economic review and policy dialogue (ERPD), was established, and the international mutual assistance system was intensified in the region so that it might present a proper countermeasure in case of international financial market instability, or prepare policy means to prevent such cases. In addition, besides the establishment of fund-raising and supervision systems, the Asian Bond Market Initiative was declared as a means of activating the bond market in the region, and the Asian Bond Fund was established as a demand-side measure to promote the Initiative.

Development of the Chiang Mai Initiative and directions for the future

The Chiang Mai Initiative (henceforth referred to as CMI) has proved to be the starting point for East Asian financial cooperation. There used to be a system called ASA (ASEAN Swap Arrangement) (Jo 2004: 11) among ASEAN member countries, in which a short-term loan was provided to countries that needed capital as a result of insufficient liquidity and current account deficit. However, after the

Asian financial crisis of 1997 the CMI became the major monetary cooperation system as Korea, China and Japan took part in the economic cooperation process under the name of ASEAN+3. Considering the characteristics of the cooperation system, it can be said that the CMI is a network of bilateral agreements, through which a specific support scale and support conditions were designated. While the ASA carries out small-scale fund support based on the multilateral agreement, the scale of financial resources committed under the CMI has reached US$120 billion.

When a funding is offered through the bilateral swap agreement network established by the CMI, 80 per cent of the total amount of swap transaction, excluding 20 per cent of the amount, is provided with the consent of the IMF. The initial swap period is 90 days, and it can be renewed six times within a maximum period of two years where appropriate (Yun 2005: 56).

A number of issues need to be addressed for the CMI system to be established as the financial cooperation scheme in the region.

First, the uncertainty of implementation of bilateral swap agreements. This meant that the fund provider took no legal responsibility for the supply of funds. Whether or not to provide fund support was a matter of the supplier's own free will, despite the existence of a bilateral agreement (Yun 2005: 56). From a legal point of view, swap agreements were not in the form of a treaty which was legally binding between the parties, but in the form of a contractual agreement between central banks. This implies that the swap agreement is not a nation-to-nation treaty, but a person-to-person contract. Accordingly, it was difficult in reality to secure the binding force of the agreement. Therefore, bilateral swap agreements had to be converted into multilateral agreements, and parts of their content related to implementation into legal obligations. At the Eighth ASEAN+3 Finance Ministers' Meeting held in May 2005, the participants agreed on conversion to CMI-Multilateralization (CMIM), and also agreed on the introduction of a collective decision-making mechanism into the CMI system as a mid-stage thereto (ASEAN+3 Finance Ministers' Meeting 2005). The official launch of CMI-Multilateralization was carried out at the Twelfth ASEAN+3 Financial Ministers' Meeting in May 2009, in Bali. In this manner, the swap agreement, which used to be characterized as contracts between central banks, can now be used as an official multilateral treaty to raise funds. Two core factors are included in the swap agreement. One is the allotted amount and the other the method of decision-making. The ratio of allotted amount may exert a great influence on the direction of funds, as it implies the influence of each country in the CMIM see Table 4.2). The legitimacy of decision-making for fund operation is secured by the adoption of consensus on fundamental issues and of majority decision on lending issues (see Table 4.3).

Based on the CMI-Multilateralization, it may be assumed that the CMI is functioning as the AMF in certain limited aspects and fields. But an operational system still needs to be put in place, including an executive office, so as to change the CMI into the AMF (Oh and Oh 2009: 3). Furthermore, in order to secure the legitimacy of the funding under the CMI-Multilateralization, it needs to be accompanied by efforts to increase transparency and avoid moral

Table 4.2 The structure of CMIM

Country	*Contribution (billion dollars)*	*Borrowing multiplier compared with contribution (borrowing multiple)*
Brunei	0.03	5
Cambodia	0.12	5
China:		
excluding Hong Kong	34.2	0.5
Hong Kong	4.2	2.5
Indonesia	4.77	2.5
Japan	38.4	0.5
Korea	19.2	1
Laos	0.03	5
Malaysia	4.77	2.5
Myanmar	0.06	5
The Philippines	3.68	2.5
Singapore	4.77	2.5
Thailand	4.77	2.5
Vietnam	1.00	5

Source: Twelfth ASEAN+3 Finance Ministers' Meeting summary (press release, Ministry of Strategy and Finance of Korea, 3 May 2009).

Table 4.3 Decision-making rules of CMIM

	Agenda	*Decision-making rule*
Fundamental issues	Total scale, contribution, benefit compared with contribution Review of borrowing multiplier Readmission and membership Conditions for financial support, etc.	Consensus (unanimity)
Lending issues	Financial support, renewal, declaration of default	By majority

Source: Twelfth ASEAN+3 Finance Ministers' Meeting summary (press release, Ministry of Strategy and Finance of Korea, 3 May 2009).

hazard. It is natural that careful reviews of the macroeconomic system of the borrowing country would provide the data on which fund support is decided. It thus follows that requesting, providing and opening up of data, in a process similar to that required by the IMF, must be carried out, and a function to analyse the provided data must be established (Yun 2005: 58). A dispute settlement unit would, additionally, be needed to handle disputes over violations of multilateralized agreements.

The small amount of fund supply is another problem. The amount has just reached US$120 billion. Given that the integration of financial markets has been accelerated thanks to the increase in financial cooperation in the region and considering the growth potential of financial markets in the region, this may be regarded as insufficient.

The condition for lending poses another problem. The amount available without consent of the IMF is a mere 20 per cent of the total swap size (ASEAN+3 2005: Article 6(IV)), and the lending of the remaining 80 per cent is accompanied by the IMF conditionality. However, bearing in mind that the purpose of establishing financial cooperation in the region was mainly related to the complicated conditionality under the existing emergency lending of the IMF, it seems contradictory that much of fund support must still comply with the conditionality. This is closely related to the problem mentioned earlier of fund amount. If this system continues to operate with the present limited amount and with conditionality, the system will function only as a subsidiary of the IMF lending. This brings another issue. The fact that the funding free from the conditionality of the IMF remains at the 20 per cent level may result in the fund's limited capability in crisis prevention. Support from the IMF is available only when a crisis becomes a reality, so when the support is ready, the market has already lost its function, and the support mainly focuses on restoration from the crisis. However, the regional monetary cooperation aims at crisis prevention in addition to restoration. The current rate of 20 per cent is, therefore, regarded as too small to achieve such goals (Sohn 2007: 3). On the other hand, it is assumed that the connection between the IMF and CMIM has a positive aspect as well. It raises the credibility of the CMIM, and it helps enhance the cooperation between the CMIM and other international financial institutions, including the IMF.

As for cooperation with other international financial institutions, including the IMF, the CMIM has clearly stated that it is carrying out a supplementary role to the existing international financial institutions, including the IMF, through cooperative relationships. It must be acknowledged that, in reality, the IMF is a core mediator in the global financial market; it is the root and the trunk of international financial cooperation. As long as regional financial support measures taken in East Asia have an effect as a result of financial globalization, it is reasonable to recognize the prestige of the IMF. However, it is still necessary to convert the relationship between the CMIM and IMF into a strategic partnership because the chief purpose of the CMIM is to get over the problems caused by the instability and the insufficiency of the programmes addressing liquidity crises provided by the existing international financial institutions. As a concrete strategy, it may be suggested that the amount of funding the CMIM can determine by itself should be expanded, and at the same time, the amount of funding, its area of application and the level of conditionality should be determined by the CMIM in which the IMF participates, according to the situation of the borrowing country. The only caveat to this strategy is that the more the amount free from conditionality increases, the greater the possibility of moral hazard, so there need to be countermeasures to prevent such moral hazards (Grimes 2006: 5).

Cultivation of the Asian bond market

The development of a bond market may form a foundation for smooth flows of funds and promotion of transnational transactions because it corresponds to the development of a fund-raising market for the relevant countries or enterprises. In the long run, it will also contribute to the cultivation of a bond market for the development of regional finance (Herring 2000: 11). One important issue to be addressed in the development of a bond market is the problem of mismatch which is contained in bonds. In reality, the Asian bond markets, except for Japan, have a double risk, defined as 'currency and maturity mismatch' because of the underdevelopment of bond markets (Sun 2004: 5). Actually the problem of mismatch was partly responsible for the Asian financial crisis of 1997 (Park 2006: 116)

Effective management of the abundant foreign exchange reserve in Korea, China and Japan was another objective of the development of a bond market in the region. The Asian Bond Markets Initiative (ABMI) and Asian Bond Fund (ABF) were discussed for the first time in 2002, by the member nations of EMEAP (Executives' Meeting of East Asia and Pacific Central Banks).

The ABMI has been playing the supply-side role in the cultivation of Asian bond markets. The ABMI aims at the establishment of the Asian Guaranty Facility, credit-rating agencies and regional settlement and clearing systems, which also aimed at eliminating transaction barriers and promoting contributions from participants as substructures.

Another important element in bond market cultivation is the demand side, purchasing power. The ABF was set up in consideration of this. Though lots of high-quality bonds are issued in the region, they will not activate the bond market unless they can be purchased. In this respect, the ABF has a different function from currency swaps, which aims at supplying liquidity to central banks in a financial crisis. The ABF is composed of the ABF1 (launched in 2003), which invests in dollar-denominated bonds, and the ABF2 (launched in 2005), which invests in local currency-denominated bonds.

The legal form of the ABF may be defined as the in-house fund of BIS, which has been entrusted with the management of the fund. There are several reasons why the ABF is the in-house fund of the BIS. Besides the consideration of security and raising its credit rating making use of the fame of BIS, the biggest reason was whether the amount invested in the ABF could be accepted as a foreign exchange reserve. The amount invested in the ABF was defined as other foreign currency assets and classified as a kind of claim (Park 2006: 129). In order to be accepted as a foreign exchange reserve, it had to meet the standards set out in the IMF's *International Reserves and Foreign Currency Liquidity* (Kester 2001: 2–3). According to this, the conditions of liquidity and marketability, financing of payment imbalance and currency convertibility must be met, but once a participant invests in the ABF, an immediate encashment is not allowed. In other words, the problem occurs in liquidity and marketability. Therefore, in order to solve this problem the EMEAP has prepared a system where redemption can be carried out by asking the BIS for the redemption of the asset at any time.

Since the ABF1 invested in dollar-denominated bonds, there was no problem in currency convertibility. However, in the case of the ABF2, which consist of local-currency-denominated bonds, problems occurred on both sides. In light of this, ABF2 also designated the BIS as a legal investment body, and the participating countries obtained shares from the investment account of the BIS. Therefore, when a participating country wants to withdraw funds, it can secure them by selling shares from the BISIP (BIS Investment Pool) of the BIS (Park 2006: 129–36). When cooperation in the East Asian bond market makes progress and the ABF comes to operate as an independent fund, not the in-house fund of the BIS, these issues of currency convertibility will have to be solved as a priority issue.

Another important issue in connection with the cultivation of the Asian bond markets is the unification of legal institutions. The uniformity of regulatory systems and rearrangement of regulations in tax laws, including accounting systems, may be regarded as preconditions (Sun 2004: 11). As for the accounting system and tax laws, the key issue is the double process of taxation on capital income and taxation on dividends. Profit sharing based on fund operation and taxation standards for capital income vary from country to country, and this functions as a barrier to free transactions of bonds. As for bond issuing for non-residents, it is not necessary to set up unified regulations as bond issuing is regulated in compliance with the domestic law of each country (Yokoi-Arai 2006: 67–9). Besides this, however, regulatory integration is difficult because the level of regulation varies considerably reflecting the degree of development of bond markets. Accordingly, it may take time to bring the regulations in the region to the same level. In addition, because provision of a settlement and liquidation function in connection with bond transactions is a compulsory requirement for the establishment of a bond market, standardization of settlement systems is also a task to be settled.

Intensification of the function of the ERPD (Economic Review and Policy Dialogue)

The ERPD is an organization established to intensify policy discussion, coordination and cooperation in the management of financial, monetary and fiscal affairs among member nations of ASEAN+3. Its main functions include macroeconomic risk management, monitoring capital flow, intensification of financial systems and promotion of cooperation in the region. It is working as a regional cooperation system, with a limited function as a regional monetary cooperation forum (B.-H. Cho 2006: 131).

One of the featured functions of ERPD is monitoring the flow of short-term capitals. This is because the movement of short-term funds will proliferate when regional financial cooperation proceeds and the regional financial market is opened up. For example, if the Asian bond market is opened up according to the cultivation scenario, inflow and outflow of non-residents' short-term capital will be permitted. This may cause a problem of capital imbalance as a result of the movement of short-term capital. Accordingly, without the introduction of a proper regulation of such capital movement that is not limited to merely monitoring transactions, it might bring about a great microeconomic setback. It follows, therefore, that monitoring the market against speculative funds, proper control of such funds and a mechanism of cooperation to deal with such funds are compulsory functions of the ERPD.

However, like other financial cooperation systems in East Asia, the ERPD is nothing but an entity based on agreement for financial cooperation in the regional market, so it neither retains a corporate personality nor has the form of an international organization. Being an entity based on cooperative agreement, a limitation is placed on the ability of the ERPD to promote positive cooperation in the macroeconomic policy and financial supervision in the region, and create normative guidelines. So, if substantial progress and intensification of Asian financial cooperation are to take place, the ERPD may need to be included in the AMF, or converted into an official organization in the region.

Establishment of the AMF and its relationship with the existing international financial institutions

There are various standpoints for or against the establishment of the AMF. Opponents' main grounds lie in the fact that it would be difficult to unify regulation of the international finance market if the AMF were to be established. They argue that if the IMF and AMF were to take opposing standpoints, the influence would be reduced by half and harm done to the international financial order. On the other hand, the major basis of arguments for the establishment of the AMF lies first in the contention that the function of the IMF as the Lender of Last Resort cannot supply enough liquidity in case of multiple financial crises; second that a foreign exchange crisis spreads through a region in the first stage and those most damaged are the countries in the region; and third that a regional institution has access to better information about the region. In short, they argue that the regional institutions can provide countermeasures that are faster and more suitable for the region than other institutions (Fukasaku *et al.* 2004: 289–345). It seems that everybody in the region recognizes the need for an AMF. However, so far there has been no concrete discussion about how to design its status, function and relationship with existing international financial institutions.

It is very important to decide how to build up the function of the AMF. This is because the role of a regional organization is decided by what function is given to it, and according to that function its relationship with the existing international organizations is defined.

As an international monetary fund, the function of the AMF seems not much different from that of the IMF. In general, compared to the function of the IMF, the functions that the AMF should have may be Lender of Last Resort in the region, carrying out various statistical surveys and offering guidelines for exchange rate stability. The currency swap based on the CMIM may be achieved by expanding the function of the AMF as Lender of Last Resort. And the function of surveillance (Y.-S. Kim 2002: 364) and statistical surveys can be achieved by expanding the function of the ERPD. However, whether to include an additional role which the IMF does not have now but is making efforts to obtain, namely financial supervision, is something that needs to be reviewed carefully.

The IMF currently shows much interest in the field of financial supervision. As there exists no integrated international organization for financial supervision, international supervision of soundness of banks and securities companies are conducted by the BIS and the IOSCO, respectively. However, as the integration of capital markets has become the worldwide trend and the need for integrated international supervision arises, imposing the role of financial supervision on the AMF may be regarded as an effective measure for the stabilization of the Asian financial market. On the other hand, if the AMF is to carry out a function similar to the IMF and other financial supervisory organizations, its relationship with such organizations will become very important. And in order to enhance financial supervision, a cooperative relationship should be established among them, rather than concentrating the supervisory function on a single organization (Y.-S. Kim 2002: 364).

Regional FTA and acceleration of financial cooperation

Today, with the degree of dependence upon trade among regional countries increasing year after year, East Asian countries, including Korea, China and Japan, are showing great interest in the conclusion of FTAs among them. So far, Korea, China and Japan have focused on the conclusion of FTAs with Southeast Asian countries, but these three countries have for several years been carrying out internal reviews of the promotion of FTAs. If Korea, China and Japan promote FTAs in the region, it will effectively bring about the establishment of a free trade area in the ASEAN+3 region. And if the financial service sector liberalization is included in the FTA, it will result in a broader scope of regional financial cooperation. This is because the opening up of the market will be accompanied by institutional cooperation, so that barriers in terms of law may be eliminated and comparable regulatory systems will naturally encourage institutional integration (Sohn 2004: 31).

If an FTA includes the financial services sector liberalization, the mutual opening of financial sectors will bring the integration of institutions into shared financial markets, as well as promoting capital movement, so it may help countries

Table 4.4 Present status of FTA promotion by Korea, China and Japan in the Asian region

	Conclusion and agreement	*Under negotiation or joint study*
Korea	Singapore, ASEAN	Japan, Thailand, Malaysia, China
Japan	Singapore, Malaysia, Philippines, Thailand, Brunei, Indonesia, Vietnam, ASEAN	Korea
China	ASEAN, Hong Kong, Macao, Singapore, Thailand	Korea

Source: Data from Asia Regional Integration center (http://aric.adb.org/FTAbyCountryAll.php) (accessed 15 June 2009).

reach the same level of regulation or regulatory policies. Moreover, financial cooperation through FTAs brings about the intensification of policy cooperation and change in systems, by presenting the need for joint actions against the side-effects of the free movement of capital in the region, namely the rapid change in capital balance caused by short-term capital movements.

Japan is promoting a CEPEA (Comprehensive Economic Partnership in East Asia), while Korea and China are promoting an EAFTA (East Asia Free Trade Agreement) of ASEAN+3 (Kim 2007: 167). They share many ideas, since both initiatives promote a comprehensive FTA in the region. However, the promotion of these initiatives is expected to face a lot of difficulties because the agricultural sector occupies a very important status in regional FTAs. In fact, when Japan thoroughly reviewed the FTA as an international trade strategy in 1999, the Ministry of International Trade and Industry reported that they would change their strategy to FTA in the White Paper, but the Ministry of Agriculture, Forest and Fisheries and JA (Japan Agricultural Co-operatives) were firmly against it (Jin 2005: 63). In the case of Korea, similar evidence exists, since agricultural issues, including US beef in the negotiation of the US–Korea FTA, have caused a lot of conflict. Therefore, in the process of expanding the FTA network within East Asia, such controversial topics should be addressed.

Discussions about the possibility of introducing a common currency system

The final stage of currency and financial cooperation would be the establishment of a common currency system like the euro. According to Mundell (1961: 509–17), the East Asian region has enough factors to build up a common currency bloc (see Asian Development Bank 2002; Rana 2002; Srinivas 2002; Lee *et al.* 2002). But there are both positive and negative evaluations as to whether to introduce a common currency system. As positive factors, there are some indications of benefits from a common currency system, such as reduction in transaction costs in regional trade and capital movement, avoidance of risks resulting from changes in exchange rate, benefits from a synergy effect based on the integration of financial markets and reduction of financial costs. In addition, the indirect function of dispute control in the region may be included in the positive evaluation. On the other hand, negative aspects are also expected, such as loss of business cycle control as a result of handover of currency sovereignty, limitation in available countermeasures in cases of economic emergency because of the loss of Lender of Last Resort function and the loss of seigniorage (Ahn 2004: 86).

The establishment of a common currency system implies that common currency credit policy, foreign exchange policy and macroeconomic policy have been achieved. In this process, currency sovereignty of each country is transferred to, and the foreign exchange reserve belongs to, the newly established Asian Central Bank. And like the Stability and Growth Pact in the European Currency Community, each country's liberty may be limited in the area of fiscal policy, including limitation in the size of fiscal deficit. It is natural, therefore, that there will be a sharp confrontation over the interests of participating countries which will require a lengthy and gradual approach to the whole question (Choi 2007: 140).

On the subject of a gradual approach, in the case of the EU, the participants proposed a transition period during which the institutional details of the currency system would be crystallized, which meant that the process could be undertaken gradually. The amendment of the legal system in each country was achieved through the EC Treaty and a series of regulations and directives (EWI 1998). In particular, the soundness of the fiscal operation, the construction of the foreign exchange rate mechanism and the independence of the central bank were the core components of the process.

Current measures for financial cooperation in Asia indirectly and directly relate to the common monetary system. Notably, the CMI-Multilateralization (CMIM) could cope with a currency crisis within the region through common financial resources, and this indicates that it could also perform a role as a Lender of Last Resort under the common monetary system. In addition, with the existence of researchers or councils related to ERPD, there is an opportunity to establish an institute like the EMI (European Monetary Institute), a temporary institute established to prepare european currency union. It has also been suggested that the bonds denominated in ACU (Asian Currency Unit) should be issued in the form of a basket currency, so as to promote an Asian bond market. So, there remains a possibility that the ACU could be used before the common currency is introduced.

As seen above, the idea of a common currency system has enough viability, and it is recognized in that way, so the necessary measures on the path to a common currency system are coming into being indirectly in the process of regional financial cooperation. However, competition between the yuan and yen as a common currency might hamper efforts to establish Asian financial cooperation, bearing in mind the rivalry of China and Japan on political and historical issues. China's efforts to make the yuan a key currency were given a boost at the international symposium hosted by the Hong Kong Currency Bureau, (15–16 October 2007) and Japan has been making similar efforts. But the choices of these countries will be the biggest issues in establishing the Asian common currency system (Choi 2006: 17).

Conclusion

The essential framework for East Asian financial cooperation may be divided into four stages. The first stage includes bilateral currency swap agreements, the second multilateral currency swap agreement, the third the Asian Monetary Fund and the last is the Asian Common Currency System. The current stage of Asian financial cooperation seems to have passed the first stage and is in transit to the second.

Looking into the four stages of development, in institutional terms we are dealing with a process where systems with different standards within financial sectors are developing a single standard. It may not be too wide of the mark to suggest that the point of contact may be found in the standard schemes of international financial institutions like the IMF. However, it must be expected that there will be a fierce debate.

On the other hand, historical and political problems constitute another obstacle to the development of financial cooperation in East Asia. In particular, the historical and political conflict between Korea, China and Japan seems to be a great obstacle to the construction of a system for Asian financial cooperation. For East Asian financial cooperation to become a reality, exchanges and close cooperation need to be brought into play, in addition to substantial financial cooperation among the three countries.

5 East Asian financial integration: a road ahead

Ross P. Buckley

ASEAN comprises ten countries: Brunei, Cambodia, Indonesia, Malaysia, Laos, Myanmar, the Philippines, Singapore, Thailand and Vietnam. Its people number some 570 million (McLean 2009: 20). Its combined GDP is only half as much again as Australia's, or about a third of China's (Basic ASEAN Indicators, June 2009). Yet it thinks big. The grouping aims to become an EU-style economic community without the common currency by 2015 (ASEAN 2007).

This, to me, is empty rhetoric. The European Union was underpinned by the need to combat profound security threats that ravaged Europe twice last century and for much of the preceding centuries. The security imperative that drove union in Europe is not present in East Asia, the decades of groundwork that paved the way for union in Europe have not been undertaken in East Asia and, as an idea, East Asian union does not appear to have anything like the profile or support that European union had even 20 years before it came to pass, let alone in the handful of years remaining until 2015.

Indeed I wonder whether the concept of 'Asia' today is as strong as the concept of 'Europe' was 30 or 40 years ago. The core European countries were bound by a common religion and a long history of fluid borders. China's borders are essentially similar today to what they were 2,000 years ago. The Vietnamese see their history as a separate people stretching back 4,000 years. 'Asia' today is perhaps a concept used more often by those outside the region seeking to define or constrain it, than by those within the region seeking to understand it.

So, for what it is worth, I think political union is a long way off. However, closer economic and financial integration is a different matter. Closer economic integration is proceeding apace. Closer financial integration is realizable and much needed; it may also, eventually, serve as part of the groundwork for political union.

Closer financial integration is realizable because East Asia has the world's largest foreign exchange reserves, highest savings rates and most dynamic economies.

Closer financial integration is much needed because the Washington Consensus policies promulgated by the International Monetary Fund (IMF) and World Bank have been a conspicuous failure in promoting development, and just when the need for economic growth is at its highest in the aftermath of the global financial crisis, there is a vacuum in the International Financial Institutions (IFIs) as to the policy settings likely to promote it. Such integration is also desperately needed because over the past two decades, 'capital-account crises have been the norm rather than the exception' (Bird and Rajan 2006: 336). Its massive savings as a region give East Asia more options in dealing with global capital than most regions have, and provide greater opportunity to interact with global capital on its own terms.

A virtuous cycle is potentially achievable here. Greater regional integration of financial systems through an Asian Monetary Fund (AMF) should lead to greater regional stability; which should lead to more of these savings, both individual and sovereign, staying in Asia; which should, in turn, lead to even more regional stability. The great paradox of the East Asian crisis of 1997 was that it was brought on by foreign capital losing confidence in a region with the world's highest savings rates. If East Asia could have kept its money at home, it never would have needed foreign capital, and there would have been no chance of a crisis provoked by an exodus of foreign capital.

The region, especially with China's rise as 'factory for the world', has seen increasing levels of trade and economic integration. Many manufacturing processes today are centred in China but combine inputs from throughout the region in a hub and spoke system in which other nations contribute in their areas of comparative advantage to the Chinese production.

Trade integration has continued apace. ASEAN and China entered into a Framework Agreement on Comprehensive Economic Cooperation in 2002 and another agreement on trade in goods in 2004. Under these agreements a free trade area came into effect between China and ASEAN's five founding members and Brunei from 1 January 2010, and will be extended to embrace ASEAN's other four members by 2015 (ASEAN 2010). In February 2009 ASEAN entered into a free trade agreement (FTA) with Australia and New Zealand covering trade in goods, services, e-commerce, the movement of persons and investment.

The region is developing a 'noodle bowl' of regional and bilateral trade agreements. For instance, in the case of Australia as well as the agreement with ASEAN and New Zealand considered above, there are bilateral agreements with Thailand, New Zealand and Singapore and ongoing negotiations for over 4 years and 13 rounds on a proposed Australia–China FTA and for 2 years and 8 rounds on a proposed Australia–Japan FTA. In the interests of trade, and especially administrative, efficiency one can but hope that one day this noodle bowl of different agreements will be replaced by one free trade area extending from New Zealand to China and South Korea to Australia and embracing all the nations within the East Asian region (and perhaps even India) (Asian Development Bank 2008a: 7, 181).

However, the financial integration of the region has lagged far behind its economic and trade integration. In the words of an IMF study:

> [I]ntraregional financial integration – for example measured directly by cross-border capital flows or indirectly by cross-border correlation of consumption growth – has been more limited than elsewhere. Consequently, Asian economies appear to have become more integrated with countries outside the region than within the region. (Cowen and Salgado 2006: 4)

The seminal event, in terms of East Asian financial integration, was the East Asian financial crisis of 1997–8. It had two immediate consequences. First, because no Asian organization was able to provide support to any Asian state it led 'to the irony that Indonesia, South Korea and Thailand faced an invasiveness towards national policymaking, especially through credit conditions, that was contrary to all ASEAN precepts' (Arner, Lejot and Wang 2009: 13). This experience caused financial cooperation to replace trade cooperation as the number-one regional priority. To this day, the changes to domestic policies which the IMF forced upon countries as the price of the bailouts, and the profound extent to which the IMF initially misdiagnosed the causes of the crisis, are deeply resented throughout the region.

Second, it brought into being the ASEAN+3 grouping, comprising the ten ASEAN nations plus China, Japan and Korea. ASEAN+3 had its first summit in Kuala Lumpur in December 1997. In a short time frame, ASEAN+3 supplanted APEC as the principal economic organization within the region (Arner, Lejot and Wang 2009: 23). Since then ASEAN+6 (which includes Australia, India and New Zealand) has been developed, in part at the urging of smaller states seeking counterweights to the potential influence of China, and to a lesser extent, Japan (Arner, Lejot and Wang 2009: 16).

In the immediate aftermath of the East Asian crisis in 1997 Japan offered to fund the establishment of an Asian Monetary Fund, but the idea met stern opposition from the United States and the IMF, and a lack of support from China, and was dropped (Lipsey 2003). In its place, the much less ambitious Chiang Mai Initiative was pursued, a series of bilateral commitments by which regional nations committed to make bilateral swap arrangements and security repurchase agreements available to each other in times of need.

Over time the size of the bilateral swap arrangements were steadily expanded, while the potentially useful repo arrangements were ignored and never really used. This slow trend received a huge boost in February 2009, when the swap agreements were multilateralized and increased by US$40 billion to US$120 billion in an agreement among ASEAN+3 finance ministers known as the Multilateralized Chiang Mai Initiative (MCMI). China, Japan and Korea are to provide 80 per cent of these commitments, with the balance to come from ASEAN nations. Recent research suggests that the pre-2008 bilateral swap agreements were used in broadly efficient ways (Kohlscheen and Taylor 2008: 330). The MCMI should be far more efficient and effective, because the commitments will be multilateral.

Under the MCMI, Indonesia would be able to draw, as of right, about five times as much as under their official IMF reserve tranches (although in practice the IMF often exceeds these official levels of lending) and the Philippines six times as much as the official IMF commitments (Kohlscheen and Taylor 2008: 324).

With the implementation of the MCMI in March 2010, regional nations will have, for the first time, what they needed in late 1997: a credible alternative to the credit lines extended by the IMF. However, the MCMI credit lines are not genuine alternatives, because 80 per cent of the amounts available for drawing thereunder are not available unless a nation has an IMF programme in place. In this case, therefore, even if the MCMI had been in place in 1997, 80 per cent of the funds could not have been disbursed when most needed, in a timely fashion, as IMF negotiations dragged on for months.

The apparent reason for conditioning MCMI credit upon an IMF programme is that to date the MCMI has not had any real surveillance capacity. The commitments made in February 2009 address this issue: 'An independent regional surveillance unit will be established to promote objective economic monitoring' (ASEAN+3 2009).

It is easy to be optimistic about the MCMI. Yet it is today nothing more than a series of commitments, by an organization, ASEAN, which doesn't have a strong record of turning commitments into concrete achievements. While the MCMI has come into effect, concrete commitments are yet to be made, with the credit and reserve pooling commitments still to be agreed (Lejot 2011). The temptation to excessive optimism is large, because the MCMI is so needed and the institution to which it would logically be the precursor, so important. For a series of substantial credit lines coupled to a serious surveillance (and thus advice-giving) capacity is very close to a monetary fund, in this case, an Asian Monetary Fund. And it is the prospect of an Asian Monetary Fund that excites the imagination of those who care about the region, and its potential to chart its own economic course and contribute to global prosperity.

So the first step is to temper our optimism and recognize that the realization of the MCMI commitments is, given ASEAN's track record, likely to take some years. Its success will require a willingness to either share sovereignty or to allow one state to design and lead the initiative (Arner, Lejot and Wang 2009: 49), and there is precious little in the history of ASEAN, in the more than four decades since its inception, to suggest either of these paths will be anything but difficult.

Still these are sound reasons to explore, analyse and invest intellectual capital into the idea of an Asian Monetary Fund, not to dismiss it as unlikely to come to pass.

An Asian Monetary Fund

The nations of East Asia have enjoyed decades of extraordinary and sustained growth. For over 20 years China has grown at an average rate above 9 per cent, Malaysia, Singapore and South Korea have all grown at annual average rates above 6 per cent and Taiwan and Thailand at 5.5 per cent and 5.9 per cent respectively (Ghosh 2005; CIA 2009; Economist Intelligence Unit 1993, 1995). When Japan was outperforming the world, from 1950 to 1965, its economy expanded on average at over 10.4 per cent per annum (Beida 1970: 12).

China is today the second largest economy in the world in purchasing power parity (PPP) terms, the terms that economists generally accept are best used for comparative purposes, and the third largest economy in unadjusted US dollar terms (Seager 2010). China's GDP on a PPP basis in 2008 was $7,916 billion and its per capita GDP on the same PPP terms was $5,963. This compares to $14,625 billion and $46,859 for the US (IMF 2009).

If the same policies had worked in each of these East Asian nations and differed from those of the Washington Consensus we would have a neat, simple story. But real life is rarely neat. As H. L. Mencken wrote, 'There is always an easy solution to every human problem – neat, plausible and wrong' (1917). Indeed, the inherent and deeply embedded diversity of nations is part of the problem with the Washington Consensus – its one-size-fits-all mindset, in truth, fits very few countries.

The policies that have delivered success to different East Asian nations over time have varied, considerably, from one another, but one of the commonalities has been a much larger role for government in most of these countries than is permitted under the Washington Consensus. Certainly Japan has consistently preferred regulatory approaches 'that rein in rather than let loose market forces' (Lipsey 2003: 100). Indeed, the only East Asian country to consistently follow Washington Consensus policies fairly closely has been Hong Kong (treating it as a separate economy for these purposes).

China has followed the classic development path of moving from an agriculture-based economy into manufacturing, initially simple manufacturing such as clothing and footwear, and then ever more sophisticated manufacturing, to the point that today China is the 'factory for the world', the way the North of England was in the early years of the industrial revolution. The 'final' stage on this classic path, followed by developed countries, is the further transition into a services-based economy.

For most of the past 25 years China has been a command economy. Even today China is perhaps best described as a soft authoritarian system. Certainly it is a very different political system to the democracies of most East Asian nations. For an example of the role of the state in China's economy consider that, as recently as 2004, state-owned enterprises accounted for over 50 per cent of China's GDP and over 40 per cent of its exports (Ghosh 2005).

These different paths and systems have been supported and reinforced by the differences between the financial systems in each country. China has retained state control of its financial sector and has used this control to manage the economic cycle and to direct funds to priority sectors of the economy, precisely as it is doing today to combat the Global Financial Crisis (GFC). Most other East Asian nations have relatively low levels of state ownership generally and of their financial sector in particular (Ghosh 2005). Accordingly, their financial sectors have not provided government with a tiller with which to direct, and control, the economy as has China's.

China has invested significantly in education of late, and is increasing this investment rapidly. According to Premier Wen Jiabao's state-of-the-nation address in March 2008, the central Chinese government quadrupled health spending in 2007 and lifted spending on education by 76 per cent. The premier promised to lift health spending a further 25 per cent and education spending a further 45 per cent in the next year, and also promised steep increases in social welfare spending. These expenditure increases were underpinned by sharp increases in government revenues, up nearly 35 per cent in 2007 (Garnaut 2008: 9). The GFC has since curtailed these revenue gains, but the direction is clear.

These funding increases in China come atop a solid base: 74 per cent of young people of school age were in school in China in 2005 (World Bank 2009).

Furthermore, in China girls are as likely to be in school as boys, which is reflected in literacy rates. In China 99 per cent of young women between 15 and 24 are literate.

Education is critical for growth. China's investment in education means that its deep pool of workers has been able to make the transition into manufacturing jobs because their education has enabled the transition. This large workforce is able to supply labour to the manufacturing industry, and equipped to do so by massive state investment in education – not a condition for development repeated in many developing states.

There are few investments that generate as strong returns for a developing nation as investing in the health and education of its children (Lustig 1998, 2000). China's current spending priorities suggest it understands this, deeply. As Susan George wrote 20 years ago, 'The IMF cannot seem to understand that investing in … [a] healthy, well-fed, literate population … is the most intelligent economic choice a country can make' (George 1990: 143, 187, 235). Recent IMF and World Bank practice suggests the IFIs are still to learn this lesson (Buckley 2009).

The Washington Consensus policies

The focus of the Washington Consensus policies has been to grow the debtor's economy, so as to alleviate poverty within the country and generate sufficient foreign exchange resources to service its debts. It has been taken as axiomatic that higher growth rates lead to less poverty, that higher growth rates are only possible once economic stabilization has been achieved and that higher growth is best achieved on the back of exports, not increases in domestic demand. The policies imposed to achieve these goals typically included:

- reductions in the budget deficit to limit inflation and the need for foreign borrowing;
- limits on domestic credit expansion to control inflation;
- exchange rate devaluations to discourage imports and encourage exports;
- liberalization of tariff and quota regimes;
- a much reduced role for government and a much increased role for markets.

Other Washington Consensus policies imposed on debtors, at times, included (i) higher income and sales taxes; (ii) higher charges for state-produced goods and services such as electricity and water; (iii) privatization of state-owned companies; and (iv) deregulation of the labour market. These policies have been criticized for their adverse effect on economic growth and their devastating effect upon the living standard of the local people, particularly the poor (Bello 1994; Green 1995; Beeson and Islam 2005; Dosi, Imoli and Stiglitz 2009).

The Washington Consensus has encouraged export-led growth for developing countries (Palley 1999). However, a reliance on exports exposes developing countries to the vagaries of demand in developed and other developing countries and to the extreme volatility of global commodity prices. A better policy admits of a larger role for domestic demand-led growth. In Palley's words, '[t]his is a strategy that lifts all boats since demand growth in one country pulls in exports from others, so that all grow together' (Palley 1999). The final word on the Washington Consensus goes to Professor Hal Scott: 'there is little evidence that IMF conditions, usually requiring contractionary fiscal and monetary policies, have worked' (Scott 2003: 115).

To understand how the IMF came to have, as its primary role, the direction of the economies of debtor nations in crisis and the implementation, therefore, of the Washington Consensus, it is necessary to understand its history.

A brief history of the IMF

According to its website, the IMF was founded, along with the World Bank, in 1945 to:

> promote international monetary cooperation, exchange stability, and orderly exchange arrangements; to foster economic growth and high levels of employment; and to provide temporary financial assistance to countries to help ease balance of payments adjustment.

This is a reasonable summary. But the website proceeds:

> Since the IMF was established its purposes have remained unchanged but its operations – which involve surveillance, financial assistance, and technical assistance – have developed to meet the changing needs of its member countries in an evolving world economy.

At best, this is spin, for the Fund's purposes have changed. They changed in the 1970s, when most developed countries moved from fixed to floating exchange rates, and the core function of the Fund, the maintenance of exchange stability, was ceded by governments to the market.

The Fund performed a useful function throughout the 1950s and 60s, which were periods of sustained growth in much of the world, but by the end of the 1970s the Fund had a much reduced mission. This all changed with the debt crisis of 1982. The crisis gave the Fund the chance to reinvent itself as the manager of developing country crises. Debtors needed new money, to at least service interest. Creditors wanted assurances that the debtor's economic policies that had contributed to the crisis had been changed, and had firm views on the need for economic austerity by countries whose debt they were rescheduling. Yet direct commercial bank involvement in the setting of local economic policies was a political impossibility. The IMF was ideally placed, as an apparently independent international financial institution, to determine and monitor the economic policies, going forward, of the debtor nations.

These policies imposed by the IMF and the World Bank, and supported by the US Treasury, came to be known as the Washington Consensus, as all three bodies are headquartered in Washington, D.C. Yet these policies flew in the face of the experience of OECD countries. Britain in the nineteenth century, and the United

States in the twentieth century, promoted free-trade 'because they were the most efficient producers of the highest value-added goods. They did not become so through free trade; they protected themselves for decades in order to achieve that end' (Castaneda 1993: 464).

The debt crisis of 1982

In the early years of the debt crisis the Fund severely underestimated its magnitude and responded with ineffective policies. IMF policy prescriptions for Africa and Latin America meant the 1980s were a lost decade, in which net capital flows were northbound, in which infrastructure crumbled and in which life expectancy at decade's end in Sub-Saharan Africa was shorter than at the beginning (Bos *et al.* 2006: 12).

The debt crisis was relieved for the banks by the Brady Restructurings of the early 1990s in which the loans were converted into tradable bonds at a discount, with security for the repayment of principal and some interest. The Brady process did less for the debtor nations than the banks but brought some modest relief and encouraged new capital inflows. Of importance for this analysis is that the Brady Plan was devised initially in São Paulo and Mexico City and then given the imprimatur and support of the US Treasury (Buckley 2004). The IMF had no substantive input into crafting the only creative measure brought to bear on the debt crisis.

The Asian crisis of 1997

Asia's was a fundamentally different crisis from the debt crisis of 1982 or Mexico's peso crisis of 1994–5 in that the great majority of the troublesome indebtedness was of the private, not the public or quasi-public, sector, and it was not a crisis of over-consumption. Latin American nations had borrowed to fund government budgets. East Asian governments had not been similarly seduced. In the words of Laurence Meyer, a governor of the US Federal Reserve System:

> By conventional standards, the monetary and fiscal policies of the developing Asian economies prior to the crisis were largely disciplined and appropriate. … consumer price inflation … was relatively subdued [and] fiscal policy also appears to have been disciplined. (Meyer 1999: 5)

Asia's crisis was primarily a crisis of inadequate local prudential regulation and inadequate confidence of global capital in the region (Buckley 2000). It was a contractionary crisis. Notwithstanding all of these differences, the IMF waded into Asia imposing the Washington Consensus policies it believed had worked in Latin America in the 1980s and Mexico in 1995 – prescriptions of budgetary tightening and austerity. Austerity is always bad policy for a contractionary crisis. It is utterly ineffective in encouraging contracting economies to expand. At the time the Nobel laureate Joseph Stiglitz was the chief economist of the World Bank and he spoke out repeatedly to highlight the fundamental error in the Fund's response to the Asian crisis (Passell 1998: D2, col. 1). Joe Stiglitz was to be proved right, but when it mattered most, the IMF wouldn't listen to him.

The IMF eventually acquiesced to requests by national governments for more expansionary policy settings, but by then considerable, unnecessary economic damage and human suffering had occurred. Furthermore, the Fund only eased its austerity policies. In the meantime, Malaysia had adopted more successful strategies that remain outside the Fund's kitbag of policy options (Buckley and Fitzgerald 2004: 96).

Malaysia refused IMF funding and advice and chose to chart its own way out of the Asian crisis, imposing capital outflow controls to keep foreign capital within the country, and pegging the ringgit to the US dollar (Buckley and Fitzgerald 2004). Malaysia was then able to ease monetary policy and pursue expansionary fiscal policies, without being hampered by concerns about the impact of capital outflows on exchange and interest rates.

Malaysia had created the nearest thing to a controlled laboratory experiment as one gets in economics. Thailand and Korea sought to exit the crisis using the Fund's policies. Malaysia followed a different course. (Indonesia is a separate case, as its high debt levels meant it was in a different type of crisis.) All three economies recovered, but Malaysia's recovery was more rapid, and its poor were harmed far less (Buckley and Fitzgerald 2004). As Kaplan and Rodrik put it, 'compared to IMF programs, … Malaysian policies provided faster economic recovery … smaller declines in employment and real wages, and more rapid turn around in the stock market' (Kaplan and Rodrik 2003).

Yet the Fund's mistakes in East Asia, so clearly highlighted by Malaysia's taking the road less travelled, paled in comparison to its egregious errors in Argentina.

Argentina's implosion in 2001

From 1991 to 1998 Argentina prospered as its GDP per capita increased 44 per cent and inflation was under control (Kiguel 2004: 84). Argentina improved its banking system, more than doubled its exports, privatized a broad range of industries, experienced significant growth in oil and mineral production and achieved record levels of agricultural and industrial output (Kiguel 2002: 101–1). It was the darling of the IMF and global financial markets and toasted as 'the best case of responsible leadership in the developing world' (*The Nation* 2002: 3).

Nonetheless in late 1998 Argentina entered a severe recession caused by excessive borrowing to support general government expenditure, the peg of the peso to the US dollar and Argentina's endemic corruption (Buckley 2003: 373). The recession was magnified by massive capital flight, so that the government had to impose harsh caps on withdrawals from bank accounts, and eventually close the banks. Still the crisis deepened when the IMF refused to extend further credit to the nation in 2001, believing its economic programmes to be unsustainable. As commercial lenders followed this lead, Argentina was forced to default on its external debt of some US$132 billion.

Argentina was exceptionally resolute in its negotiations with its external creditors and refused to accept conventional levels of debt relief. President Kirchner refused to service the debt from the 'suffering and hunger of the people'. He had good grounds: Argentina's poverty rate, 27 per cent in 1999, by 2003 had doubled to 54.7 per cent; per capita GDP, US$7,800 in 1999, by 2004 had fallen to $3,800; and debt that represented 47.4 per cent of GDP in 1999, by 2004 was 140 per cent of GDP (Hornbeck 2004: 4).

In early 2005, 76 per cent of Argentina's creditors accepted its offer to exchange its debt for bonds at the unprecedented discount of some 66 per cent on a net present value basis. Argentina emerged from its default on the most advantageous terms ever secured by a middle-income country in a debt restructuring. In the words of the *Financial Times*, 'Argentina gambled, and the gamble paid off' (*Financial Times* 2005: 20).

In contrast, the IMF emerged with its credibility in tatters. Never before had a country that had so faithfully followed the Fund's policies collapsed so severely, never before had the Fund's image been so badly damaged by a sovereign default.

An Asian consensus

Other nations should be grateful that China and the other nations of East Asia have ignored IMF advice and taken their own paths, because for decades the stellar economic growth of East Asia has lifted that of the world. China's capacity to produce manufactured goods, clothing and other items ever more efficiently and cheaply has kept a lid on inflationary pressures in virtually all developed economies. For Australia, Brazil and other commodities exporters China's growth has provided a massive market for minerals and other commodities. Indeed, the rise of East Asia generally underpinned global prosperity in the two decades leading up to the global financial crisis.

East Asia is uniquely placed in terms of domestic savings rates and foreign exchange reserves. China and Japan hold nearly 20 per cent each of worldwide official foreign currency reserves (Kohlscheen and Taylor 2008: 323). For many years, China and Japan have been the principal buyers of US Treasury bonds. The Chinese and Japanese have saved and lent, so Americans can borrow and spend.

China has amassed massive foreign exchange reserves, on the back of a most probably undervalued currency. These reserves serve as splendid insurance against global financial instability. Recent research suggests that while China may well be manipulating the value of its currency, it is not in breach of its obligations under the Articles of Agreement of the IMF or the various WTO treaties (Mercurio and Leung 2009). A nation cannot maintain an under-value for its currency and control its interest rates if it needs global capital (Obstfeld and Rogoff 1995; Obstfeld, Shambaugh and Taylor 2005). It is only the independence that high domestic savings rates give a nation which allows the long-term manipulation of the value of its currency. China has started to allow the yuan to appreciate. It announced on 19 June 2010 that the 23-month freeze on the yuan against the US dollar would be relaxed and gradual change in the value of the yuan would be allowed within a daily trading band of 0.5 per cent (Rich 2010).

The success of Asia, East and South, highlights the weaknesses of the Washington Consensus policies. China and India are two very different nations, with different political systems, development paths, financial systems and economic policy settings. Yet both nations have far outperformed those implementing Washington Consensus policies. It is arguable that China and India have unique advantages not available to other developing nations. China's advantages include a massive supply of relatively well-educated, cheap labour and a huge potential domestic market which China has used adroitly to lure inbound foreign direct investment (and ensure high technology comes along with it). India's advantages include a similarly large, cheap workforce coupled to widespread facility with the English language, the English common law legal system and other institutions and its tradition of excellence in mathematical and scientific education.

So comparisons between China or India on the one hand with other developing countries on the other may not be fair or informative. However, comparisons between China and India suggest the policies of the Washington Consensus are misguided. For of the two nations, India's policies are closer to those of the Washington Consensus than China's. Government has a much smaller role in the Indian economy than in China's. The market is the major allocator of financial and other resources in India, much less so in China. Yet China has consistently outperformed India, and, given the increased investment in its human capital which China's economic growth has made possible, it is likely to continue to outperform India in the foreseeable future.

Conclusion

For years Western experts have been predicting that China's high growth rates could not be sustained (Krueger 2005; Gailbraith and Liu 2000; Prasad 2004; Dekle 2005). The weakness of its institutions, such as the rule of law and independent courts, militate against sustained growth in Western eyes. But China's continued growth, far beyond the limits the experts were certain would constrain it, suggests that China may have crafted its own paradigm in which the lessons of institutional economics need to be revised. Whether that system is transferable to other nations with different work ethics and cultures and levels of entrepreneurship is another matter. What is clear is that Washington Consensus policies have not worked in most countries to which they have been applied, and the policies that engendered such dramatic and sustained periods of growth in China, Japan, South Korea, Singapore, Malaysia, Taiwan and other countries are quite different from those of the Washington Consensus.

An Asian Consensus would, logically, be an amalgam of the policies that have worked to empower East Asian economic growth and lift massive portions of the region's population out of poverty: policies that allow a larger role for government, that prioritize inbound equity investments over debt and focus on investments that bring with them high technology and management expertise, and policies that emphasize nation building through investment in the education and health of the local people rather than the repayment of foreign debt.

An Asian Monetary Fund could develop and promulgate this Asian Consensus and thereby pioneer new approaches to the development challenge. It could serve the region far more effectively than the IMF and its Washington Consensus policies ever have.

The second reason an AMF represents a great opportunity is that presently the region is not benefiting, as a region, as much as it could from its massive foreign exchange reserves. An AMF could work to more fully develop regional bond markets and take other initiatives to keep the region's savings in the region. Greater regional financial self-sufficiency would serve to insulate the region from the volatility that comes with a dependence upon foreign capital.

A decade ago, Eichengreen and Bayoumi concluded about East Asia that 'there is little sign, comparable to the evidence which has existed in Europe for nearly 50 years, of a willingness to subordinate national prerogatives to some larger regional entity' (Eichengreen and Bayoumi 1999: 11). A decade later this is less true than it was, but is still not wrong.

So the road to an Asian Monetary Fund will likely be long and difficult. But the first major steps have been taken. An AMF represents the chance to move away from a development model that is focused primarily upon ensuring poorer nations are able to service their debts and move towards a model that is genuinely focused upon the development of the nations themselves and their people. An AMF also represents the chance to use the region's foreign exchange reserves to insulate the region against the destabilizing effects of global capital and the capital account crises that currently accompany globalized international finance. The people of East Asia deserve nothing less.

Sincere thanks to the Australian Research Council for the Discovery Grant that supported this research, and to Lara Hall for her invaluable research assistance. All responsibility is mine.

6 Open accession provisions in FTAs

A bridge between regionalism and multilateralism?

Meredith Kolsky Lewis[1]

This chapter suggests adopting a pragmatic approach to the Article XXIV problem that would entail (a) clarifying the meaning of 'substantially all the trade' in Article XXIV; (b) holding new FTAs to the agreed-to definition; and (c) permitting existing FTAs to either conform to the new definition or to amend their agreements to include an open accession provision, if one is not already in place. The chapter first briefly discusses the nature of the Article XXIV problem. Second, it discusses the potential for an FTA to be declared inconsistent with Article XXIV in WTO dispute settlement and the ramifications such a decision would have. Third, it suggests a pragmatic approach is needed to stave off the possibility of undesirable dispute settlement proceedings. In this section the chapter acknowledges and addresses some of the difficulties with the proposed approach, and also identifies some systemic benefits of the open accession option.

The Article XXIV problem

Free Trade Agreements (FTAs) are endemic, yet they are problematic for the multilateral trading system. While the WTO notionally permits only FTAs that cover 'substantially all the trade' between the FTA parties,[2] in practice the vast majority of FTAs among WTO members exclude some portion of trade – often entire sectors – from their coverage. As a result, the balance envisioned by the framers of the General Agreement on Tariffs and Trade (GATT) – whereby FTAs and their trade-diverting effects will be tolerated so long as the agreements fully liberalize trade among the FTA parties – has not been realized.[3] Even though the WTO has a mechanism for reviewing FTAs,[4] there is still no institutional method or practice of regulating whether FTAs comply with the conditions set out in GATT Article XXIV, and no consequences for FTAs that do not so comply.[5]

Furthermore, the overlapping commitments and inconsistent rules existing between the various FTAs – commonly referred to as a 'spaghetti bowl'[6] – further diminish the potential for FTAs to serve as stepping stones to multilateralism rather than stumbling blocks. Finally, the proliferation of WTO-inconsistent FTAs is threatening the ability of World Trade Organization (WTO) members to conclude the current Doha Round of trade negotiations.

This troubling situation has led many to identify the spread of WTO-inconsistent FTAs as undermining the MFN principle and threatening the continuing vitality of the WTO as an institution.[7] These concerns are not new; indeed nearly 40 years ago Ken Dam was writing about the flaws in Article XXIV and the problems that could arise out of the inability to ensure that FTAs would satisfy the Article.[8] As well as identifying the problems with Article XXIV and the proliferation of FTAs that do not cover 'substantially all the trade', academics and other commentators have proposed a range of potential solutions to this problem.[9] However, most commentators are sceptical about the likelihood that WTO members will ever reach agreement as to what 'substantially all the trade' should mean, or that members will agree to discipline FTAs in any meaningful way. This scepticism is understandable – in fact it seems quite justified in light of the seeming inability of the WTO membership to make any substantive progress towards resolving these issues. Indeed, members have not shown a strong interest in negotiating new substantive provisions to ameliorate the current problems. This is logical. Presumably WTO members that are party to relatively few FTAs – or to 'clean' FTAs that would likely comply with any interpretation of 'substantially all the trade' would balk at the idea of implementing stricter rules prospectively only. This would give a free ride to hundreds of agreements, and would institutionalize and legitimize the overbroad use of this significant exception to the MFN principle. On the other hand, the vast majority of WTO members are party to at least one FTA that would be unlikely to satisfy any measure of 'substantially all the trade', and these members have reason to resist any change that isn't solely prospective as they would need to revisit the terms of agreements that have already been negotiated and implemented.

The nuclear option: challenging Article XXIV-consistency in WTO dispute settlement

While members may in large part be willing to disregard noncompliant FTAs because their own agreements suffer the same flaws, it is possible that at some point a member will put Article XXIV to the test substantively in WTO dispute settlement.

To date dispute settlement panels and the Appellate Body have assiduously avoided making a substantive determination as to the WTO-consistency of a given FTA.[10] Some have argued that it should not be possible for members to challenge the consistency of FTAs with Article XXIV;[11] however, it seems clear that this is a justiciable issue, and it therefore could arise at some point in WTO dispute settlement. Section 12 of the WTO Understanding on Article XXIV GATT provides that: 'The provisions of Articles XXII and XXIII of GATT 1994 … may be invoked with respect to any matters arising from the application of those provisions of Article XXIV relating to customs unions, free-trade areas or interim agreements leading to the formation of a customs union or a free-trade area.' The Appellate Body in the *Turkey – Textiles* case also made clear that it would expect a panel to require the country defending the FTA as falling within the Article XXIV exception to prove the conditions of Article XXIV (paragraphs 8(a) and 5(a)) are met.[12] A dispute settlement panel, faced with the issue of whether the North American Free Trade Agreement was consistent with Article XXIV, found that the United States had made a prima facie case that NAFTA was consistent with Article XXIV. However, no counter-evidence was offered by the complainant, Korea, and the panel did not engage in a detailed review of this issue.[13]

Thus a panel would very likely have the jurisdiction to determine whether a given FTA was consistent with Article XXIV. However, in the first instance, one might ask what WTO member could bring such a challenge? The answer is likely 'plenty of members'. Standing likely would not present an obstacle, at least not for many challenges. The Appellate Body has stated that any WTO member that is a 'potential exporter' has standing – framed as 'sufficient legal interest' – to initiate a panel proceeding.[14] It is not necessary for the member initiating the dispute to demonstrate a specific trade effect in order for a measure to be found to be inconsistent with WTO obligations.[15] Thus it has been said that 'the burden of persuasion allocated to complainants is relatively low'.[16] Indeed there have been a number of successful 'as such' challenges to measures of WTO members. In these cases the laws have been challenged as being inconsistent with WTO commitments even though such laws had not actually been applied as yet in a WTO-inconsistent manner.[17] In the context of Article XXIV-consistency, the complaining member could simply argue that it was not being given MFN treatment by the parties to the FTA, and the burden would then fall upon the respondent member or members to demonstrate that MFN did not need to be provided because the Article XXIV exception was applicable.[18]

A further question one might ask is, even accepting that many WTO members *could* initiate such a dispute, what WTO member *would* bring such an action? Thus far this has been why the dispute settlement system has not been forced to address the issue – cases are not being brought; there appears to be little appetite for the pot to call the kettle black. The reasons for this are likely severalfold and a number of rationales have been suggested.[19] For purposes of this chapter the reasons are not important – what matters is that there is no bar on members from utilizing the dispute settlement system to challenge the Article XXIV-consistency of an FTA, and that it is not impossible to imagine that a panel will eventually be faced with this sort of complaint and have to address the issue substantively.

The implications of such a complaint would be potentially quite destabilizing for the WTO. Were a panel ever to determine that a given FTA does not comply with Article XXIV, the question would arise as to how the offending member should comply with the decision – would it have to renegotiate its FTA or alternatively provide the terms of the FTA on an MFN basis to all WTO members? Either of these possibilities would likely be quite difficult for WTO members to accept. There would also be significant ripple effects for the dozens if not hundreds of other FTAs that could equally have been challenged. WTO members presumably have little interest in sparking this form of chaos and have therefore been in a holding pattern of accepting each other's non-compliant agreements. However, this state of affairs may not continue indefinitely. A member may feel that it is losing trade liberalization ground as a result of the proliferation of FTAs, and if its own agreements are largely defensible, could take its chances by initiating a dispute. While there is no reason to think either member would initiate such a dispute, New Zealand and Singapore are examples of members that have relatively 'clean' FTAs and that may see their most significant market opportunities as being those obtained via the WTO rather than via FTAs, where any comparative advantage gained is soon lost as a result of the creation of other FTAs.

Thus, although at present only hypothetical, it is certainly possible that a dispute could be brought that would require a panel to make a substantive determination as to the Article XXIV-consistency of an FTA. Should this possibility become a reality, the WTO would face serious threats to its institutional stability. As a result, although members are not particularly interested in addressing the Article XXIV problem, they should nonetheless consider whether there are any modifications that could be made to the current rules that would assist in ameliorating the FTA problem and would therefore reduce the threat of the 'nuclear solution' of a WTO dispute settlement action.

A pragmatic path forward?

It is easy enough to identify the problems with FTAs and Article XXIV, but identifying a potential solution that is realistic is far more difficult. Entrenched interests of WTO members mean that reaching consensus on change will be very challenging.

Given the very large number of FTAs already in existence, it would be highly unlikely members would agree to reform the process in a way that would apply retroactively to their agreements. At the same time, it would be unsatisfactory to develop new rules that would give a free pass to the existing agreements, as there are so many of them covering such a large amount of trade.[20]

Commentators have proposed a range of solutions. These include focusing efforts on reducing all tariffs to as close to zero as possible to negate the preferential effects of FTAs (Bhagwati);[21] clarifying the meaning of 'substantially all the trade' and having non-compliance trigger an obligation to extend MFN treatment to affected third parties (Cottier);[22] abandoning efforts to preference the WTO over FTAs and to treat the two as of equal status and encouraging multilateralization by including MFN provisions in FTAs (Pauwelyn);[23] and deeming WTO rules to be supreme over any RTA provisions that conflict with them (Picker).[24]

This chapter proposes another approach, whereby new disciplines would be proposed and implemented with respect to *future* FTAs, while *existing* agreements would have the option of following the new rules or of making their agreements open to accession to any member that is willing to accede to their terms or terms deemed equivalent. This part will first discuss the proposal, and then argue that the proposal proffered may also assist in bridging the gap between regionalism and multilateralism.

The proposal

The aim is to offer a pragmatic suggestion, in recognition of the entrenched nature of this problem and the difficulties that will arise in attempting to enact a modification to GATT Article XXIV. Although this suggestion could not possibly resolve all of the many difficulties caused by the proliferation of noncompliant FTAs, the hope is that it may be gentle enough to be acceptable to WTO members while still improving the situation currently at hand.

As noted above, the proposal has two parts. First, for *future* agreements, members should agree to substantive criteria to be applied in determining an agreement's consistency with GATT Article XXIV. In other words, consensus needs to finally be reached as to the meaning of 'substantially all the trade'. Because this standard would only be applied as a matter of course on a prospective basis, members would not necessarily have to alter pre-existing agreements. Second, for *existing* agreements, parties to those agreements would have two options. First, they could conform their agreements to the substantive criteria agreed to for future agreements; or second, avail themselves of a 'grandfathering' provision which would deem their agreements unchallengeable on 'substantially all the trade' grounds so long as the agreement adopted an open accession policy if it did not already have one.

In addition, a failure to adopt either option would render the FTA susceptible to challenge in WTO dispute settlement. It is suggested that if an FTA were found to fall afoul of the newly clarified rules, the remedy should be that the terms of the FTA have to be offered on an MFN basis to the WTO membership. If an FTA does not cover 'substantially all the trade' it should not be entitled to exempt itself from the general Article I obligations.

Thus 'clean' agreements would not require any change. For members with agreements that come close to meeting the 'substantially all the trade' requirement, perhaps this rule would nudge them to liberalize a bit more so as to satisfy the newly clarified Article XXIV. And for members with dodgier FTAs, they wouldn't have to radically change their FTAs if they did not want to, so long as they opened their agreement up for others to join if they so wished.

With respect to the open accession provision requirement, this could prove difficult to monitor and administer, because accession would still need to be negotiated. Thus it would need to be clear on what bases a potential new member could legitimately be excluded. In addition, this might be seen as being too soft on the existing FTAs and therefore not be attractive enough to newer participants in bilateral agreements. Notwithstanding these difficulties, open accession provisions would at least provide the potential for further liberalization and for a degree of multilateralization of existing regionalism.

It bears examining whether an agreement that does not cover 'substantially all the trade' but that is open to all members to join is even in need of special treatment (such as a special status under Article XXIV), or whether it is instead consistent with GATT Article I in that the terms are open to all. It would seem that such an agreement would not satisfy the requirements of GATT Article I because even if the agreement were open to accession by any member, the terms of accession would need to be negotiated at least to some degree and thus would not be being offered 'immediately and unconditionally' as required by GATT Article I. Therefore permitting such agreements would require a waiver. Enacting such a waiver – which could be seen as a form of 'grandfather clause' for existing FTAs – would be an improvement over the status quo and might be pragmatic enough to be a credible proposal. This would only be offered as a way of grandfathering the existing inconsistent FTAs. Future notified FTAs would need to satisfy the Article XXIV requirements.[25]

As noted above however, careful consideration would have to be given to how to monitor whether open accession clauses were being administered in good faith.

Open accession provisions and multilateralizing regionalism

In the debate over whether FTAs are stepping stones or stumbling blocks, those who tout regionalism sometimes argue that FTAs have the effect of chipping away at barriers and ultimately will be aggregated into bigger and bigger blocks of liberalization. Jagdish Bhagwati has criticized as unrealistic this notion that FTAs could be aggregated to lead to increasingly multilateralized trading blocks. In particular, he notes that the 'spaghetti bowl' of differing rules of origin and differences in levels of tariff reduction commitments and other FTA provisions makes it unlikely that FTAs will be able to be amalgamated into agreements comprising more parties.[26]

Bhagwati's argument seems unassailable with respect to FTAs that have very different terms and coverage. But the situation may be less hopeless with respect to highly comprehensive FTAs. If two different FTAs both reduce tariffs on all goods to zero for example, it would seem to be easier to join these FTAs than two that featured significant sectoral exclusions and differed from one another in terms of what specifically was excluded. Indeed this has long been the vision of Singapore – that its FTAs would 'pave the way for APEC-wide trade area'.[27]

A further way that regional trade could contribute to rather than hinder multilateral trade liberalization is through policies of open regionalism such as those espoused by APEC. At the 1994 APEC summit in Bogor, members agreed to a policy of open regionalism as an objective. Open regionalism, while not fully defined, would entail members liberalizing unilaterally and on an MFN basis rather than by pursuing bilateral free trade agreements.[28] As FTAs nonetheless began to proliferate in the Asia-Pacific, the Pacific Economic Co-operation Council, an entity associated with APEC that provides it with policy guidance, submitted Best Practice Recommendations for APEC's FTAs to the 2004 APEC meeting. These practices, which were adopted at the meeting, included one which provides that FTAs should have open accession clauses.[29] This is consistent with the open regionalism concept. Prior to the agreement on the Bogor goals, Senior Minister Lee Kuan Yew of Singapore even suggested that the United States should open NAFTA to accession by all APEC members. He used the concept of competitive liberalization to support his idea, arguing that some APEC members would quickly accept such an offer, and this would then impel the rest of the APEC membership to do so as well.[30]

This raises the question, what is the value of open accession provisions? These clauses feature in a minority of FTAs and generally provide that other members may accede to the agreement on terms to be negotiated and agreed to.[31] While most such provisions are never acted upon, they at least provide an opportunity for broadening or multilateralizing regional arrangements. Most of the FTAs that do have open accession provisions are FTAs that are comparatively comprehensive in their coverage. For example, New Zealand and Singapore frequently use open accession provisions, and both countries have highly liberalized economies and tend to enter into high-quality comprehensive trade agreements. It also bears noting that Taiwan has proposed that it be a WTO requirement that FTAs contain open accession provisions.[32]

As a general proposition I believe that FTAs are stumbling blocks in the path of multilateral trade liberalization. And competitive liberalization seems unlikely to materialize as a result of the proliferation of the usual non-comprehensive FTAs. However, comprehensive, open accession agreements may provide the best possibility to prove the exception to the rule as they provide a more realistic opportunity to 'multilateralize' regionalism.[33] This could particularly take hold in the APEC context, where open regionalism has long been a central tenet, even if never fully defined.[34] It has been suggested that APEC's open regionalism experience may serve as a useful model for making trade agreements more susceptible to being multilateralized, and in turn to defragmenting the world trading system.[35]

The process of multilateralizing regionalism may become more realistic if the growth arises not out of the combination of disparate bilateral agreements, but rather from particular open accession agreements expanding to become larger and larger, as is contemplated by the expansion of the P-4 Agreement into a broader Trans-Pacific partnership.

The Trans-Pacific Economic Partnership Agreement (P-4 Agreement) between New Zealand, Singapore, Brunei and Chile is a highly comprehensive trade agreement which has an open accession provision. The goal of the P-4 countries was to negotiate a strategic agreement that could serve as a template for a broader Asia-Pacific agreement. In the past some have suggested that the P-4 could serve as a 'dock' for other interested APEC members, with resultant scepticism that the P-4 'is clearly too small to provide a foundation for APEC-wide arrangements'.[36] However, this scepticism may soon give way, because negotiations have been initiated to expand that agreement into a new agreement that will include the United States, Australia, Malaysia, Peru and Vietnam alongside the original P-4 partners. This new agreement, currently under negotiation, is being called the Trans-Pacific Partnership or TPP. If the United States does accede, the enlarged agreement's prospects to serve as a gateway agreement will seem much stronger. Technically, the TPP is not an expansion of the P-4 but a new agreement. However, the fact that the P-4 Agreement contains an open accession provision and was designed for expansion has spurred the creation of the new, enlarged agreement. The TPP itself will likely contain its own open accession provision which will in turn facilitate its expansion to include more and more countries.

Conclusion

This chapter has suggested a pragmatic method for breaking the current deadlock regarding Article XXIV-inconsistent FTAs. A solution of some sorts should be pursued, no matter how difficult, because it is a real possibility that a member could challenge such an FTA in WTO dispute settlement, with potentially significant destabilizing ripple effects for other members. The solution offered here provides non-compliant FTA members with a choice – conform their agreements to the to-be-clarified 'substantially all the trade' requirement, or add an open accession clause to their existing agreements. The latter option may be perceived as too soft, but open accession clauses have an independent benefit in that they may assist in multilateralizing regionalism, as is currently being seen with the open accession P-4 Agreement serving as the starting point for a broader Trans-Pacific Partnership Agreement that will include, *inter alia*, the United States and Australia.

Notes

1 An expanded version of this chapter has been published as 'The Prisoners' Dilemma Posed by Free Trade Agreements: Can Open Accession Provisions Provide an Escape?' *Chicago Journal of International Law* 11, 2011: 631.
2 GATT Article XXIV.
3 See, e.g., Cone 2005: 567 (examining the history of Art. XXIV and describing it as representing an effort to encourage a European customs union while requiring most-favoured nation (MFN) treatment).
4 This is the Committee on Regional Trade Agreements (CRTA). See World Trade Organization, 'Work of the Committee on Regional Trade Agreements'. Online. Available HTTP: <http://www.wto.org/english/tratop_e/region_e/regcom_e.htm>. The CRTA is tasked with examining the specific regional trade agreements and with considering the systemic ramifications of such agreements. However, the CRTA's findings are not to be used as evidence with respect to the WTO-consistency of any particular agreement. Thus while it may speed up the review of agreements, it is still a mechanism with little obvious impact on the bigger Article XXIV problems.
5 The WTO has taken some steps in this direction. The General Council's Decision of 14 December 2006 regarding transparency mechanisms for RTAs calls for the Secretariat to prepare factual presentations on FTAs that have been notified to the WTO and for the CRTA to implement this mechanism. Although the Decision states that these factual presentations cannot be used for dispute settlement, it also provides that this mechanism will be replaced with a permanent mechanism to be adopted as a part of the Doha Round. In this context, members will review the legal relationship between this mechanism and relevant WTO provisions relating to RTAs. WTO Negotiating Group on Rules, 'Report by the Chairman to the Trade Negotiations Committee' (13 July 2006), TN/RL/18.
6 Bhagwati 1996: 2–3.
7 See, e.g., Bhagwati 2008; Limão 2006: 896 (finding that FTAs have impeded multilateral trade liberalization); Picker 2005: 267; Lewis 2008; 2005: 554, 557–9; Cottier 2005: 595, 597 (noting problem of noncompliant FTAs as stumbling blocks); WTO Consultative Board Report to the Director-General Supachai Panitchpakdi, 'The Future of the WTO: Addressing Institutional Challenges in the New Millennium' (WTO Geneva, 2005).
8 For example, Dam 1970.
9 See, e.g., Picker 2005; Cottier 2005: 599 (clarifying the meaning of 'substantially all the trade' through negotiations or case law).
10 In the GATT era three panels were faced with claims arguing that a given FTA was inconsistent with the GATT. One of these panels was never activated; the other two (*EC – Tariff Treatment on Imports of Citrus Products from Certain Countries in the Mediterranean Region* and *EEC – Import Regime of Bananas*) resulted in unadopted panel reports. For a discussion of these GATT Panels see Mavroidis 2006: 187, 204–5; see also discussion in Cho 2001: 419, 437–8.
11 Roessler 2000, cited in Mavroidis 2006:194.

12 *Turkey – Textiles*, WT/DS34/AB/R, 22 October 1999 at paras 58–9.
13 *United States – Definitive Safeguard Measures on Imports of Circular Welded Carbon Quality Line Pipe from Korea*, WT/DS202/R, 29 October 2001 at Section 7.142–4.
14 See *EC – Bananas III*, WT/DS27/AB/R, adopted 25 September 1997 at para. 136; see also discussion in Kwak and Marceau 2006: 467.
15 See Kwak and Marceau 2006 and Dispute Settlement Understanding (DSU) Article 3.8.
16 See Mavroidis 2006: 187.
17 For example *United States – Antidumping Act of 1916*, WT/DS136, 162/AB/R, adopted 26 September 2000.
18 See Mavroidis 2006: 208.
19 See Pauwelyn 2007: 2 n.4. Pauwelyn identifies various reasons why WTO members may refrain from challenging regional trade agreements in WTO dispute settlement: that because RTAs are ubiquitous it is in no member's interests to tighten up the rules as it may affect one's own arrangements; that members may not trust panels with the complicated analysis of conformity with Article XXIV; and that third parties may not want to challenge agreements that don't cover 'substantially all the trade' as the solution may be that more of the areas in which they compete with one of the FTA partners become covered by the agreement, rather than less. See further Pauwelyn 2007. See also Mavroidis 2006: 211–12.
20 See, e.g., Picker 2005: 306 ('the sheer number and coverage of existing RTAs suggests that reform of Article XXIV must apply to extant agreements, not just to future agreements').
21 Bhagwati 2008: 97–100.
22 Cottier 2005.
23 Pauwelyn 2007.
24 Picker 2005: 307.
25 In general, however, open-access FTAs should be encouraged. These are the types of FTAs that could best serve as building blocks rather than stumbling blocks. Cooper 2006: 14; Bergsten 1997.
26 Bhagwati 2008: 92–7.
27 Singapore Prime Minister Goh Chok Tong in 2001, quoted in Dent 2006: 227.
28 See, e.g., Dent 2006: 45–7.
29 Dent 2006: 221.
30 Bergsten 2007: 14n.16.
31 Open accession provisions are somewhat unusual but not unheard of. They are more common amongst APEC partners than elsewhere. Agreements featuring such provisions include the Thailand–New Zealand FTA (Article 18.5); the Thailand–Australia FTA (Article 1905); the North American Free Trade Agreement (NAFTA) and the Armenia–Moldova FTA (Article 18). Within APEC, agreements centred in Oceania all have open accession provisions; of the agreements centred around the United States, some have open accession provisions (e.g. the United States–Australia FTA and the United States–Singapore FTA) but others do not (e.g. the United States–Chile FTA); and among agreements centred in East Asia, very few FTAs contain open accession provisions. See Dent 2007: 447, 459, Table 1.
32 TN/RL/W186, August 3 2005; see also discussion in Schaefer 2007: 585, 595.
33 See generally Cho 2006: 39, 77–8; Cho 2001: 454–7; Pauwelyn 2007. See also Lawrence 2007: 494 ('dynamics of regional groups that are open to all newcomers will differ from those of exclusive or selective ones').
34 For example Chatterjee 1999.
35 S. Cho 2006: 77–8.
36 Bergsten 2007: 14n.16.

7 Dynamic process of a transnational dispute settlement as an autopoietic system?

Lessons from cases in North America involving the WTO, NAFTA and domestic laws

Tomohiko Kobayashi

> If you govern the people legalistically and regulate people's behavior by punishment, they will try to avoid it without having a sense of shame. If you govern them by means of virtue and regulate people's behavior with propriety, they will have a sense of shame, and correct themselves.
>
> Confucius, *Lunyu* (fifth century BC), Chapter 2, Verse 3.

Introduction

Potential conflict between the Regional Trade Agreements (RTAs) and the Agreement Establishing the World Trade Organization (the WTO Agreement) has long been a subject of academic as well as practitioner concerns (Pauwelyn 2006: 197). While this is a typical example of the 'fragmentation' of international law, the 'difficulties arising from the diversification and expansion of international law (International Law Commission, Study Group 2006) are what states make of it. Instead of focusing solely on its negative effects, we should look more carefully into the state practice, that is, how states actually deal with overlapping norms and fragmented dispute settlement (DS) mechanisms, absent a hierarchical order or coordinating mechanism.

From this perspective, recent experience in North America provides an interesting example. In the recent three trade disputes among contracting parties of the North American Free Trade Agreement (NAFTA), a single measure triggered a multidimensional complex dispute. While parties sought solution of the dispute through multiple DS proceedings under the NAFTA and the WTO in sequence, after years of dispute they reached a comprehensive agreement that settled the dispute across the board. In two of them, the comprehensive deal was done *after* the issuance of binding DS rulings under the WTO and/or the NAFTA in order to override them.

It would be difficult to identify exact *reasons* why the parties in conflict at last reached a settlement, since a number of different factors may come into play under the specific circumstances of each case. Instead, this paper tries to explore the architecture and possible *reconfigurations* of the process in which parties managed to settle these multidimensional complex disputes. It will help us to understand the role of the DS mechanism for the settlement of disputes among East Asian countries.

The primary objective of this paper is to unveil the process of dispute settlement between two out of three NAFTA partners, which go through sequencing and parallel DS proceedings and result in a comprehensive deal. While a mutually agreed solution among the parties in conflicts is generally encouraged, it raises important questions as regards the effectiveness of the settlement of international disputes. Two questions now arise. The first one relates to the relationships between separate DS proceedings: do these fora operate separately, without any connection between each other? If the answer is affirmative, the fragmentation of the dispute settlement mechanism would apparently do more harm than good, if any, to the effective settlement of a dispute, which asks us to pursue the reduction of fragmentation. The second question relates to the role of separate DS proceedings in the settlement of the dispute. Do the DS rulings become useless where the parties finally reach a comprehensive deal? If the answer is affirmative, again, this means that a fragmented DS mechanism has only a limited effectiveness. The secondary objective of this paper is to find lessons for East Asian countries from the North American experience.

Under the heading 'Experiences in North America', this paper outlines the framework of the process of dispute settlement, then looks into three major trade disputes fought between two out of the three NAFTA countries: the *Sweeteners* dispute (US and Mexico), the *Cement* dispute (Mexico and the US) and the *Lumber* dispute (Canada and the US). While making few additional inputs in terms of facts and specific DS rulings, this chapter tries to illustrate the holistic picture of the disputes at hand. The section on 'Possible rationales' offers a theoretical investigation of the relationship between segmented DS proceedings and the relationship between the comprehensive agreement and the previous DS rulings. The chapter's final section summarizes the analyses in the preceding chapters. In addition, we take a brief look at how the lessons of these analyses could affect the future of dispute settlement among East Asian countries.

Summing up, first of all, our answer is 'no' to both of the above two questions. By focusing on the dynamic process of dispute settlement, we find spontaneous normative networks that stimulate comprehensive settlement of multifaceted disputes. It is in this kind of mutual supportiveness of DS proceedings and negotiated deals that the experiences in North America provide East Asian countries useful insights for developing a future framework for the effective settlement of disputes within the region. This finding confirms Professor Nakagawa's analysis on the positive role of negotiated deals for the settlement of trade disputes in East Asia (Nakagawa 2007: 867).

Experiences in North America

Structures of dispute settlement

The relevant structure of the DS mechanisms is illustrated in Figure 7.1. In each case, the cause of the international dispute is a single act, that is, the anti-dumping (AD) or countervailing duty (CVD) measures introduced by a NAFTA country against imports from a NAFTA partner. It is usually the case that trade disputes involving AD measures are complex, multidimensional and multifaceted, since they involve a variety of actors (including private firms and governments) as well as a variety of norms (including municipal laws, the NAFTA and the WTO Agreement).

While all NAFTA countries are members of the WTO as well, the WTO Agreement and the NAFTA are independent of each other. Needless to say, each WTO member is required to make their domestic laws and regional agreements in conformity with the WTO Agreement according to Article 16.4 of the Marrakesh Agreement Establishing the WTO, Article XXIV of the GATT 1994 and Article 5 of the General Agreement on Trade in Services. On the other hand, however, the NAFTA has a priority over the WTO Agreement among the NAFTA partners according to Article 103(2) thereof. See horizontal opposing arrows between two ellipses in Figure 7.1. Moreover, there is no effective allocation of jurisdiction between the DS mechanisms under the WTO and the NAFTA. Even if we assume that the relevant provisions of domestic law and the NAFTA are consistent with the WTO Agreement, there is a risk of conflict between the NAFTA rulings and the WTO rulings. For example, a dispute arising from an identical action may be divided into parts, once they are filed to different tribunals that apply different laws to different aspects of the dispute according to the legal formulation of each segment. Then, that measure may be found inconsistent with the NAFTA but consistent with the WTO Agreement in a contradictory manner, since the NAFTA dispute settlement panel is independent of its counterpart under the WTO Agreement. Thus, a measure taken by a NAFTA country can be subject to duplicate jurisdiction between the WTO and the NAFTA DS mechanisms (see two downswing arrows in Figure 7.1).

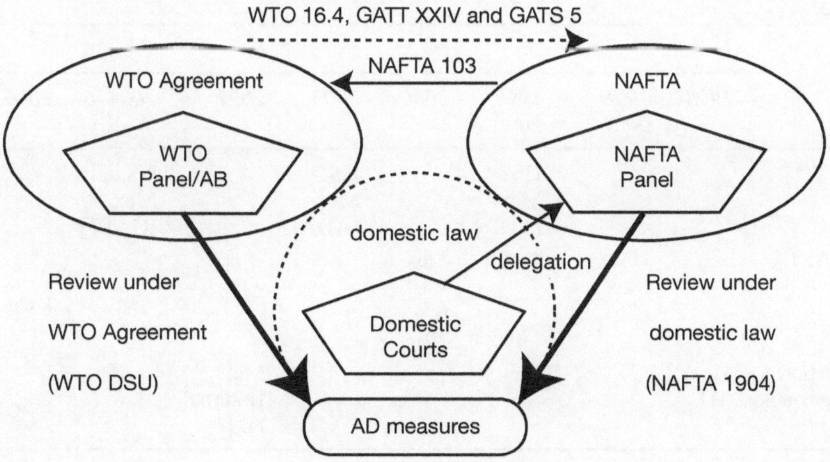

Figure 7.1 Multidimensional jurisdictions for NAFTA countries

From the above description of the complex structure for settling disputes, it is clear that there are considerable risks of conflict in the application of the NAFTA and the WTO Agreement. This brings us to the next question, that is, how, in reality, NAFTA countries manage the risks associated with the lack of coherence in DS mechanisms.

Process of dispute settlement

Our first mandate is to examine how (not why) long-lasting complex disputes resulted in solution through a comprehensive agreement, notwithstanding a series of preceding DS proceedings and rulings. We look into the process of each dispute in the following subsections. The numbers listed in Figures 7.2 to 7.4 indicate phases of the dispute. Each item represents measures in dispute or cases filed to the DS mechanisms. Bracketed items represent DS proceedings that did not result in the issuance of final rulings before reaching the comprehensive agreement. Phases are aligned in chronological order according to the time the procedure started.

Sweeteners dispute

The sequence of this dispute is shown in Figure 7.2. An anti-dumping measure Mexico imposed in 1998 on sweeteners (High Fructose Corn Syrup: hereinafter HFCS) (Mexican SECOFI 1998) from the US was the trigger for another long and complex trade dispute (Phase 1).

In response to the AD measure, the US requested consultations on the NAFTA DS procedure under Chapter 19 of the NAFTA (NAFTA 1998b) (Phase 2). The reason the US brought actions under the NAFTA is that the Mexican measure intended to counteract the US's alleged breach of the NAFTA commitments to

	1	*2*	*3*	*4*	*5*	*6*	*7*	*8*
	1998	*1998–2001*	*1998–2000*	*2000–*	*2000–1*	*2002*	*2004–6*	*2006*
WTO			US > Mex. [ADA]		US > Mex. [ADA]		US > Mex. [GATT]	
NAFTA		US > Mex. [Ch. 19]		Mex. > US [Ch. 20]				Deal
Disputed measures	Mex. AD					Mex. [Internal tax]		

Figure 7.2 Process of the Sweeteners dispute (*the United States v. Mexico*) domestic law

open its market to Mexican sugar products (Vacek-Aranda 2006). However, a series of hold-ups in procedural matters led to considerable delays in the hearings and postponed the final decision until 2001. Thus, the US shifted its focus to the WTO dispute settlement procedure (Phase 3), and won the case in 2000 (WTO 2000).[1] While Mexico filed a separate motion against the US under the Chapter 20 of the NAFTA concerning the US obligation on market access (Phase 4), the procedure did not make progress either owing to technical problems regarding the composition of the panel. The US also won another WTO panel case later, concerning Mexico's implementation of the first WTO recommendations (WTO 2001) (Phase 5).

In accordance with the WTO rulings, Mexico lifted the AD measure, but introduced an internal tax on certain sweeteners, including HFCS, instead (WTO 2005) (Phase 6). While the internal tax is different from the original AD duty, they have a similar effect in practice. Swiftly responding to that measure, the US filed another case under the WTO DS procedure, and the WTO panel and Appellate Body found in favour of the US (WTO 2006a) (Phase 7). Following the adoption of the third WTO recommendations in March 2006, both parties reached an agreement on its implementation in June 2006 (WTO 2006b). After that, both parties reached a comprehensive agreement to resolve the dispute across the board (Sweeteners Agreement of 2006) (Phase 8).

Cement dispute

The US imposed AD duties on imports of gray Portland cement from Mexico in 1990, upon request from its domestic industry (USDOC 1990) (see Figure 7.3, Phase 1). Mexican producers filed a case with the US courts against the ITC's injury determination, in vain (USCIT 1993) (Phase 2). In parallel, the Mexican

	1	*2*	*3*	*4*	*5*	*6*	*7*
	1990	*1990–2*	*1990–2*	*1995–6*	*1998–2001*	*2003–6*	*2006*
GATT/WTO			Mex. > US [ADC]			Mex. > US [GATT]	
NAFTA				Mex. > US [Ch. 19]	Mex. > US [Ch. 19]		
Domestic courts		Mex. > US [AD statute]					Deal
Disputed measures	US AD						

Figure 7.3 Process of the Cement dispute (*Mexico v. the United States*)

government made recourse to the DS procedure under the GATT Tokyo Round Anti-Dumping Code (Phase 3). Although the GATT panel found DOC's initiation of the AD investigation as defective and recommended the US to revoke the AD measure (GATT 1992), the panel report was never adopted.

Mexico then filed another case under the NAFTA DS procedure upon its entry into force in January 1994 (Phase 2). While the NAFTA panel found in favour of Mexico with regard to administrative review determinations, it rejected Mexico's main claim regarding the validity of the original determination for the following three reasons: that the Mexican producers failed to raise claims against the DOC's determination promptly; that the NAFTA panel does not have authority to revoke the determinations issued before the NAFTA came into force; and that GATT DS rulings, whether adopted or not, do not have a binding effect (NAFTA 1996) (Phase 4). Mexico continued to bring the case under every administrative review determination to the NAFTA panel, in vain based on similar reasoning (NAFTA 1998a) (Phase 5).

Thus, Mexico filed a case before the WTO DS panel (WTO 2003) (Phase 6). Nearly at the end of the WTO panel proceeding, in March 2006, both governments reached a comprehensive agreement to resolve the *Cement* dispute across the board (Cement Agreement of 2006) (Phase 7).

Above all, the Cement Agreement settled or suspended the litigations before the NAFTA and the WTO. Accordingly, the WTO panel was suspended in 2006 and finally lapsed as of 14 January 2007 (WTO 2007). In addition, in accordance with the Agreement, US domestic industries requested rescission of the administrative review for the most recent period. The US Department of Commerce compromised pending claims to AD duties for entries during that period, as well as entries of Mexican cement that entered the US from 1 August 2005 to 2 April 2006. On the other hand, the Agreement provides mechanisms of export restriction and export licence under Mexican government regulations.

The Cement Agreement provided in its Article XI that if all interested parties had abided by its terms, the US Department of Commerce (USDOC) would terminate the Cement Agreement on 31 March 2009. Since all the obligations of the Cement Agreement were fulfilled, the USDOC terminated the Cement Agreement on 31 March 2009, accompanied by the revocation of AD measures in force at that time and the expiration of the export licensing scheme on 12 May 2009 (USDOC 2009).

Lumber dispute

It was the AD and CVD measures imposed by the US authorities in May 2002 on softwood lumber from Canada (USDOC 2002) that triggered another round of the long-lasting dispute between the US and Canada (Carmody 2006: 664) (see Figure 7.4 below, Phase 1). The imposition of the AD/CVD measure followed the expiry of the Softwood Lumber Agreement 1996 (SLA of 1996), which was the result of a previous dispute, commonly known as the *Lumber II* dispute. This paper deals with the so-called Lumber III dispute as a distinct one from the preceding disputes.

	1	*2*	*3*	*4*	*5*	*6*	*7*	*7*
	2002	*2002–6*	*2002–4*	*2005–6*	*2005–6*	*2004–7*	*2005–6*	*2006*
WTO DS			Can. > US [ADA]	Can. > US [ASCM]				
NAFTA DS		Can. > US [Ch. 19]				Can. > US [Ch. 11]		
Domestic courts		Can. firm > US [AD statute]			Can. > US [APA]		US firm > US [US Const.]	Deal
LCIA arbitration	–	–	–	–	–	–		
Disputed measures	AD/ CVD							

Figure 7.4 Process of the *Lumber* dispute (*Canada v. the United States*)

Soon after the imposition of the measures, from June 2002, Canada filed litigations to the NAFTA DS panels addressing three factors (dumping determination, injury determination and CVD determination) (Phase 2). It was the beginning of the third round of US-Canadian disputes on softwood lumber. Canada eventually obtained three binding rulings that are favourable to it in part. On the other hand, however, it also filed six parallel cases to the WTO DS procedures in April 2003 (Phases 3 and 4), pending the NAFTA DS proceedings. Canadian industries and the government of Canada also filed a lawsuit to the Court of International Trade (USCIT 2006) (Phase 5).

Canadian producers further filed separate cases to the investor-state arbitration under Chapter 11 of the NAFTA (Simpson 2007) (Phase 6). On the other hand, the Coalition for Fair Lumber Imports, filed a case arguing that the NAFTA panel review provisions under the NAFTA Implementation Act of 1993 violated the Due Process Clause, the Appointments Clause, Article III and other provisions of the US Constitution (USCA 2006) (Phase 7). After the coming into effect of the comprehensive agreement, the US Court of Appeals (D.C. Circuit) declared its lack of jurisdiction over the claim.

Finally, in September 2006, the two governments reached a comprehensive agreement, the so-called Softwood Lumber Agreement (SLA) 2006 to resolve the *Lumber* dispute across the board (Phase 8). Under this agreement, the US agreed to terminate the AD/CVD measures in question retroactively and refund duties collected after 2002. Canada agreed to establish export monitoring system including quotas to support export volume and price of Canadian lumber. Both countries agreed to terminate six pending WTO cases (DS236, DS247, DS257, DS264, DS277 and DS311) (WTO 2006c). On the other hand, the SLA did not require termination of NAFTA Chapter 11 claims, according to the amendment of 12 October 2006 added as Annexe 2A to the Amended SLA 2006.

SLA 2006 has its own dispute settlement mechanism assigning the London Court of International Arbitration (LCIA) as the exclusive forum, which the US used as early as October 2007, slightly over a year after the entry into force of the SLA 2006. The legal place of arbitration is London, the UK, as set forth in Article XIV:13 thereof. The US requested arbitration first, arguing that Canada violated the SLA in calculating export quotas. The LCIA issued arbitral awards in March 2008 for the first request in favour of the US (LCIA 2008). It then ordered Canada to provide compensatory remedy to the US (LCIA 2009a). An additional award was issued in September 2009 that rejected lump-sum payments offered by the Canadian government (LCIA 2009b). In parallel, in January 2008, the US posted a second request for arbitration concerning the anti-circumvention clause, which is still under way.

As is shown above, the conclusion of a comprehensive deal in the *Lumber* case does not necessarily mean the end of the story (Bowman *et al.* 2010: 587). However, it definitely integrated the fragmented disputes into one single regime. This is the remarkable feature we cast light on here.

Possible rationales

Common features in the three disputes

The process of dispute settlement shown in this chapter illustrates interesting phenomena in the settlement of international disputes. The three trade disputes have several common features: they are disputes arising from AD/CVD measures; each of them caused a serious, decades-long confrontation between the NAFTA partners; political and economic stakes were so high that parties were not able to settle the dispute by negotiation or consultation, without using the DS proceedings; the dispute was divided up in the course of parallel DS procedures under the WTO Agreement or the NAFTA; and, finally, each resulted in a comprehensive agreement that settled the dispute as a whole, without regard to the preceding DS proceedings.

The following two sections deal with two questions raised in the introductory section, namely, the relationship between plural DS proceedings and their role in the settlement of disputes, respectively.

Relationship between concurrent DS proceedings

Can there be a relationship?

The first question is as follows: how do the DS proceedings relate to each other during the course of back-to-back, parallel recourse to the different fora?

Before looking into the specific theoretical framework, we should determine whether there exists a 'process' in the first place. DS procedures under the WTO and the NAFTA may have no bearing on one another. If we stick to the formal separation of treaties and DS proceedings without looking into the actual process of dispute settlement, it leads to the approach that the sequence of the DS proceedings is just a coincidence and has no direct influence to other DS proceeding or the comprehensive deal.

It is true that DS procedures under the WTO and the NAFTA are independent of each other. However, there are significant linkages between them and cross-references in their rulings. First of all, in the cases where DS rulings were issued, many of them referred to the relevant rulings of their counterparts. Secondly, while Article 2005 of the NAFTA prohibits forum shopping, NAFTA panels and the WTO panels do not reject their jurisdiction based on this provision (Pauwelyn 2006: 201). Thus, to see concurrent DS procedures irrelevant to each other does not fit the reality. We need some theoretical framework that explains the phenomenon that was shown above.

Possible reconfigurations

POLITICAL SCIENCE APPROACH

The first possible approach sees the selection and escalation of the dispute as the result of rational calculation. According to Busch, complaining states choose whether or not to file cases to the appropriate fora on the basis of their estimates of the rulings (Busch 2007: 737). As indicated by the auxiliary lines added to

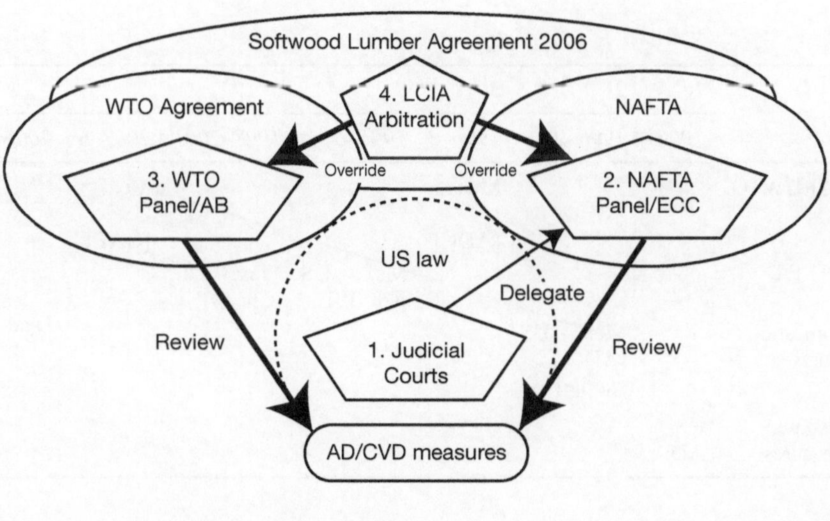

Figure 7.5 Multidimensional jurisdictions in the *Lumber* dispute

Figures 7.6 to 7.8, it seems as if the escalation in the dispute from the NAFTA DS procedures to the WTO DS procedures led to the comprehensive agreement between the disputing parties.

At first sight, this approach may explain the process of dispute settlement in the first two cases. If this is the case, to make recourse to the WTO proceeding before going to the NAFTA proceeding is the answer to avoiding complexity in the process of dispute settlement. However, this approach does not fit the process in the *Lumber* case, especially when DS rulings are inconsistent with each other. More specifically, there are inconsistencies between the WTO and NAFTA

	1	*2*	*3*	*4*	*5*	*6*	*7*	*8*
	1998	*1998–2001*	*1998–2000*	*2000–*	*2000–1*	*2002*	*2004–6*	*2006*
WTO			US > Mex. [ADA]		US > Mex. [ADA]		US > Mex. [GATT]	
NAFTA		US > Mex. [Ch. 19]		Mex. > US [Ch. 20]				Deal
Disputed measures	Mex. AD					Mex. [Internal tax]		

Figure 7.6 Process of the *Sweeteners* dispute (*the United States v. Mexico*)

	1	*2*	*3*	*4*	*5*	*6*	*7*
	1990	*1990–2*	*1990–2*	*1995–6*	*1998–2001*	*2003–6*	*2006*
GATT/WTO			Mex. > US [ADC]			Mex. > US [GATT]	
NAFTA				Mex. > US [Ch. 19]	Mex. > US [Ch. 19]		
Domestic courts		Mex. > US [AD statute]					Deal
Disputed measures	US AD						

Figure 7.7 Process of the *Cement* dispute (*Mexico v. the United States*)

	1	*2*	*3*	*4*	*5*	*6*	*7*	*7*
	2002	*2002–6*	*2002–4*	*2005–6*	*2005–6*	*2004–7*	*2005–6*	*2006*
WTO DS			Can. > US [ADA]	Can. > US [ASCM]				
NAFTA DS		Can. > US [Ch. 19]				Can. > US [Ch. 11]		
Domestic courts		Can. firm > US [AD statute]			Can. > US [APA]		US firm > US [US Const.]	Deal
LCIA arbitration	–	–	–	–	–	–		
Disputed measures	AD/ CVD							

Figure 7.8 Process of the *Lumber* dispute (*Canada v. the United States*)

dispute settlement panel findings in the evaluation of injury determination and the implementation measure in response to the original findings. These inconsistent findings generate 'conflict' in the sense that the subject country cannot obey these rulings simultaneously. In addition, the WTO procedure does not override the NAFTA counterpart or resolve the dispute as a whole, as the disputing parties are well aware. Thus, this approach does not fully explain the process we saw earlier (see the section above on 'Experiences in North America'), since the superiority of the WTO it assumes does not exist.

NORMATIVE INTEGRITY APPROACH

The second approach sees the absence of integrity as the main reason for complexity. According to Pauwelyn, the WTO Agreement and the NAFTA should be interpreted in a coordinated manner to allocate proper jurisdictions to one or the other forum in dealing with each dispute. In addition, he argues for the application of international 'comity' on the part of both panels under the WTO and the NAFTA (Pauwelyn 2006: 202).

On the one hand, WTO members are required to ensure the conformity of its laws with the obligations in accordance with Article XVI:4 of the WTO Agreement. In the course of the WTO DS proceedings as well, provisions of the member country applicable to that measure are deemed to be consistent with the WTO Agreement unless the provisions themselves are subject to review. On the other hand, the NAFTA panel under its Chapter 19 applies the law of the country that introduced the contested measures. Thus, according to this approach, both the WTO panel and the NAFTA panel apply substantially the same norm, that is, the WTO Agreement and the domestic law referred to by the NAFTA that is deemed to be compatible with the WTO Agreement, respectively. It sees the processes of the three recent cases as an anomaly.

It is true that, in each case before us, the language of the relevant provisions of US antidumping law is identical or at least closely similar to the GATT/WTO Agreement. Thus, according to this approach, WTO panels and NAFTA panels should have reached consistent reasoning and rulings in evaluating the same action. Further, the NAFTA panel might have referred to the WTO Agreement in interpreting relevant domestic law, and even given way to the WTO panel's interpretation of that Agreement.

However, it does not mean the DS panels are required to reach consistent rulings in every case in accordance with the WTO and the NAFTA. While the WTO panels and NAFTA panels sometimes referred to one another's proceedings or rulings, they do not defer to the other tribunal, or try to interpret their applicable laws in a consistent manner. Thus, we cannot adopt this approach, since it tries to explain the DS process on the basis of a relationship between substantive norms that is preferable but not existent.

NETWORKING APPROACH

Another alternative is to see these phenomena as dynamic 'networks' elaborated by Gunther Teubner. In the context of seeking the role of law in the era of globalization (Jenks 1953: 403), this approach is based on his earlier scrutiny of 'autopoietic', which literally means 'self-producing', systems (Mingers 1995: 11). The reason why this paper takes up the concept of autopoiesis of law is not that several scholars apply it to the international legal system (D'Amato 2005: 335), but because it consciously deals with a systemic conflict of laws within or among legal systems (Teubner 1993: 100).

The networking approach does not assume the hierarchical or harmonized integrity of the different legal systems, but focuses on 'double reflexivity' among individual subsystems or 'networks' among state parties which are in a double-bind situation between different norms (Teubner 1997a: 160). According to Fischer-Lescano and Teubner:

> Following the collapse of legal hierarchies, the only realistic option is to develop heterarchical forms of law that limit themselves to creating loose relationships between the fragments of law. This might be achieved through a selective process of networking that normatively strengthens already existing factual networks between the legal regimes. (Fischer-Lescano and Teubner 2004: 1017)

and:

> Beyond the alternative of either central coordination or autarky of closed regimes, we are left with a *network* logic. It is characterized by combining two conflicting demands with one another. On the one hand one finds in networks the autonomous and decentralized reflections of networks nodes which seek compatibility with their human and natural environments. On the other, in networks linkages exist between these decentralized reflections in the sense that nodes observe each other closely. (Fischer-Lescano and Teubner 2004: 1033)

It focuses on the linkage *process* rather than the substantive relationship of decentralized norms (Teubner 1997b: 8, 2006: 42). According to this approach, it is not institutional settings but the process of interactive connections between actors that provide operative order in the fragmented world (Fischer-Lescano and Teubner 2004: 1039). It finds the maintenance of 'weak compatibility' and lines of communication to be useful and appropriate, in order to deal with coexisting legal systems including treaty regimes (Fischer-Lescano and Teubner 2004: 1045).

This approach applies to the dispute settlement process of the above three cases in the North American region. Knowing the risk of incompatibility between the separate DS mechanisms, parties in conflict pursue an operational compatibility in the course of the DS process as a whole. While panels in the course of DS proceedings under the WTO Agreement and the NAFTA do not defer to the arguments and rulings of their counterparts, they take due notice of other systems by referring to rulings of one another.

Having that said, as we saw in the previous section, interactive connections between the parties do not necessarily occur in all cases. Networking theory is descriptive but not prescriptive: it does not provide logic about how different DS panels pursue compatible rulings with one another during the course of the DS proceedings.

Conclusion

As far as our analysis above has shown, neither approach fully explains the actual process of dispute settlement in the cases we refer to in this paper. On the other hand, each approach provides us certain clues for further investigation. Informal linkages among DS panels as well as among parties in conflict are generated in the course of sequential DS proceedings to address fragmentation of international norms. In this sense, sequencing DS procedures under different treaties did not exist or operate in an isolated manner. Thus, our answer to the first question we dealt with in this section is negative. Back-to-back DS proceedings are connected to one another, as shown in some DS rulings that refer to findings of their counterparts, owing to the parties' desire for managing fragmented norms.

Role of the dispute settlement rulings

Are formal DS proceedings inefficient?

The second question to be addressed is whether or not the settlement of disputes through mutual agreement impairs the role of DS proceedings or the rulings. Put differently, is it a waste of time and money to conduct separate DS proceedings if parties finally reach a comprehensive agreement to resolve the dispute?

After the conclusion of the comprehensive agreement, it was no longer necessary to implement preceding DS rulings and ongoing DS proceedings were terminated through mutual withdrawal of the claims. If the sequencing DS proceedings have some linkages between each other, as we found in the previous section, what is the role of these DS proceedings for the settlement of the dispute? This question lingers especially in cases where the formal DS procedures have only limited jurisdiction to deal with complex dispute involving multiple treaty obligations.

Possible reconfigurations

Needless to say, amicable settlement of the dispute is encouraged under both the WTO and the NAFTA DS procedures. It is not surprising that parties in conflict reach a compromise after the filing of DS procedures but *before* the issuance of the final rulings of the dispute settlement bodies (Busch and Reinhardt 2000: 164), because of the uncertainty of judicial outcome. On the contrary, once the ruling is issued, at least the prevailing party does not have to concede. We must look for a more suitable rationale elsewhere. In addition, any agreed solution of dispute is required to be consistent with the international obligations of disputing parties, as set forth in Article 3.7 of the WTO Understanding on Rules and Procedures Governing the Settlement of Disputes (DSU). Also, NAFTA panel decisions are binding, as set forth in Article 1904, paragraph 9 thereof, as are the adopted WTO panel reports that are binding in substance.

While several authors indicate certain effect of the DS rulings on the subsequent comprehensive agreements (Busch and Reinhardt 2006: 31; Carmody 2006: n.674), they do not pay attention to the situation where the settlement was reached after the issuance of DS rulings. In this context, again, Teubner's networking theory is a useful clue to understanding the role of DS rulings for the settlement of the fragmented dispute (see the subsection on the 'Networking approach', above).

While one can argue that both the WTO Agreement and the NAFTA are 'autopoietic', there is no coherence between them or higher normative framework to coordinate them. In the context of North American practice, the coexistence of the DS mechanisms under the WTO Agreement and NAFTA produced an alternative 'network' between state parties of both treaties that finally facilitated comprehensive agreements among parties in conflict to settle complex disputes involving the WTO, NAFTA and domestic laws.

Under the situation of fragmented coexistence of DS mechanisms, each DS mechanism deals with specific disputes in accordance with its internal logic. While DS panels refer to other rules and findings of their counterparts, it is solely the applicable laws which DS panels build their decisions on. Findings of each DS panel aim at an effective settlement of the dispute at hand, with potential conflicts between one another. When a conflict occurs between the findings of different DS panels in terms of the application of different rules, the parties are forced to find a way out of this 'double bind' situation. It is at this moment that the fragmentation of DS mechanism creates conflicts and provides parties with an opportunity for a comprehensive settlement of disputes, which 'allows for the transformation of external incompatibilities into internally-manageable contradictions' (Teubner 2009: 16). According to Teubner, 'Under certain conditions, however, hybrid arrangements provide for an institutional environment in which paradoxical communications is not repressed; not only is it tolerated, it is also invited, institutionally facilitated and sometime, rendered productive' (Teubner 2009: 17). In this sense, conflicts in norms or findings act as a catalyst for parties to settle the dispute at hand by overriding rules or DS findings that are in conflict with each other. More specifically, the assignment of the LCIA as the exclusive forum in the *Lumber* dispute can be seen as a result of a hybrid network between the parties in conflict.

In addition, in the *Lumber* and *Sweeteners* case, it was the conflicts between the findings resulting from separate DS proceedings before the WTO and the NAFTA panels that affected the settlement of the dispute through negotiation. Absent the superior court to coordinate conflicting rulings, the parties in any case have to resolve conflicts arising from the fragmented proceedings. At first glance, this kind of contradiction is to be eliminated in order to deal with complex disputes involving more than one treaty (Nakagawa 2007: 858). However, from a different perspective, it indicates rather the positive role of formal DS procedures. There is potential for conflict in any case, since the roots of conflicts reside in the fragmentation of substantive norms (the WTO, NAFTA and domestic laws). And a back-to-back recourse to multiple DS proceedings helped them to grasp overall picture of the complex dispute in its totality, only after they got enmeshed into the mud of fragmentation.

Conclusion

To address the fragmentation of international law, this paper has examined recent experiences in the North American region concerning the use of multiple DS fora for settling single economic disputes that have complex features involving more than one norm. Apparently, the fragmentation of DS mechanisms caused a sequence of litigations before multiple DS fora. Even if states do not originally intend to get stuck in the mud of repetitious DS proceedings, the losing party tends to take the other side to another tribunal, hoping to take something back. However, fragmented DS proceedings helped them to grasp the overall picture of the complex dispute in its totality, once they got enmeshed in them.

The role of fragmented DS mechanisms should thus be evaluated against this background. The process of dispute settlement may help parties to realize and sort out their stake and the essence of the dispute at hand. Even the winning party comes to realize that a victory in intergovernmental DS proceedings is not the end of the story. Effective remedies are required for the private actors who are directly involved in the dispute (Emerson and Bernier's statement 2006; Wilson's statement 2006).[2] It affected the parties' motivations to settle the dispute in a comprehensive manner through negotiation. This led to the comprehensive agreement that overrode earlier DS rulings and lawsuits, providing private parties with side payments.

The 'conflict' in international obligations brings the implementing country a double-bind situation when that country is to implement both treaties at the same time. In other words, the DS panels served to expose conflicts and to build a momentum for a comprehensive settlement of the dispute that is effective in the sense that it dispenses with the double-bind situation. Therefore, from this analysis, the answer to the second question is negative.

Conclusions

Let us sum up our observations by answering the two questions raised at the beginning of the paper. First of all, are the DS proceedings isolated when each of them deals with respective segment of a dispute? The answer is negative. Then, does the settlement of the dispute through comprehensive agreement impair the role of formal DS procedures? The answer is negative, again, as far as these three cases are concerned.

The fragmented process of dispute settlement took a significant role in all three interesting cases dealt with in this paper. The term 'process' is not limited to formal DS proceedings, but covers a progressive development as a whole to settle a complex and multidimensional dispute. The analysis of the dynamic process of dispute settlement indicates an evolution of an allopoietic system out of plural autopoietic systems such as the WTO and the NAFTA regimes, without formal integration of dispute settlement mechanisms under the WTO and the NAFTA. While Teubner's argument does not directly focus on conflicts among international agreements, and is not free from criticism (Perez 2006), it gives us a useful insight into the process of settling fragmented and complex international disputes. Further research is necessary to scrutinize its applicability to other disputes or in other areas.

This finding has implications to other regions as well. There is already a study that shows even East Asian countries proactively use the WTO DS mechanism in order to solve trade disputes among them, while still relying on negotiated deals (Nakagawa 2007: 841). What if there are more DS mechanisms available within the East Asian region? In this regard, the experience in North America also tells us that an increase in DS mechanisms does not necessarily lead to the legalization of dispute settlement. As long as the fragmentation of norms and coexistence of overlapping DS mechanisms remain, legalistic actions sooner or later face paradoxical double-bind situations, which require mutual reference, or double reflexivity, among independent DS mechanisms.

Finally, it is not an either–or question between legalism and negotiated settlement of disputes. What is required to comprehend the proper role of the fragmented international DS system is to seek a multidimensional and process-oriented perspective that provides parties with options for reaching the effective and flexible settlement of disputes. Finding networks or functional collaboration among separate DS mechanisms is a step forward.

Notes

1 *Mexico – Anti-Dumping Investigation of High-Fructose Corn Syrup (HFCS) from the United States*, WT/DS132/R, adopted 24 February 2000.

2 Announcement by the Honourable David Emerson, Canadian Minister of International Trade, and the Honourable Maxime Bernier, Canadian Minister of Industry, 14 December 2006; Opening Statement of Ambassador Michael Wilson before the Canadian Parliament Standing Committee on International Trade, 21 August 2006.

8 APEC's role in rationalizing international investment obligations

J. Anthony VanDuzer

Introduction

The world is girdled by an increasingly dense web of international investment agreements (IIAs) involving more than 170 countries. Despite widespread participation in investment treaties, however, many countries, including developing countries in particular, have steadfastly opposed the development of a multilateral regime for investment. Investment was removed from the Doha Round negotiating agenda in 2004 as part of efforts by members of the WTO to increase the likelihood of a positive outcome for the round.[1]

In this context, we will see continuing expansion in the number of bilateral and regional IIAs worldwide. Continued growth in IIAs, however, will make it even more difficult for countries to understand the precise nature and impact of their multiple obligations and to ensure that their international obligations and their domestic policy are consistent. The famous spaghetti bowl of treaties will increasingly threaten the ability of states to develop and implement a coherent policy on foreign investment that contributes to economic growth and development. At the same time, firms that seek to take advantage of the protections offered by IIAs will be impeded by the difficulty of understanding what protection they will receive from the tangle of overlapping, but not always consistent commitments undertaken by host states. The result may be to undermine the essential investment-inducing objectives of these agreements.

This paper analyses the challenges to coherence created by the current complex web of IIAs and explores the role that can be played by Asia-Pacific Economic Cooperation (APEC) in helping to develop a more coherent, comprehensible and effective international investment regime. APEC is well placed to contribute to resolving these challenges. Despite its promise, however, so far it is not clear to what extent APEC has contributed to coherence in the IIAs negotiated by its members and more generally to the coherence of international investment law.

The challenge of diversity in international investment obligations

Strands in the spaghetti bowl

In the absence of multilateral rules, bilateral and regional arrangements relating to investment have mushroomed. Since the Germany–Pakistan bilateral investment treaty (a BIT) signed in 1959, developed and developing countries have been actively negotiating BITs and other international agreements relating to investment. Historically, the primary purpose of these treaties has been to provide protection to developed country investors from discrimination, uncompensated expropriation and other unfair measures of host developing country governments. For host countries, the hope is that by committing to the protections guaranteed in these treaties, they will attract investment. The number of these treaties began to expand rapidly in the 1990s and the early part of this century. In 2009, UNCTAD estimated that there were more than 5,900 treaties dealing with investment issues worldwide, representing an increase of almost 40 per cent in the last decade alone (UNCTAD 2010a: 81).[2] The region leading the world in the expansion of IIAs is Asia. In 2008 and 2009, most of the new BITs concluded involved Asian countries, many of them with neighbours in the region (UNCTAD 2008b, 2009b).[3] The ASEAN member states and Japan concluded a comprehensive agreement covering trade in goods and services and investment in 2008.[4] China concluded a Free Trade Agreement (FTA) with New Zealand in April 2008 that includes a chapter on investment protection.[5] And in February 2009, ASEAN members concluded a Comprehensive Investment Agreement (ASEAN 26 February 2009).

While the more than 2,750 BITs involving 179 countries comprise the largest single group of investment treaties, an increasingly diverse variety of other treaties deal with investment issues, including preferential trade and investment agreements (PTIAs) negotiated bilaterally and regionally. Indeed the rate of growth in BITs has been declining since 2001 and there is a shift toward treaties combining investment rules with trade liberalization in free trade agreements, economic partnership agreements and other forms of preferential trading arrangements (UNCTAD 2007b: 17). The number of PTIAs doubled between 2003 and 2008 (UNCTAD 2008c: 26).[6] Some of these agreements provide protection equivalent to BITs, while others provide only a framework for cooperation.[7] PTIAs deal with trade in goods and services, labour issues, the movement of people, the environment and other issues not typically addressed in BITs. IIA obligations also overlap with the trade commitments of WTO Members. Obligations under the WTO's General Agreement on Trade in Services (GATS) (Annexe 1b 15 April 1994), Agreement on Trade-Related Investment Measures (TRIMs) (Part of Annexe 1A 15 April 1994) and Agreement on Trade-Related Aspects of Intellectual Property (TRIPS) (Annexe 1C 15 April 1994), among others, can all apply to host state rules related to investment.

Studies of these many strands of the global IIA web have found that there is an emerging consensus on the key categories of substantive obligations for investor protection that should be included in IIAs (UNCTAD 2008a).[8] At the same time, however, there is considerable variation in the ways in which these obligations are expressed and the exceptions and reservations to these obligations that different IIAs permit. In part, this is due to the recent adoption by some developed countries, like Canada[9] and the United States,[10] of new model agreements[11] that respond to the world's experience with investment obligations, including the explosion of investor-state arbitration cases.[12] New treaty provisions also reflect changing policy preoccupations, including greater concern regarding environmental and social issues related to investor activities and greater respect for the host country's right to regulate to achieve development objectives (UNCTAD 2010a: 87, 88). For example, the recent EU–CARIFORUM Economic Partnership Agreement (EPA) expressly permits the parties to take measures to prevent investors from engaging in bribery and corruption, and to ensure compliance with core labour standards.[13]

Variations in treaty content are also driven by a shift in the context in which investment obligations are being negotiated. While traditionally BITs were entered into between developed countries seeking protection for their investors and developing countries hoping to attract investment, increasingly developing countries are signing investment agreements among themselves, reflecting their increasing importance as capital exporters. Nineteen of 82 BITs signed in 2009 (23 per cent) were such south–south agreements. While China is the overall leader among developing countries, India led the way in 2008 with six new agreements with other developing countries (UNCTAD 2009b). South–south treaties sometimes do not mirror investment treaties traditionally negotiated between developed and developing countries (UNCTAD 2008c). The 2005 India–Singapore Comprehensive Economic Cooperation Agreement, for example, does not include some provisions that have been thought of as core IIA provisions, like most favoured nation treatment and 'fair and equitable treatment'.[14] The 19 member states of the Common Market for Eastern and Southern Africa (COMESA) entered into the COMESA Common Investment Agreement in 2007. This Agreement contains a variety of innovative features, including a mandate for a committee created under the agreement to make recommendations to member states with respect to 'the development of common minimum standards relating to investment in areas such as: (i) environmental impact and social impact assessments; (ii) labor standards; (iii) respect for human rights; (iv) conduct in conflict zones; (v) corruption; and (vi) subsidies' (COMESA 2007: art 7.2(d)).[15]

In addition, though they are relatively few in number, some recent treaties between developed countries also contain distinctive features. Unlike US investment treaties with developing countries and the North American Free Trade Agreement (NAFTA 1993), the US–Australia Free Trade Agreement does not provide for investor-state dispute settlement in its investment chapter.[16]

Finally, there has been a significant increase in the number of investor-state arbitrations under investment treaties. Fifty-seven per cent of known cases have been commenced in the last five years (UNCTAD 2010a: 83). In 2009 alone, at least 32 new cases were filed, bringing the total of known treaty arbitrations to 357 (UNCTAD 2010a: 83).[17] These cases involve 81 states. In most cases (over 90 per cent), claims have been by investors from developed countries against developing countries. About 43 per cent of the cases decided so far have found in favour of the investor, in some cases based on broad interpretations of vaguely worded IIA provisions, especially the obligation commonly imposed on host states to provide investors with 'fair and equitable treatment' (UNCTAD 2010a: 83).[18] Another troubling aspect of these cases has been a lack of consistency in tribunal awards creating uncertainty regarding the scope of IIA obligations (UNCTAD 2009a: 12, 2010a: 83).

An attractive solution to the chaotic proliferation of IIAs would be a multilateral agreement, but the prospects for such an agreement appear remote. Investment was added to the WTO agenda at the Singapore ministerial conference in 1996 with the creation of a working group on trade and investment (WTO 1996). When the Doha Round of negotiations was initiated in 2001, the members agreed that negotiations on investment would take place after the 2003 ministerial meeting on the basis of a decision to be taken at that meeting on the modalities of negotiations (WTO 2001: para. 20). After much study and discussion, however, investment was formally removed from the negotiating agenda in 2004 as part of efforts by members of the WTO to narrow the focus of the negotiations with a view to increasing the likelihood of a positive outcome for the round.

In summary, the global network of IIAs has several important characteristics. It is rapidly expanding at both the bilateral and regional level. While there is general agreement on the kinds of protections for investors that may be included in an IIA, there is increasing variation in the content of these protections, and exceptions and reservations are more frequently found. Further, new types of provisions addressing a range of new issues in some agreements seek to better preserve the ability of countries to regulate foreign direct investment to achieve development and other public policy goals. This is particularly true in the burgeoning number of south–south IIAs. There is a growing trend for investment protection provisions to be integrated into much more comprehensive treaties dealing with trade in goods and services and other issues. Finally, investment arbitrations are becoming more frequent and, sometimes, have resulted in some surprising and conflicting decisions. As a result of all of these characteristics, the universe of IIAs is becoming more diverse and complex, presenting a serious challenge to policy coherence, as discussed in the next section.

The policy coherence challenge

Introduction

The adoption of new treaty models and new approaches to investment protection in some treaties demonstrates one of the benefits of the current practice of independent, uncoordinated bilateral and regional negotiation of IIAs: the prospect for experimentation and innovation. In principle, this gives countries choices when determining what international investment obligations they undertake and allows them to customize their obligations to their particular situations. Often, especially for developing countries, this is not the case in practice. When negotiating with developed countries, negotiations may begin and end with a model agreement drafted by the developed country and offered on a take-it-or-leave-it basis.

There is also a tension between, on the one hand, the need to ensure that the international investment regime can adapt to our evolving understanding of the nature and effect of investment obligations and to the differential development needs of host countries and, on the other, the coherence of the international investment regime. More importantly, the complex and varied international investment rules to which countries have committed themselves can create a serious challenge to policy coherence for individual countries. This policy coherence challenge operates on at least two different levels for each country: coherence between a country's domestic policy and its international obligations and coherence between its different international obligations. For developing countries this challenge is often compounded by limited capacity to fully engage in a careful assessment of what treaty provisions are optimal for them as well as compatible with their domestic policy and their other international obligations. For all countries, the coherence challenge is growing as a result of innovation in the terms of IIAs, the incorporation of investment rules in more broadly focused economic integration agreements and the evolution in our understanding of IIA provisions through the decisions by investor-state arbitration tribunals.

Coherence between domestic policy and international commitments

For many countries, it is difficult to ensure that their multiple diverse IIAs are compatible with their current foreign investment policy. As well, since IIAs typically operate for long terms with lengthy notice requirements for termination, states need to be able to forecast their future foreign investment policy and ensure that the treaties that they sign do not constrain their ability to implement that policy. Throughout the term of the treaty, states need to constantly bear in mind their obligations as domestic policy evolves to ensure that they remain in compliance over time (UNCTAD 2008c). These challenges can only be met if a state has a developed domestic policy on foreign investment to which it is prepared to make a long-term commitment. In many developing countries, this degree of policy development, certainty and commitment simply does not exist. In these circumstances, it is extremely difficult to make effective choices regarding what level of international obligation to undertake.

For example, a threshold domestic policy issue for each state negotiating an IIA to consider in relation to commitments it proposes to undertake is how open its domestic markets should be to foreign investment. If a country has already adopted a policy of opening the domestic economy to foreign investment with limited restrictions, the effect of an IIA provision guaranteeing that access (often called a 'right of establishment') would not require any change in government policy. However, such a provision in an IIA would preclude a future return to a policy of excluding or limiting foreign investment. It is precisely this limitation on future policy change by the host state that is the mechanism by which the IIA commitment encourages foreign investment. By contrast, if a state does not permit foreign investment, either generally or in particular sectors, if it does not have a robust system in place to make decisions about permitting particular foreign investments, or if it lacks the capacity to regulate foreign investors who enter the country, a commitment to a right of establishment would force a substantial, and likely inappropriate, shift in domestic policy on foreign investment. This simple example shows the importance of establishing domestic foreign investment policy before a country can make appropriate choices about what IIA commitments to undertake.

Another specific domestic policy area that may be affected by international trade and investment commitments is performance requirements imposed by states as a condition of permitting an investment or granting a subsidy, such as a requirement to hire a minimum number of local employees. Some performance requirements that affect trade in goods, such as requirements for foreign manufacturers to source inputs locally, will be inconsistent with the obligations of WTO members in the General Agreement on Tariffs and Trade (GATT 30 October 1947) to provide national treatment and not to impose quotas on goods. The application of these GATT rules to performance requirements imposed in connection with investments is confirmed by the WTO TRIMs Agreement, which provides an illustrative list of trade-distorting investment measures. A small but growing minority of IIAs impose further restrictions on states' resort to performance requirements (UNCTAD 2003: 119-120). While constraints on use of performance requirements in an IIA may be beneficial in terms of attracting foreign investment, the point here is simply that a well-developed domestic policy and a sophisticated appreciation of the impact on domestic policy of international trade and investment rules is needed to avoid conflicts between domestic rules and international commitments. This is a challenge for most countries.

Coherence between international commitments

A second policy coherence challenge for states is the complex interaction between the IIAs they have entered into as well as between their IIAs and any trade commitment they have undertaken that may have implications for investment. If a state is a WTO member, for example, it will have to consider the relationship between IIA commitments and its obligations under the WTO's GATS. A country's GATS obligations may be relevant because GATS applies to the supply of services through a commercial presence, which includes some forms of investment. The possible interaction between IIAs and GATS is complex and will vary significantly from one country to the next.[19] To the extent that states already have obligations under GATS, they must evaluate whether the obligations entered into under investment agreements are consistent with their GATS obligations. If a state has already agreed to a certain obligation under GATS, a similar commitment in an IIA may not represent a substantial additional commitment. For example, accepting an obligation to admit foreign investors in an IIA may seems to have only a marginal effect if the state has already committed through GATS to an unlimited national treatment obligation in relation to that country's services suppliers operating through a commercial presence. Even if an IIA commitment seems identical to a state's prior GATS commitment, however, the IIA provision applies more broadly in fact because it is not limited to investors supplying services through a commercial presence as defined in GATS. A wider variety of investors in all sectors are protected. As well, if the IIA contains investor-state dispute settlement procedures, the IIA commitment differs from the GATS obligation, because it can be enforced directly by the investor through those procedures.[20]

Most-favoured nation (MFN) obligations, which appear in some form in most IIAs and GATS, raise particular problems for policy coherence. Though they vary in scope, MFN clauses in IIAs generally oblige each state party to treat investors from the other party states no less favourably than investors from any other country. MFN clauses in existing IIAs can have the effect of committing a state to extend the benefit of commitments undertaken in new IIAs to investors from states party to those existing agreements. By importing obligations agreed to in one negotiation into another treaty context, an MFN obligation might effectively harmonize obligations to the highest level negotiated in any treaty. For many states who have signed multiple IIAs, the operation of the MFN clause in this way might result in unanticipated consequences. In the arbitral decision in *Maffezini* v. *The Kingdom of Spain*,[21] the tribunal held that, subject to certain limitations, an MFN obligation could apply to treaty-based dispute settlement procedures, meaning that an investor protected by an MFN clause in an IIA could use the most favourable process found in any IIA to which the host state is a party, rather than the specific dispute settlement process provided for in the treaty to which the investor's home state is a party. Subsequent cases have come to differing conclusions, and some recent model treaties have provisions that specifically address this problem. The model treaties of Canada and the United States now limit the MFN obligation to specific kinds of activities in relation to an investment, with the result that MFN treatment does not apply to dispute settlement procedures. They also specifically exclude the application of MFN to most other international obligations and dispute resolution procedures. Most existing treaties, however, do not contain such protections.

Increasing challenges to policy coherence over time

INTRODUCTION

The challenges related to policy coherence are getting harder as a result of a number of contemporaneous trends. One is the proliferation of increasingly diverse IIAs, including in particular PTIAs. As well, while the core of investment protection obligations are well established, the content of IIAs is evolving in a number of ways: (i) with a view to better preserving host state policy space for the regulation of investment, the content of core obligations is being expressed in more specific terms and more treaties are including increasingly extensive exceptions and reservations; (ii) IIAs are beginning to include new kinds of provisions designed to facilitate the contribution of foreign direct investment to development in the host state and the achievement of other public policy objectives; and (iii) some investor-state arbitration tribunals have adopted unexpectedly broad and inconsistent interpretations of core IIA provisions.

CHANGING CONTENT OF CORE OBLIGATIONS AND INCREASED USE OF EXCEPTIONS AND RESERVATIONS

Some countries have modified the core provisions in their more recent investment treaties to ensure that their IIA obligations strike an appropriate balance between protecting investors against state action and preserving sufficient regulatory flexibility for states. At least in part, these modifications have been in response to arbitral decisions adopting broad interpretations of those provisions. Another approach has been to add exceptions and to permit reservations to protect the policy space for states to regulate in areas like the protection of health, the environment and national security and to take prudential measures to protect the host state's financial system. Both these approaches were adopted by Canada and the United States in the most recent versions of their bilateral investment treaties (DFAIT 2004; USDS 2004).[22] Similar provisions have been adopted in recent treaties entered into by a number of countries, including Japan, Korea, China, Singapore, Jordan and Peru (UNCTAD 2007a, 2010a: 87).

Adopting new, more nuanced versions of provisions like those guaranteeing national treatment or prohibiting expropriation without compensation bolstered by exceptions may be desirable in terms of preserving domestic policy space, but this trend raises new policy coherence challenges. For example, what are the implications of these new more balanced provisions for the interpretation of different versions of the same provision in older treaties? Should the older provisions be interpreted to provide broader protection for investors because either their language is not as specific or because the inclusion of exceptions in newer treaties implies that the exceptions did not exist previously? There is no straightforward answer to these questions. It is not clear to what extent the scope of IIA obligations in older agreements may be different from newer versions of the same provisions or whether the MFN obligations in existing treaties may effectively guarantee investors the best protection available in any treaty. There is no doubt, however, that the introduction of different versions of core provisions and exceptions has rendered IIA obligations less predictable and increased the policy coherence challenge for host states.

NEW PROVISIONS TO FACILITATE THE CONTRIBUTION OF FOREIGN DIRECT INVESTMENT TO DEVELOPMENT IN THE HOST STATE AND TO ACHIEVE OTHER PUBLIC POLICY OBJECTIVES

There is a debate about whether even these new IIA models referred to above reflect the right balance between investor protection and the interests of host countries. A number of countries have re-evaluated the benefits of IIAs in light of weak empirical evidence of their investment-inducing effects (Sachs and Sauvant 2009)[23] as well as some surprisingly broad interpretations of IIA obligations by arbitral tribunals. One result is that there is increased interest in investment promotion commitments from developing country parties to IIAs. Such provisions are seldom found in existing IIAs (UNCTAD 2008d). Where they have been included, investment promotion provisions contain vague, non-binding commitments or merely confirm the continuation of existing programmes.[24]

More fundamentally, academics and governments are asking whether there is a need to change the content of IIAs to address more directly the development issues that are so vital to developing countries. Attracting investment is necessary but not sufficient for development. Effective host country regulation is also needed (VanDuzer 2008: 359). One way to achieve this would be to require greater investment by developed countries in technical assistance to support the creation of the kinds of robust, transparent and effective regulatory regimes that are likely to both encourage investment and facilitate the achievement by host states of their development objectives. Few treaties have provisions on technical assistance, though, like investment promotion, technical assistance is more often addressed in recent agreements (UNCTAD 2008b).

The adoption of investment promotion and technical assistance provisions in IIAs would not represent a threat to policy coherence for host states since they do not limit their policy-making flexibility, in most cases. Indeed, at least with respect to technical assistance, such commitments may even assist host countries to better ensure policy coherence. Other new kinds of provisions do raise coherence issues.

Very recently, a few treaties have begun to include provisions that are designed to assist host states to achieve development and other policy goals more directly and effectively. For example, some provisions in recent treaties support host state efforts to curtail bribery and corruption, meet minimum labour standards and protect the environment. In some cases, these kinds of provisions may be attractive to host developing countries as ways to ensure that FDI leads to sustainable development. At the same time, some developed countries are interested in imposing standards for social responsibility on their investors in connection with their actions abroad.[25] Countries like Canada and the USA now routinely seek commitments regarding the maintenance of labour and environmental standards in their trade and investment agreements.[26] While a few countries have taken some limited steps toward incorporating these kinds of provisions,[27] so far at least, no agreement has done so in a thoroughgoing way.[28] Nevertheless, going forward, the changing assessment of the costs and benefits associated with IIAs and changing policy preoccupations in developed and developing countries are likely to combine to drive further innovation in IIA provisions supporting an effort to achieve development and other policy goals. However desirable such provisions may be, overall, these innovations will further aggravate the problem of policy coherence. As well, since development needs vary across countries, adapting IIAs to take such needs into account may reduce coherence across IIAs.

INVESTOR-STATE DISPUTE ARBITRATION CASES

As noted, one consequence of the expansion of IIAs that provide for investor-state arbitration is that increasing numbers of cases are being brought. In each such case, an arbitral tribunal must decide how treaty obligations apply to a specific government measure. Decisions in individual cases can clarify the nature and content of a particular obligation in a treaty as well as identical or similar obligations in other treaties. So far, however, investment arbitrations have not greatly contributed to coherence in investment rules through a progressive refinement of our understanding of what IIA provisions require. One reason is that some decisions have adopted novel interpretations of vaguely worded treaty provisions. Also, decisions have not always been consistent. While arbitral tribunals frequently rely on previous decisions for guidance, typically there is no requirement for a tribunal's decision in a particular case to be consistent with decisions in previous cases. There are numerous examples of inconsistent decisions (UNCTAD 2008c: 35, 2010a: 85). Novel interpretations of IIA provisions may mean that IIA commitments apply in unexpected ways. Inconsistent interpretations reduce certainty regarding the scope of treaty obligations. Both pose challenges for governments seeking to ensure that their actions comply with their international obligations on an ongoing basis.

Another challenge to coherence is that the dispute settlement procedures are not the same in all treaties and are evolving in new treaties, both as a result of innovations in procedures adopted by states in their investment treaties[29] and changes to the arbitral rules that govern arbitration proceedings (UNCTAD 2010a: 88, 89).[30] Varying procedures make it harder for states to manage their participation in dispute settlement and their exposure to liability effectively.

The role of APEC

Introduction

APEC is well placed to respond to the challenge of improving coherence in international investment obligations. APEC is a grouping of developed and developing countries whose overall goal is to facilitate sustainable economic growth in the Asia-Pacific region though trade and investment liberalization. To achieve this goal, APEC has adopted a number of instruments that are intended to contribute to greater coherence in IIA practice, including its Non-Binding Investment Principles (APEC 1994). APEC also promotes understanding of international investment issues and the development needs of its members through research and capacity-building programmes. In this way, APEC facilitates domestic policy development and informed choices regarding compatible IIA obligations. Despite its promise, however, so far it is not clear how significant APEC's contribution has been to coherence in the IIAs negotiated by its members.

The advantages of APEC

The nature of APEC

APEC possesses several characteristics that should allow it to contribute effectively to the development of a more coherent international investment regime. APEC operates on the basis of non-binding commitments, open dialogue and equal respect for the views of all participants. Unlike the WTO, APEC is not a forum for negotiating treaty obligations. Decisions made within APEC are reached by consensus, and commitments are undertaken on a voluntary basis. While a multilateral treaty undoubtedly represents the most effective way to achieve coherence in international investment law, attempts to develop a multilateral treaty on investment have foundered.[31] The efforts to support coherence though a variety of other 'soft' strategies employed by APEC, as described below, represent a second-best solution. Nevertheless, APEC's activities can contribute to a more coherent regime for international investment and are likely the only feasible approach in the present environment.[32]

As a broadly representative group, APEC is well placed to work toward investment rules that support the interests of countries at different stages of development. APEC's 21 members[33] include China, Japan, Australia, New Zealand, Russia, the three NAFTA states and a number of smaller developing countries. APEC involves two of the three major trade and investment groups in the world – North America and Asia-Pacific – the latter being the region that is most actively engaged currently in the negotiation of IIAs. Together, APEC countries account for approximately 40 per cent of the world's population, 54 per cent of world GDP and 44 per cent of world trade (APEC 2009).

APEC also has the capacity to link discussions about investment with other issues, such as corporate governance and social responsibility, anti-corruption, labour standards and the movement of people. Going forward, investment rules will have to be more responsive to these social dimensions of globalization and the development needs of host countries. APEC, with its broad range of members and its programmes on all of these issues, is well placed to support the development of rules that meaningfully address them. As well, it seems clear that the next generation of investment rules will need to be much more closely integrated into rules relating to international trade in goods and services. APEC is engaged on all of these issues as well.

One final aspect of APEC that deserves mention is its engagement with the private sector. The APEC Business Advisory Council was created in 1995 to provide a business sector perspective on the various initiatives and activities undertaken by APEC. Business leaders from every country, representing large and small businesses from a wide variety of sectors, make up its membership. The participation of the business community is an important element of developing effective domestic policy on investment as well as workable international investment rules.

APEC goals

Another advantage of APEC is that it has strongly embraced the goal of policy coherence in investment rules as part of its efforts to facilitate sustainable economic growth in the Asia-Pacific region through trade and investment liberalization. APEC ministers expressly accepted 'high quality, consistent and comprehensive' FTAs that include investment provisions as a goal of APEC at its meeting in November 2008 (APEC 2008b).[34]

APEC activities

The 'three pillars' of APEC's activities are: (i) trade and investment liberalization; (ii) business facilitation; and (iii) economic and technical cooperation. Activities in these three areas form the foundation of a broad-based approach that supports greater coherence in international investment law.

In terms of activities directly related to IIAs, APEC has developed three major investment instruments that are useful policy tools for countries seeking greater coherence in their international investment obligations.

1 'Non-binding Investment Principles' (APEC 1994).[35] Adopted in 1994, these 12 general principles broadly correspond to the core provisions that are found in most IIAs and are intended, where adopted, to facilitate investment inflows.
2 'Menu of Options for Investment Liberalization and Business Facilitation to Strengthen the APEC Economies' (APEC 1997). Adopted in 1997, the Menu sets out a broad range of options for regulatory reform at the domestic level. The Menu addresses a variety of policy areas with a view to assisting countries to identify measures that would liberalize their domestic investment regime and facilitate private sector investment. Some of these correspond directly to core provisions of IIAs, such as those dealing with non-discrimination and expropriation, while others cover related policy areas, like competition policy and intellectual property. Progress on implementation is regularly reported by APEC members.
3 'Investment Transparency Standards' (APEC 2003). Adopted in 2002 by the economic leaders of APEC, these standards provide detailed transparency benchmarks for governments related to: (i) trade and investment liberalization and facilitation; (ii) monetary, financial and fiscal policies; (iii) services; (iv) investment; (v) competition policy and regulatory reform; (vi) standards and conformity assessment procedures; (vii) intellectual property; (viii) customs procedures; (ix) market access; and (x) business mobility.

These instruments facilitate the development of domestic investment policy, which was identified above as a prerequisite for countries to be able to negotiate coherent international obligations. At the same time, their non-prescriptive character recognizes the diversity among APEC's membership, in terms of level of development and openness to foreign investment, while encouraging common approaches to negotiating investment treaties amongst APEC member economies.

APEC is also directly involved in providing technical assistance and capacity building in relation to investment through a variety of programmes in a wide range of areas related to investment.[36] APEC's Investment Experts Group of the Committee on Trade and Investment (IEG), which has representatives from every APEC member government as well as other investment experts, is actively engaged in programmes designed to improve the transparency of investment regimes, in:

- promoting dialogue with the APEC business community on ways to improve the investment environment;

- enhancing investment promotion and facilitation;
- improving technical cooperation;
- training, and;
- other forms of capacity building.

It also carries out research on issues like the relationship between investment and development and how to foster a more favourable investment environment through IIAs.

To take just one specific example of APEC's activities, as part of APEC's efforts to develop a comprehensive business facilitation programme, a project entitled 'Capacity Building for Investment Liberalization and Facilitation' was proposed by Japan and endorsed by the APEC Human Resources Development Working Group Capacity Building Network in 2006. The project was implemented in collaboration with the IEG. One component of the programme was to develop a series of case studies on investment to assist business and government stakeholders to more successfully carry out investment transactions. These case studies were published by APEC as *Opportunities and Challenges for Foreign Investment in the APEC Region: Case Studies* in December 2008 (Akatsu 2008).[37] Another component of the project consisted of capacity-building workshops and other training programmes for stakeholders based on the case studies. These and similar programmes on investment policy generally, as well as myriad industry-specific issues, assist not only governments seeking to enhance their capacity to develop effective investment policy, but also businesses seeking to invest in APEC member countries.

Another important initiative is APEC's ongoing work to develop a model Free Trade Agreement chapter dealing with investment. Following APEC's ministerial meeting in Santiago, Chile in 2004, APEC's Committee on Trade and Investment was charged with developing a non-binding set of best practices for FTAs. By November 2008, 15 chapters had been endorsed by APEC members. An investment chapter has been drafted, but only a majority of APEC members have so far endorsed it (APEC 2008b). A model investment chapter, if used by parties in practice, could be an effective source of harmonized rules for APEC members and other countries. In the past, the OECD's Draft Convention on the Protection of Foreign Property served as the model for many of the BITs negotiated in the 1970s and 1980s, which resulted in a high degree of consistency of investment obligations during that period (OECD 1967). Greater consistency in investment treaties based on an APEC model would facilitate greater policy coherence. APEC model provisions could contribute, as well, to redressing the chronic inequality of bargaining power between developed countries and developing countries resulting from unequal economic and political power. Model provisions supported by APEC capacity-building activities could also contribute to redressing asymmetries in information and experience with IIAs and in the resources available to evaluate the impact of IIAs on the domestic investment environment, and on social and economic policies. Even if not adopted, an investment chapter would have a positive educational impact, helping governments learn from the experience of others and providing a useful reference point for negotiations.

APEC's success to date in promoting policy coherence

Despite APEC's activities directed to promoting coherence in the IIAs negotiated by its members, substantial differences remain in those agreements. A recent study of APEC IIAs found that there was considerable uniformity regarding categories of core investor protections, but increasing variation in their content (UNCTAD 2008a). Also, while APEC's investment instruments have been substantially followed at the level of the general structure and intent, there remains significant inconsistency between the instruments and IIA practice in the APEC region. What the situation would be in the absence of APEC's efforts, however, is not obvious. It seems likely that APEC has been able to assist some of its members in the formulation of more effective domestic policy regarding foreign investment and has enhanced their capacity to negotiate compatible IIAs, though success in this regard is hard to measure.

The failure by APEC to adopt a model investment chapter for FTAs at its meeting in November 2008 may point to a limit on what APEC can achieve. While APEC's broad-based cooperative approach may facilitate understanding, enhance domestic policy making and accommodate the differing development needs of its members, the diversity in its membership is likely to be a substantial impediment to real progress in achieving coherence in the IIAs they negotiate (Hufbauer and Schott 2007).[38]

Conclusions

The complex and expanding web of agreements to which countries are committed poses serious challenges to coherence between their domestic policy and their international obligations. A threshold problem for some countries is that they lack domestic capacity to formulate and implement domestic policy on foreign investment and to ensure that their international obligations are compatible with and supportive of their domestic policy. APEC's work directly addresses the shortfall in domestic capacity, supporting learning and sharing of experience on a wide range of investment policy issues. At the same time, APEC is actively working toward improved coherence through its research and other programmes and by developing common principles, practices and treaty provisions relating to investment. In light of the current impracticality of negotiating multilateral investment rules, efforts like APEC's that are not linked to specific treaty negotiations are needed if coherence is to be advanced. Nevertheless, it remains unclear whether APEC's efforts will substantially improve coherence in the international investment rules that bind its members in light of the many factors currently encouraging diversity in IIA obligations.

Notes

1 See the discussion of the history of investment in the WTO in Singapore Ministerial Declaration 1996 and Doha Ministerial Declaration 2001.

2 In 2008, UNCTAD estimated that only 76 per cent of IIAs are in force and 2,700 are agreements limited to commitments to reducing double taxation (UNCTAD 2008c). By the end of 2007, 120 BITs were renegotiated treaties between parties who were already parties to BITs (UNCTAD 2008c). Also, some existing agreements have been

terminated recently. In January 2008, Ecuador announced that it would terminate its BITs with nine countries. Venezuela recently denounced its BIT with the Netherlands and some BITs between member states of the European Union have been terminated (UNCTAD 2010a: 85, 86).

3 The Asia-Pacific region has the largest number of BITs, with 1,050 by the end of 2007. China alone has signed more than 120 (UNCTAD 2008b: 36).

4 Japan–ASEAN Comprehensive Economic Partnership Agreement, signed 26 March to 14 April 2008, entered into force 1 December 2008.

5 New Zealand–China Free Trade Agreement, signed 7 April 2008, entered into force 1 October 2008.

6 The more than 250 PTIAs remain a small fraction of the number of BITs.

7 For example, 'ASEAN–US Trade and Investment Framework Agreement' (USTR 25 August 2006).

8 This report analyses a sample of 28 IIAs between and/or involving APEC member economies. These comprise 14 BITs and 14 PTIAs. In *International Investment Rule-Making: Stocktaking, Challenges and the Way Forward* (UNCTAD 2008c: 2), the current state of affairs is described as 'unity at the core' and 'variation at the periphery'.

9 Canadian Model Foreign Investment Promotion and Protection Agreement, 2003.

10 United States Model Bilateral Investment Treaty, November 2004.

11 UNCTAD recently reported that eight countries are currently revising their model agreements and six have completed revisions in the past few years (UNCTAD 2010a: 85).

12 By the end of 2009, at least 357 investor-state cases had been initiated (UNCTAD 2010a: 83).

13 EU–CARIFORUM Economic Partnership Agreement, signed 15 October 2008, OJ L289/1/3, 30 October 2008. (CARIFORUM includes the states of the Caricom and the Dominican Republic.)

14 India–Singapore Comprehensive Economic Cooperation Agreement, signed 29 June 2005, entered into force 1 August 2005, ch. 6.

15 See, generally, *International Investment Law: Understanding Concepts and Tracking Innovations* (OECD 2008: c.3).

16 Australia–US Free Trade Agreement, signed 18 May 2004, entered into force 1 January 2005, ch. 11.

17 This represents a slight increase from 2008, when 30 new cases were initiated. Increased awareness regarding the existence and nature of investor-state proceedings resulted, in part, from increased transparency. A few large, high-profile awards may also be responsible.

18 UNCTAD recently reported that 164 known cases have been concluded. Of these 62 were decided in favour of host countries, 47 were decided in favour of investors and 55 were settled (UNCTAD 2010a: 83).

19 The scholarly literature on this subject is just beginning to develop. See Adlung and Molinuevo (2008) and Houde and Yannaca-Small (2004).

20 Ensuring coherence is also more complicated where, as is the case for most WTO members, a country has committed to providing national treatment for only some sectors in its national schedule of commitments. Also, in practice, GATS commitments are currently being negotiated as part of the Doha Round.

21 Subsequent decisions reaching varying conclusions are *Salini* v. *Jordan*; *Siemens* v. *Argentina*; and *Plama Consortium Limited* v. *Bulgaria*.

22 See, generally, *World Investment Report 2007: FDI in Extractive Industries* (UNCTAD 2006b). In 2009, a subcommittee to the Advisory Committee on International Economic Policy (ACIEP) had been asked to review the US Model BIT. ACIEP is a committee of non-government advisers to the US government on international economic policy (Vis-Dunbar 2009a). Its report was presented to the State Department and the US Trade Representative on 30 September 2010 (Advisory Committee on International Economic Policy 2009).

23 Sach and Sauvant provide an up-to-date survey of the evidence. They conclude that 'it is difficult to establish firmly the effect of BITs on foreign direct investment flows', citing data problems, variability in BITs and the challenge of isolating the effect of IIAs from other variables affecting investment flows.
24 For example, 'Agreement on Partnership and Cooperation Establishing a Partnership between the European Communities and Their Member States and the Russian Federation' (European Commission 24 June 1994: Art. 58).
25 Host states may legitimately view the extraterritorial application of home state regulation as an unwelcome intrusion on host state sovereignty. They may even view it as neo-colonialist or racist interference (Seck 2008). It is also possible that part of the motivation of developed countries seeking commitments in relation to labour rights and the environment may be a reduction in the outflow of capital to treaty partners with lower effective standards in these areas.
26 See, for instance, 'Free Trade Agreement between Canada and Peru' (DFAIT 29 May 2008).
27 See the discussion of the COMESA Common Investment Agreement and the EU–CARIFORUM Economic Partnership Agreement.
28 A model BIT that does so has been proposed by the International Institute for Sustainable Development (Mann *et al.* 2005).
29 See, for example, the extensive provisions in 'Canada's Model FIPA' (DFAIT 2004: Arts 20–47) that provide for, among other things, the issuance of binding treaty interpretations by a commission of ministerial representatives of the party states, transparency of proceedings and detailed rules for the participation of *amicus curiae*. 'The Treaty between the United States of America and the Oriental Republic of Uruguay Concerning the Encouragement and Reciprocal Protection of Investment' (Trade Compliance Center 4 November 2005: Annexe E) obliges the parties to discuss the desirability of an appellate body to promote consistency in arbitration decisions.
30 Most international investment arbitrations take place under the arbitration rules in the 'Convention on the Settlement of Investment Disputes between States and Nationals of Other States' (ICSID Convention 18 March 1965) and the rules created by the ICSID Administrative Council pursuant to Arts 6(1)(a) to (c) of the 'ICSID Convention' (Administrative and Financial Regulations, Rules of Procedure for the Institution of Conciliation and Arbitration Proceedings (Institution Rules); Rules of Procedure for Arbitration Proceedings (Arbitration Rules) Doc. ICSID/15 (ICSID Arbitration Rules)). On 5 April 2006, the Administrative Council approved significant amendments to the ICSID Arbitration Rules. These amendments came into effect on 10 April 2006 (ICSID 5 April 2006).
31 Including, for example, the attempt by the members of the Organization for Economic Cooperation and Development (OECD) to negotiate a multilateral agreement on investment, which failed in 1998 (OECD 1998). On the history of investment and the WTO, see the Singapore Ministerial Declaration 1996 (WTO 1996) and Doha Ministerial Declaration 2001 (WTO 2001).
32 In light of the dim prospects for a multilateral agreement, UNCTAD recently endorsed the development of a forum for consensus building, sharing experiences and best practices on investment treaties (UNCTAD 2010a: 90).
33 Australia; Brunei Darussalam; Canada; Chile; People's Republic of China; Hong Kong, China; Indonesia; Japan; Republic of Korea; Malaysia; Mexico; New Zealand; Papua New Guinea; Peru; The Republic of the Philippines; The Russian Federation; Singapore; Chinese Taipei; Thailand; United States of America; and Vietnam.
34 The role of model FTA chapters in promoting coherence was also acknowledged in the '2008 Leaders' Declaration' (APEC 2008b).
35 A comparison of the APEC principles and other major international investment obligations, including those in the WTO, NAFTA and BITs, is undertaken in Gugler and Tomsik (2006).
36 Many examples may be found on the APEC website, such as 'Market Liberalization and its Relationship with Market Structure, Conduct and Performance of the Food

Processing Industry in ASEAN Economies' (Ahmad and Shamsudin 2008). APEC adopted an Investment Facilitation Action Plan in 2007, the implementation of which is to be monitored by the new APEC Policy Support Unit. APEC members also have Individual Action Plans for trade and investment liberalization, the implementation of which is subject to peer review.

37 The project was led by the Institute for International Studies and Training, a non-government organization, under the supervision of Japan's Ministry of Economy, Trade and Industry.

38 Hufbauer and Schott are also skeptical that it will be possible to agree on a draft investment chapter.

9 Vertical allocation of competences for investment treaties in the European Union

Markus Burgstaller[1]

Introduction

The era of modern investment treaties began when Germany and Pakistan concluded a bilateral agreement that entered into force in 1962. Germany's interest in investment treaties was grounded in the loss of its earlier foreign investment in negotiated settlements after 1949 as a result of the damage it had brought in World War II. In an investment treaty the host state renounces part of its sovereignty in order to attract foreign investment. In turn, for an investor an investment treaty provides legal protection against state interference, which can come in a range of different forms, including expropriation, conversion and transfer of assets or any forms of unfair, inequitable, discriminatory or arbitrary treatment. Today, these investment guarantees are contained in large part in the approximately 2,000 bilateral investment treaties (BITs) that are currently in force worldwide. Germany has the most comprehensive network with 126 BITs in force, while other EU member states also concluded a great number of BITs and continue to conclude such treaties.[2]

Prior to the entry into force of the Treaty of Lisbon the then European Community had never concluded an investment treaty or an international agreement that was predominantly regulating investment with third states. Indeed, from Opinion 1/94 issued by the European Court of Justice (ECJ) it followed that the Community competence for the common commercial policy (CCP) did not extend to foreign direct investment (FDI) involving third states.[3] The Community and the member states together, however, concluded several international agreements with third states that contain provisions in the field of FDI.[4] Regardless of these agreements, the member states have been the dominant factor in shaping the EU's investment relations with third states. Nevertheless, even prior to the entry into force of the Treaty of Lisbon certain developments casted doubt on member states' competence to conclude, amend and uphold their BITs.

In particular, on 3 March 2009 the ECJ rendered its judgments in infringement cases brought by the European Commission (the Commission) against Austria and Sweden. The cases concern some BITs entered into by the two member states, on the one hand, and various third states, on the other hand, under which investors are guaranteed the free transfer of capital connected with their investments. All of the BITs concerned predate the accession of the member states to the EU and were therefore governed by Article 307 EC (= Article 351 TFEU). Under this provision, member states are obliged to take all appropriate steps to eliminate any incompatibility with the EC Treaty contained in such agreements. The Commission contended that Austria and Sweden infringed that obligation inasmuch as their agreements do not provide for the restrictions on the free movement of capital to and from third states envisaged in Articles 57(2), 59 and 60(1) EC and they have not acted to rectify that situation. In its judgments the ECJ declared that the member states failed to fulfil their obligations under Article 307(2) EC.[5] On 19 November 2009 the ECJ confirmed its view in its judgment in the parallel infringement proceedings against Finland.[6] With a view to the Court's jurisprudence on Article 307 EC, in effect, Austria, Finland and Sweden may have to terminate the BITs in question. In its judgments, the ECJ clarified that the incompatibilities with the EC Treaty to which the BITs with third states give rise are not limited to the defendants in these cases.[7] Therefore, the ECJ's judgments may have consequences for BITs of all EU member states.

The major shift in the vertical allocation of competences for investment treaties, however, occurred on 1 December 2009, when the Treaty of Lisbon entered into force.[8] The Treaty of Lisbon shifts the allocation of competences between the EU and its member states in the field of FDI towards the EU. Article 207(1) TFEU states:

> The common commercial policy shall be based on uniform principles, particularly with regard to changes in tariff rates, the conclusion of tariff and trade agreements relating to trade in goods and services, and the commercial aspects of intellectual property, *foreign direct investment*. [emphasis added]

The extension of the CCP to FDI under the Treaty of Lisbon means that the EU has exclusive competence to negotiate and conclude investment treaties with respect to FDI.[9] Member states will lose the competence to negotiate and conclude treaties covered by the Union competence. But while the extent of the Union's competence is not yet clear, it would seem that the continued applicability of BITs of member states in force with third states is not endangered,[10] subject to possible infringement proceedings commenced by the Commission against member states.

This chapter will analyse the vertical allocation of competences for investment treaties in the EU following the entry into force of the Treaty of Lisbon in two steps. First, it will discuss the extent of the Union's exclusive competence to conclude investment treaties under the Treaty of Lisbon. Second, it will outline the approach taken by the Commission to implement this major shift in the allocation of competences.

The Union's foreign direct investment competence under the Treaty of Lisbon

Limitation to foreign direct investment

The extension of the CCP under the Treaty of Lisbon has one significant limitation: the Union competence is limited to foreign *direct* investment.[11] Thus, agreements which cover forms of investment other than FDI are not covered by the exclusive EU competence. The TFEU, however, does not define the term direct investment. Neither was the term defined in the EC Treaty. The term is referred to in Article 64 TFEU (= Article 57 EC). The explanatory notes of Council Directive 88/361/EEC, the secondary legislation passed with respect to Article 57 EC, define the term in the following:

> Investments of all kinds by natural persons or commercial, industrial or financial undertakings, and which serve to establish or to maintain lasting and direct links between the person providing the capital and the entrepreneur to whom or the undertaking to which the capital is made available in order to carry on an economic activity. This concept must therefore be understood in its widest sense.[12]

Annex I to Directive 88/361/EEC gives some examples for direct investments such as '[e]stablishment and extension of branches or new undertakings belonging solely to the person providing the capital, and the acquisition in full of existing undertakings', '[p]articipation in new or existing undertakings with a view to establishing or maintaining lasting economic links',[13] '[l]ong-term loans with a view to establishing or maintaining lasting economic links'[14] and '[r]einvestment of profits with a view to maintaining lasting economic links'.[15]

The ECJ summarized the scope of direct investment in the following terms:

> [T]he concept of direct investments concerns investments of any kind undertaken by natural or legal persons and which serve to establish or maintain lasting and direct links between the persons providing the capital and the undertakings to which that capital is made available in order to carry out an economic activity. As regards shareholdings in new or existing undertakings ... the objective of establishing or maintaining lasting economic links presupposes that the shares held by the shareholder enable him, either pursuant to the provisions of the national laws relating to companies limited by shares or otherwise, to participate effectively in the management of that company or in its control.[16]

The court also ruled that a participation of 25 per cent would constitute direct investment. At the same time, the court was willing to adopt a flexible approach.[17] Overall, however, it is not entirely clear what 'effective management' or 'control' of a company means under EU law.

It seems therefore sensible to look at other definitions of the term 'direct investment' in international legal instruments. Notably, the IMF defines foreign direct investment as 'an incorporated or unincorporated enterprise in which a direct investor, who is resident in another economy, owns 10 per cent or more of the ordinary shares or voting power (for an incorporated enterprise) or the equivalent (for an unincorporated enterprise)'.[18] Similarly, pursuant to the OECD's definition foreign direct investment is characterized by a long-term participation of at least 10 per cent in a foreign enterprise.[19] Consequently, there appear to be good reasons that foreign direct investment means participation in a company through an investment of at least 10 per cent in that company.[20]

Further limitations to the Union's foreign direct investment competence?

The wording of Article 207 TFEU does not contain any further limitation to the Union competence. Some commentators, however, argue that further restrictions to the Union's competence would apply. For example, it has been argued that the Union's competence would be limited in a sense that FDI has to be connected to international trade law. This limitation would be justified because the CCP traditionally concerned trade agreements and because the Convention deliberations would support such a reading.[21] But it is unclear why the traditional scope of the CCP should limit the Union competence for FDI. Rather, it would seem that precisely because the drafters intended to broaden the Union competence such a limitation can hardly be justified.[22] Indeed, the Convention deliberations show that several representatives proposed the exclusion of FDI from the draft chapter on the CCP.[23] One representative emphasized the need for a clarification in the Treaty to the extent it was not the intention to remove the competence of member states to conduct bilateral investment activity.[24] No clarification, however, was made. Neither was any limitation made. This reinforces the view that the Union's competence is not limited to the extent that FDI has to be connected to international trade law.

Another possible limitation may flow from the parallelism clause contained in Article 207(6) TFEU, which reads as follows:

> The exercise of the competences conferred by this Article in the field of the common commercial policy shall not affect the delimitation of internal competences between the Union and the Member States, and shall not lead to harmonisation of legislative or regulatory provisions of Member States insofar as the Treaties exclude such harmonisation.

The most important question with regard to international investment law is to what extent this clause may limit the scope of investment treaties which the Union is competent to conclude. It has been argued that by virtue of Article 207(6) TFEU substantive treatment standard provisions against expropriation would be excluded from the Union's competence.[25] Indeed, Article 345 TFEU (= Article 295 EC) states that '[t]he Treaties shall in no way prejudice the rules in Member States governing the system of property ownership'. But the better interpretation of this Article is that it does not preserve exclusive powers for member states to determine expropriation. According to the ECJ's settled case law, the right to property is one of the general principles of EC law. However, it is not absolute, but must be viewed in relation to its social function. The exercise of the right to property may be restricted, provided that those restrictions in fact correspond to objectives of general interest pursued by the Community and do not constitute in relation to the aim pursued a disproportionate and intolerable interference, impairing the very substance of the rights guaranteed.[26] More specifically, the ECJ has interpreted Article 295 EC narrowly so that its scope does not reserve for member states the power to decide the conditions under which an expropriation takes place.[27] In *Kadi and Al Barakaat*, the court emphasized that even temporary measures which entail a restriction of the exercise of the right to property need to be justified under Community law. There must exist a reasonable relationship of proportionality between the means employed and the aim sought to be realized.[28] There is one more reason why expropriation is covered by the Union's competence for FDI. Before the Treaty of Lisbon was opened for signature, a footnote to Article 207 TFEU excluded expropriation from the scope of the reference to FDI.[29] The footnote, however, does not appear in the final text of the Treaty of Lisbon. For these reasons, the better view is that the Union competence extends to expropriation.

Neither does the parallelism clause in Article 207(6) TFEU mean that the lack of exercise of Union internal competence limits the existence or the exercise of Union external competence. As said, the drafters of the Treaty deliberately extended the scope of the CCP to all sectors of the service economy. To interpret the clause as a limitation to the external and internal competences of the Union would limit the Union's external competences. Such an interpretation would contradict the express intention of the drafters of the Treaty. Therefore, the better interpretation is that Article 207(6) TFEU may limit the internal, but not the external competence of the Union. As a consequence, the Union's external competence extends beyond the scope of the internal competence.[30] This interpretation is in line with the jurisprudence of the ECJ[31] and Article 3(2) TFEU.[32] An external competence may exist without a parallel internal competence.

In conclusion, under the Treaty of Lisbon the EU is competent to conclude comprehensive investment treaties. The competence covers market access; pre- and post-establishment standards of treatment; performance requirements; investor-state dispute settlement provisions and the terms of the conditions under which expropriation may take place.[33] The major apparent limitation of the Union's competence results from the term 'foreign direct investment'. Because of this limitation the Union's competence does not cover portfolio investments. The limitation is mitigated as a result of the broad interpretation which this term should be given. Nevertheless, because of this limitation investment treaties that cover *all* forms of investments will have to be concluded as mixed agreements. Mixed agreements have to be ratified by the EU and all 27 member states. Therefore, the EU and its member states will have to sign and ratify agreements with coverage beyond the exclusive Union competence for FDI.[34] In the process of negotiation, conclusion and application of mixed agreements, member states are bound by the duty of cooperation. They are under a duty, if not to abstain from action, at the very least to cooperate closely with the Union's institutions in order to 'facilitate the achievement of the [Union] tasks and to ensure the coherence and consistency of the action and its international representation'.[35] Consequently, the result of the vertical allocation of competences under the Treaty of Lisbon may be an increased cooperation on foreign investment policy between the Union and the member states.

Consequences of the Union's foreign direct investment competence for the BITs of member states and European foreign investment policy

Upon the entry into force of the Treaty of Lisbon existing BITs of member states with third states remain valid under international law.[36] Further, without further qualification, these BITs are compatible with EU law since they were concluded before the new Union competence for FDI entered into force and thus do not violate the vertical allocation of competences between the Union and its member states. The issue of compatibility with EU law cannot arise because the supervening external Union competence in matters previously regulated by BITs of member states does not suffice in itself to render those agreements incompatible with the rules and principles governing the division of powers.[37] However, under Article 351(2) TFEU (= Article 307(2) EC) member states will be under an obligation to terminate these BITs. Following the ECJ's judgments in the infringement cases and the entry into force of the Treaty of Lisbon it remains to be seen whether the Commission moves on to challenge comprehensively the compatibility of BITs between member states and third states with EU law. Until the Commission does, from its point of view, successfully challenge these BITs, they remain in force, at least until the Union exercises its new competence in this field under the Treaty of Lisbon. Thus, investors may rely upon and commence arbitration under such BITs.

From an EU policy perspective, an enhanced EU competence is to be welcomed because the negotiating power of the Commission is likely to be stronger than that of individual member states, in particular smaller ones. A strengthened EU competence will also contribute to the development of an integrated policy approach concerning trade and investment. As has been recognized by the drafters of the Constitutional Treaty (and, thus, by implication the drafters of the Treaty of Lisbon), there are strong linkages between these two areas and an increased EU competence for investment might make it easier for the EU to conclude combined international agreements on trade and investment. Indeed, the main rationale for including investment into the CCP was to strengthen the EU as an actor in multilateral negotiations on foreign investment.[38] Thereby, the drafters followed a proposal which the Commission has made for many years.[39]

An extension of the CCP to investment will also lead to efficiency gains, since an investment treaty between the EU and a third state will cover 27 member states at once. The multiplying effect will be particularly beneficial for those member states with few BITs.[40] An EU competence for investment will also reduce distortions between EU investors in third states through replacing the existing BITs of member states with EU BITs. This will remedy a comparative advantage which a few member states enjoy compared to other member states. Such competence will also improve the transparency at the global level, as the total number of BITs will be reduced significantly. A common EU investment policy will further increase the attractiveness of the EU as a location for FDI from third states because a harmonized investment scheme on an EU level will create an equal level playing field for foreign investors in the EU. Economies with more transparent trade and

FDI regimes attract more FDI compared to those economies with less transparent trade and FDI regimes.[41]

Implementation of the Union's foreign direct investment competence

On 7 July 2010 the Commission took the first step in implementing the Union's FDI competence with two initiatives. First, a draft regulation sets up transitional arrangements offering guarantees on existing BITs between EU member states and third states (Draft Regulation).[42] Second, a policy paper lays out the Commission's strategy for exercising the new competence in negotiations of BITs with third states in the future (Communication).[43] These two documents will be summarized, followed by a brief assessment in the context of the development of a common European foreign investment policy.

The Draft Regulation

The 'Explanatory Memorandum' to the Draft Regulation clarifies that BITs of EU member states remain binding as a matter of public international law. However, in the light of the entry into force of the Treaty of Lisbon the obligations in these BITs 'should be addressed from the perspective of the EU's exclusive competence on foreign direct investment'.[44] The Draft Regulation states that the objective of the proposal is 'to authorise the continuation in force of [BITs of EU Member States with third states] and to establish conditions and a procedural framework for the negotiation and conclusion by Member States of such agreements'.[45] The Draft Regulation is divided into four Chapters, each of which consists of one or more Articles. These are outlined in the paragraphs that follow.

Chapter I of the Draft Regulation sets out the subject matter and scope of the Regulation.

Article 1 provides that the Regulation covers agreements between EU member states and third countries relating to investment.

Chapter II of the Draft Regulation provides for authorization for existing BITs that EU member states have concluded with third countries to remain in force.

Article 2 requires EU member states to notify to the Commission all agreements that they wish to maintain under the terms and conditions of the Regulation. Agreements which have been concluded but not entered into force equally fall under Article 2.

Article 3 authorizes the maintenance in force of all existing agreements between EU member states and third countries relating to investment that have been notified by EU member states, starting upon the entry into force of the Regulation. This authorization is without prejudice to the obligations of EU member states under the law of the Union.

Article 4 provides for the annual publication of all notified agreements in the Official Journal, to ensure that the exact scope of the legal coverage provided by the Regulation is known by all stakeholders.

Article 5 provides for the review of agreements which have been notified. The review will identify quantitative and qualitative aspects of the agreements in place, as well as the possible obstacles the agreements could present to the implementation of the CCP. In particular, the Commission will assess whether the agreements or provisions thereof conflict with the law of the Union, undermine negotiations or agreements relating to investment between the Union and third countries, or undermine the Union's policies relating to investment, including in particular the CCP. No later than five years after the entry into force of the Regulation, the Commission will present a report based on the review of the agreements and any possible recommendations to discontinue the application of the provisions of Chapter II or to modify these provisions.

Article 6 details the possible withdrawal of the authorization granted under this Chapter. A withdrawal of authorization may be necessary for one or more agreements with a given third country when these agreements conflict with the law of the Union. Second, authorization could be withdrawn where an agreement overlaps, in part or in full, with an agreement of the Union in force with that third country and this specific overlap is not addressed in the latter agreement. Finally, the authorization of one or more agreements could be withdrawn where an agreement undermines the Union's policies relating to investment, including in particular the CCP or where the Council has not taken a decision on the authorization to open negotiations concerning investment within one year of the submission of a recommendation by the Commission pursuant to Article 218(3) TFEU. Article 6 provides for consultation between the Commission and EU member state(s) concerned through which the concerns giving rise to a possible withdrawal of authorization are to be addressed.

Chapter III provides for the modification of existing agreements and the conclusion of new agreements.

Article 7 provides for the general framework under which EU member states may conclude or modify bilateral agreements relating to investment.

Article 8 requires the notification to the Commission of an EU member state's intent to modify an existing or to conclude a new bilateral agreement with a third country. EU member states are requested to provide all relevant documentation relating to the renegotiation or negotiation of an agreement, which can be made available to other EU member states and the European Parliament subject to the requirements of confidentiality.

Article 9 details the substantive grounds on the basis of which the Commission would not authorize the opening of formal negotiations by EU member states, which include notably the ground that a member state initiative could undermine the objectives of EU negotiations or EU policy. The Commission may require a member state to include in a negotiation appropriate clauses, for example with respect to (a) the termination of the agreement in the event of the conclusion of a subsequent agreement between the Union, or the Union and its member states, on the one hand, with the same third country on the other hand; (b) transfer provisions; or (c) most-favoured nation treatment with a view to ensuring equal treatment of all EU investors in the relevant third country.

Article 10 requires that EU member states keep the Commission informed of (re)negotiations that have been authorized. In addition, the Commission may request to participate as an observer in the negotiations concerning investment between the member state and the third country, to ensure full transparency and consistency with the Union's investment policy.

Article 11 deals with the end of the negotiating process and provides for the procedure and conditions under which member states can be authorized to sign and conclude an agreement. Further to the notification of the agreement, which is to be submitted to the Commission before it is signed, the Commission assesses whether the agreement does not undermine imminent or ongoing EU investment negotiations or conflict with the obligations of EU law.

Article 12 provides for the review of authorizations that would be made pursuant to Chapter III of the Regulation. By reviewing the quantitative and qualitative aspects of the negotiations and agreements authorized, the Commission will assess the appropriateness of continuing the application of the provisions of Chapter III. The report and any possible recommendation to discontinue the application of the provisions of this Chapter or to modify these provisions will be presented no later than five years after the entry into force of the Regulation.

Chapter IV sets out certain requirements regarding the conduct of member states with regard to agreements covered by this Regulation.

Article 13 requests EU member states to provide information with respect to meetings which take place under the auspices of covered agreements. Furthermore, member states are requested to inform the Commission of any request for dispute settlement lodged against themselves under the auspices of their agreements as soon as they become aware of such request and to cooperate with the Commission as regards the activation of dispute – which they would be allowed to lodge against another third country party to such agreement – or consultation mechanisms under an agreement.

Article 14 provides that EU member states may indicate whether any of the information they provide in accordance with Articles 8 and 11 is to be considered confidential and whether it can be shared with other member states.

Article 15 creates a new committee which shall assist the Commission in the management of the Regulation and stipulates the procedures under which this committee shall operate.

Article 16 provides that the Regulation enters into force 20 days following the day of its publication, which means that Chapter II applies to agreements in force before that date.

Pursuant to Article 207(2) TFEU the Draft Regulation has to be adopted by the European Parliament and the Council, acting by means of regulations in accordance with the ordinary legislative procedure. In essence, this means that the Council (composed of EU member states) has to adopt the Regulation by qualified majority together with the approval of the Parliament.[46] It seems likely that there will be considerable resistance against the Draft Regulation in the Council as member states will be reluctant to cede power to the Commission. Further, the enhanced role of the Parliament as a result of the entry into force of the Treaty of Lisbon is likely to further complicate the process of obtaining approval for the Commission. At the same time, investors will pressurize European policy-makers to find a compromise in order put an end to a time of legal uncertainty in a crucial policy area. At the time of writing it cannot be safely predicted when the transitory regime as foreseen in the Draft Regulation (or amended) will enter into force. Preferably, in the interests of EU investors in third countries and in the interests of third country investors in the EU, this entry into force will be sooner rather than later.

The Communication

The Draft Regulation is accompanied by the Communication, which 'explores how the Union may develop an international investment policy'.[47] Several features of the Communication are worth mentioning.

First, while the Communication differentiates between FDI and other forms of investment, in particular portfolio investment, the Commission appears to be of the view that the Union's competence is broad enough to conclude comprehensive investment treaties on its own, without the need to conclude mixed agreements. The Commission argues that Articles 63–6 TFEU provide that, in principle, all restrictions on payments and capital movements, including those involving direct as well as portfolio investments, both between member states and between member states and third countries, are prohibited. The Commission says that:

> [t]hat chapter does not expressly provide for the possibility to conclude international agreements on investment, including portfolio investment. However, to the extent that international agreements on investment affect the scope of the common rules set by the Treaty's Chapter on capitals and payments, the exclusive Union competence to conclude agreements in this area would be implied.[48]

It is not entirely clear whether the Commission is of the view that this competence derived from Articles 63–6 TFEU is broad enough so as to provide a basis for exclusive Union investment treaties. Such a view, however, is likely to face resistance from member states. Most member states seem to adhere to the position that future European investment treaties have to be concluded as mixed agreements.

Second, the Commission is well aware of the fact that the Union will face severe practical constraints in the exercise of its new competence for FDI under the Treaty of Lisbon. It is clear that the Union does not have the resources to enter into BIT negotiations with third states on a broad scale upon the entry into force of the Treaty of Lisbon. Rather, the Union will have to focus on selected third states, thereby adopting a piecemeal approach. In the Communication the Commission notes that in the short term the prospects for realizing the integration of investment into the CCP arise in ongoing trade negotiations, where the Union has so far focused only on market access for investors.[49] Pursuant to the Communication, in the short to medium term, the Union should also consider under which circumstances it may be desirable to pursue stand-alone investment agreements.[50]

Third, as regards the standards of investment protection, the Communication makes reference to and appears to endorse the inclusion of both relative standards such as most-favoured nation treatment and national treatment as well as absolute standards such as fair and equitable treatment, full protection and security and umbrella clauses in future European investment treaties. The Commission is also firmly of the view that expropriation provisions are covered by the exclusive Union competence.[51]

Fourth, as regards dispute settlement, the Communication contains a commitment of the EU to investor-state arbitration, noting that 'investment involves the establishment of a long-term relationship with the host state which cannot be easily diverted to another market in the event of a problem with the investment'.[52] The Commission stresses that the Union has not historically been a significant actor in this field and favours the principles of transparency and consistency in the interpretation of international investment law. Rather optimistically, the Commission says that it 'will explore with interested parties the possibility that the European Union seek to accede to the ICSID Convention'.[53] The International Centre for Settlement of Investment Disputes (ICSID) is the most important arbitral institution in the field of investment disputes. The availability of ICSID presents numerous advantages for the settlement of investment disputes.[54] According to its Article 67, the ICSID Convention is open 'for signature on behalf of States members of the Bank'. Notably, the Convention is not open for signature for a supranational organization such as the EU. It is doubtful, at least, whether Article 67 of the ICSID Convention would allow for the Union to sign 'on behalf of States'. Rather, it would seem that the EU cannot become a member of the ICSID Convention. Until and unless it may do so, however, the EU may not offer its treaty partners to arbitrate under the ICSID arbitration rules. Moreover, according to Article 66(1) ICSID Convention each amendment to the Convention requires that all contracting states have ratified, accepted or approved the amendment. Therefore, in practice such an amendment is unlikely. Potentially, the non-availability of the ICSID dispute settlement mechanism may be a drawback for investors protected only under an EU investment treaty.

Fifth, the Commission clarifies that the EU, represented by the Commission, will defend all actions of EU institutions. The Commission says that:

> [g]iven the exclusive external competence, the Commission takes the view that the [EU] will also be the sole defendant regarding any measure taken by a Member State which affects investments by third country nationals or companies falling within the scope of the agreement concerned.[55]

Conclusion

Upon the entry into force of the Treaty of Lisbon, the continued fragmentation of competences between the Union and its member states, in particular as a result of the limitation of the Union competence to FDI under the Treaty of Lisbon, is likely to cause confusion both within the EU and with the EU's treaty partners. Because the Union's exclusive competence to conclude investment treaties with third states does only cover FDI, but not portfolio investments, BITs comparable to the US Model BIT covering all kinds of investments will have to be concluded as mixed agreements. In this context, it is doubtful whether EU member states will endorse the Commission's broad interpretation of the Union's exclusive competence in the Communication.

It remains to be seen whether the Commission comprehensively challenges the BITs of member states with third states following the ECJ's judgments in the infringement cases and the entry into force of the Treaty of Lisbon. Until the Commission does successfully challenge these BITs, they continue to be applicable. Further, given the limitation of the Union's exclusive external competence to FDI under the Treaty of Lisbon, member states will continue to play a role in shaping the EU's external investment policy. In this context, the Commission is likely to face severe opposition from EU member states as regards its proposals in the Draft Regulation. Member states are unlikely to accept a rapid cession of their powers. Rather, it is likely that the transition of power from the member states to the Union will take considerable time.

As the Communication states, the two documents 'are only first steps in the development of a European international investment policy, which will be gradual and targeted and will also take into account responses to this Communication'.[56] It is to be expected that there will be numerous responses.

Notes

1 This contribution draws on Burgstaller: 2010 and Burgstaller: forthcoming.

2 Other European states with a comprehensive BIT programme are the United Kingdom, Italy and France, all of which have around 100 BITs in force. In 2007 the Netherlands (five), Finland, Germany and Spain (three each) together accounted for the majority of the new BITs concluded by EU member states (UNCTAD 2008a).

3 ECJ, Opinion 1/94.

4 The EU–Chile Association Agreement is the most advanced bilateral free trade agreement currently in force including investment issues. On the multilateral level, the most important agreement is the Energy Charter Treaty (ECT), a multilateral treaty with 47 Contracting Parties, including the European Communities and all member states. Both the European Communities and all member states are Contracting Parties to the ECT as it was concluded as a mixed agreement, falling within the scope of both Community and member state competence. See Council and Commission Decision 98/181/EC, ECSC, EURATOM.

5 ECJ, C-205/06; ECJ, C-249/06.

6 ECJ, C-118/07.

7 ECJ, C-205/06, para. 43; ECJ, C-249/06, para. 43; ECJ, C-118/07, para. 34.

8 Treaty of Lisbon amending the Treaty on European Union and the Treaty establishing the European Community.

9 Article 2(1) TFEU states: 'When the Treaties confer on the Union exclusive competence in a specific area, only the Union may legislate and adopt legally binding acts, the member states being able to do so themselves only if so empowered by the Union or for the implementation of Union acts.' The TFEU put an end to the three-pillar-structure of the EU. Reference in the context of the TFEU is therefore made to 'Union', 'EU' and 'EU law' rather than 'Community' and 'EC law'.

10 BVerfG, para. 380.

11 In the Draft Articles of the Convention's Praesidium it was explained that foreign direct investment was included in the scope of the CCP 'in recognition of the fact that financial flows supplement trade in goods and today represent a significant share of commercial exchanges'. European Convention, Draft Articles on external action in the Constitutional Treaty, CONV 685/03. The Treaty of Lisbon did not change the

Constitutional Treaty's provisions in respect of the Union's competence for FDI, which is why the Convention's deliberations are a useful point of reference for the interpretation of the Union's competence for FDI.

12 Council Directive 88/361/EEC. The ECJ has endorsed this definition of direct investment. See ECJ, C-446/04, paras. 179–82; ECJ, C-157/05, paras. 33 and 34; ECJ, C-112/05, para. 18; ECJ, C-101/05, para. 46.

13 According to the explanatory notes 'there is participation in the nature of direct investment where the block of shares held by a natural person of another undertaking or any other holder enables the shareholder, either pursuant to the provisions of national laws relating to companies limited by shares or otherwise, to participate effectively in the management of the company or in its control'. Council Directive 88/361/EEC.

14 The explanatory notes explain that the term 'long-term loans' means 'loans for a period of more than five years which are made for the purpose of establishing or maintaining lasting economic links. The main examples which may be cited are loans granted by a company to its subsidiaries or to companies in which it has a share and loans linked with a profit-sharing arrangement. Loans granted by financial institutions with a view to establishing or maintaining lasting economic links are also included under this heading.' Council Directive 88/361/EEC.

15 See also ECJ, C-463/00.

16 ECJ, C-446/04, paras. 181 and 182.

17 ECJ, C-492/04, paras. 22–4.

18 IMF 1993: 86.

19 OECD 1999: 7.

20 Tietje 2009: 16.

21 Krajewski 2005: 113–14.

22 The fact that Article 207 TFEU, unlike Article 133 EC, does not distinguish between trade in goods and other areas of the CCP supports the view that the Treaty of Lisbon put an end to the traditional approach of the CCP which henceforth expands towards other areas of economic activity.

23 Fischer 2003; De Villepin 2003; Palacio 2003.

24 Hain 2003.

25 Ceyssens 2005: 279–81; Tietje 2009: 14–15.

26 ECJ, C-306/93, para. 22; ECJ, Joined Cases C-37/02 and C-38/02, para. 82; ECJ, C-347/03, para. 119; ECJ, Joined Cases C-402/05 P and C-415/05 P, para. 355.

27 See ECJ, 4/73; ECJ, C-84/95.

28 ECJ, Joined Cases C-402/05 P and C-415/05 P, paras 358 and 360.

29 In addition, this very footnote also excluded investor-state arbitration from the Union's foreign direct investment competence.

30 Krajewski 2005: 116–17.

31 ECJ, Case 22/70; ECJ, Opinion 1/75.

32 Article 3(2) TFEU states: 'The Union shall also have exclusive competence for the conclusion of an international agreement when its conclusion is provided for in a legislative act of the Union or is necessary to enable the Union to exercise its internal competence, or in so far as its conclusion may affect common rules or alter their scope.'

33 It should not be overlooked that the Union's action on the international scene has to respect some non-economic principles enshrined in Article 21 Treaty on European Union (TEU). Article 21(1) TEU states: 'The Union's action on the international scene shall be guided by the principles which have inspired its own creation, development and enlargement, and which it seeks to advance in the wider world: democracy, the rule of law, the universality and indivisibility of human rights and fundamental freedoms, respect for human dignity, the principles of equality and solidarity, and respect for the principles of the United Nations Charter and international law.' Further, Article 21(2) TEU states: 'The Union shall define and pursue common policies and actions, and shall work for a high degree of cooperation in all fields of international relations, in order to [*inter alia*] foster the sustainable economic, social and environmental development

of developing countries, with the primary aim of eradicating poverty; … help develop international measures to preserve and improve the quality of the environment and the sustainable management of global natural resources, in order to ensure sustainable development.' It is unclear, however, to what extent these principles may in effect limit the Union's competence to conclude investment treaties with third states.

34 As far as negotiation is concerned, the division of competence under a mixed agreement does not, generally, influence participation in negotiations. While the practice is decided on a case-by-case-basis, it is accepted that the Commission may act as a sole negotiator for the whole agreement according to the mandate given to it by the Council. Craig and de Burca 2008: 198–9; Article 218 TFEU.

35 ECJ, C-266/03, para. 60; ECJ, C-433/03, para. 66; ECJ, C-459/03, para. 174. The principle of cooperation can be seen as a constitutional principle within EU external relations law.

36 Eeckhout 2004: 335; but see Manzini 2001: 785.

37 ECJ, C-466/08, para. 113.

38 European Convention, Draft Articles on external action in the Constitutional Treaty, CONV 685/03.

39 The Commission made proposals to that effect for example during the Intergovernmental Conferences leading to the Treaty of Amsterdam and the Treaty of Nice. See European Commission, Report on the Operation of the Treaty on European Union, SEC(95)731, 57–60 and European Commission, Commission Opinion in accordance with Article 48 EU, COM(2000)34, 27.

40 On the other hand, member states might have different priorities in the respective third state, depending how extensively their investors are engaged in that state and how strongly they are interested in attracting investors from there. Individual member states may also have different preferences for political and historical reasons. See the discussion by Karl 2004: 425–6.

41 Drabek and Payne 2001.

42 Proposal for a Regulation of the European Parliament and of the Council Establishing Transitional Arrangements for Bilateral Investment Agreements between Member States and Third Countries, COM(2010)344 final.

43 Communication from the Commission to the Council, the European Parliament, the European Economic and Social Committee and the Committee of the Regions – Towards a Comprehensive European International Investment Policy, COM(2010)343 final.

44 Draft Regulation 2010: 2.

45 Draft Regulation 2010: 3–4.

46 For details on the ordinary legislative procedure see Article 294 TFEU.

47 Communication 2010: 1.

48 Communication 2010: 8.

49 Communication 2010: 7. The Communication singles out ongoing negotiations with Canada, India, Singapore and the Mercosur.

50 Communication 2010: 7. The Communication singles out China and Russia in that regard.

51 Communication 2010: 9.

52 Communication 2010: 9.

53 Communication 2010: 10.

54 For example, the rules of procedure for arbitral proceedings are specifically tailored for arbitration with the participation of a government party; oversight by the ICSID Secretariat and the availability of the institution's resources and experienced personnel represent a major asset in investment arbitration; and the self-contained enforcement regime of the ICSID Convention means that enforcement of ICSID awards will generally be smoother than enforcement of non-ICSID awards. See McLachlan, Shore and Weiniger 2007: 4–5; Muchlinski 2008: 4–48; Dolzer and Schreuer 2008: 20–1; Schreuer 2009: 1117–50.

55 Communication 2010: 10.

56 Communication 2010: 11.

10 Investment treaties and public goods

Daniel R. Kalderimis

Introduction

It is a truism that multinational business operates in a global environment. In getting products to market, firms move seamlessly between importing and exporting goods, providing cross-border services and making use of an international production and distribution network. All of these activities form part of a single commercial operation.

It is, therefore, an interesting quirk of legal history that the international economic law which regulates these activities is divided along the tenuous boundary of trade and investment. Although the practical difference between trade in services through commercial presence and foreign direct investment (FDI) investment may be slight, the regulatory disparity remains significant. This is not merely a distinction between World Trade Organization (WTO) and bilateral investment treaty (BIT) regulation. It is a distinction discernible in most, if not all, free trade agreements (FTAs) which include both trade and investment chapters.

There are a number of well-understood differences between the two regimes. In this chapter, I want to focus on one particular difference: the absence, for the most part, in BITs of broad general exception provisions such as those found in the WTO system.

This is not a technical issue, but an issue of basic concept – how best to balance investor rights against state police powers. It has been highlighted, albeit indirectly, by the swathe of investment treaty cases taken against Argentina. It has been given renewed emphasis by the possibility of action against developed countries for their own responses to the global financial crisis (see for example Van Aaken and Kurtz 2009). And it is worth particular attention because it has been marginalized in recent years by the more vocal debate over whether the investment treaty system lacks transparency, legitimacy or is simply biased towards investors.

The wider legitimacy debate is both interesting and important. Gus Van Harten's thesis that investment arbitration is really a species of international administrative law raises serious systemic questions (see Van Harten 2007; Van Harten and Loughlin 2006). Susan Franck has recently progressed the debate by reference to evidence that developing countries are not statistically disadvantaged by investment treaty arbitration (Franck 2009). But even if this is so, it tells us that international investment law as written is applied neutrally and fairly. It does not confirm that international investment law is itself neutral and fair.

It is surprisingly easy to conflate the two propositions. Indeed, someone as clear-sighted as Jan Paulsson wrote over 20 years ago that developing countries should recognize 'international [investment] arbitration as it is: a neutral means for the resolution of conflicts … to be mastered rather than complained about' (Paulsson 1987: 20). Such advice puts me in mind of Anatole France's dry observation that '[t]he law, in its majestic equality, forbids rich and poor alike to sleep under bridges, to beg in the streets, and to steal their bread' (France 1894). As a leading international politics text points out: '[r]ules shore up power not just because they are biased or enforced unequally … but by singling out for prohibition or restriction the strategies available to some actors and not the strategies available to others … The rules themselves are therefore a major focus of contention' (Janoski *et al.* 2005: 46).

Few would contend that BITs have traditionally reflected a balanced deal. As José Alvarez has recently written, '[i]n the early days of the U.S. BIT program, the treaty's references to "reciprocal" investment flows was something of a fraud' (Alvarez 2009: 3). The majestic equality of US–Mongolia BIT, for instance, permits Mongolian investors in the USA the same legal protections as American investors in Mongolia. Indeed, as Alvarez himself candidly remarked in 1992:

> A BIT negotiation [with the US] is not a discussion between sovereign equals. It is more like an intensive training seminar conducted by the United States, on U.S. terms, on what it would take to comply with the U.S. draft. The result is an instrument that is not by any means balanced as between the rights and responsibilities of multinational corporations. (Alvarez 2009: 4)[1]

We all know the situation is changing. Canada has habitually included general exception provisions in its BITs, the USA's 2004 Model BIT seeks to strike a different balance between investor rights and state regulatory autonomy from the 1994 version (see Vandevalde 2009: 283) and China's first FTA, with New Zealand, specifically incorporates a general exception modelled on GATT Article XX (New Zealand–China Free Trade Agreement 2008). We also know, from Burke-White and Von Staden's study of non-precluded measures clauses in BITs (Burke-White and Von Staden 2008) that there is some scope, particularly in BITs with the USA and Germany, for invoking these clauses to protect state interests. But most BITs do not contain any form of exception or non-precluded measures clause (Newcombe and Paradell, 2009: n.29; Brower 2009: 347, 372n.116) and those which do are usually drafted more narrowly and for a more limited purpose than their GATT equivalents.

There is, as yet, no clear consensus as to whether recent moves to 'rebalance' the international investment regime are for the better or will have lasting effect.

This chapter makes three suggestions.

First, what international investment law needs above all else is treaty text which expressly grapples with the hard questions. The absence of adequate treaty language in older BITs has led to tribunal reasoning which, whilst well-meaning, is unanchored and unconvincing. In the long run, this can only erode the credibility and legitimacy of the emerging system.

Second, we must continue the wider debate as to the proper objectives of BITs and the linkages between investment law and other areas. It is obviously easier to draft appropriate treaty language onto a firm jurisprudential foundation.

Third, although agreement as to whether BITs should be simple instruments of investor protection (Schwebel 2006; Vandevalde 1998) or linked to broader issues of development (Muchlinski 2009: 35, 48) is not likely to be reached soon, this is no excuse for new BIT language to avoid reference to public goods. Even without untying the Gordian knot which proved fatal to the 1998 Multilateral Agreement on Investment (MAI) and in June 2009 put paid to Norway's progressive Draft Model BIT (Vis-Dunbar 2009b), it should still be possible to create an express and circumscribed allowance in BITs for the provision by states of public goods. This is especially so when the alternative is tribunals crafting their own solutions through exegesis.

In these respects, I believe the investment treaty regime has something to learn from the more mature GATT/WTO regime. In what follows, I ask four – admittedly basic – questions:

1 What is the rationale for the general exception provisions in international trade law?
2 What is the rationale for the typical absence of general exception provisions in international investment law?
3 Is international investment law able to strike the right balance between enforcement of investor rights and state regulatory power in the absence of general exception provisions?
4 What implications might follow from the answers to the above questions?

Public goods

First, however, I should say a few short words about public goods in economic theory.

The distinction between private and public goods goes back to Adam Smith's *An Enquiry into the Nature and Causes of The Wealth of Nations*, in which Smith recognized that, powerful though the market was, it did not create incentives to create 'public institutions and public works [even] though they may be in the highest degree advantageous to a great society' (Smith 1776: vol. 1, 69). Our modern understanding of public goods comes from economist Paul Samuelson, who in 1954 defined public goods as those which are non-rival (i.e. the use by X does not preclude the opportunity of use by Y) and non-excludable (i.e. it is impossible or impracticable to limit use of the good to X) (Samuelson 1954). It is easy enough to think of goods which manifestly (though not absolutely) bear these qualities. Numerous intangible social benefits come to mind, such as clean air and potable water, national defence, law enforcement and a stable political and financial system. Tangible examples also exist, such as lighthouses (Coase 1974), public highways and streetlights.

It is recognized that adequate provision of public goods usually requires non-market mechanisms, such as public budgets and taxes (Musgrave and Musgrave 2003: xiii) and that, in practice, solutions are identified not by technical analysis but mediated through the vicissitudes of domestic politics (Desai 2003: 69). As many have pointed out, globalization has added a new layer of complexity to this process. For the purposes of this chapter, I make the simple claim that public goods are a critical part of a state's political economy. International economic instruments should therefore be – and be seen to be – compatible with the adequate provision of public goods.

The general exception provisions in WTO law

The issue of combining economic liberalization with the adequate provision of public goods has been addressed carefully – though inevitably imperfectly – by the WTO system. In simple terms, the WTO represents an explicit compromise between trade liberalization and regulatory autonomy. In the more nuanced terms of John Ruggie, the 1947 GATT – and hence the 1994 WTO regime – is characterized by a political commitment to 'embedded liberalism' (as opposed to 'laissez-faire liberalism') (see, generally, Lang 2006). That is, the GATT struck a balance between two competing policy objectives – the first to liberalize trade, and the second to enable intervention in support of domestic stability. The notion was that the desire to liberalize international trade was 'embedded' within a larger vision: a shared commitment to social stability as part of the post-World War II order.

This shared vision is written into the text of the GATT through numerous provisions and mechanisms, including the wording of primary obligations such as Article I (MFN) and Article III (national treatment) and the rules on trade remedies and safeguards. But none of the mechanisms is as important as the general exception provision in Article XX, a version of which also appears in GATS as Article XIV. This is augmented by a specific security exception provision in GATT Article XXI and GATS Article XIV *bis*. It is also reflected elsewhere in the WTO system, for example in Article 2 of the GATS Annex on Financial Services, which permits a member to take measures for prudential reasons.

Early GATT case law adopted a narrow interpretation of Article XX – and in particular of the word 'necessary' in some of its paragraphs (see, e.g., *United States – Section 337 of the Tariff Act of 1930*, GATT Panel Report 1989: para. 5.26). Infamously, the first *Tuna/Dolphin* panel found that the USA's embargo on Mexican tuna was not justified as other potential options, such as negotiating an international convention relating to purse seine-net fishing, could have been pursued instead (GATT Panel Report (not adopted) 1991; see also *United States – Section 337 of the Tariff Act of 1930*, GATT Panel Report, 1989). The public outcry following the *Tuna/Dolphin* panel decision was considerable. This outcry was part of the context for the Appellate Body's own early interventions on Article XX, such as the *Shrimp/Turtle* case which related to Article XX(g) and in which the Appellate Body held that the USA's environmental legislation was not necessarily inconsistent with Article XX(g), although its particular application was not justified (Appellate Body Report 1998).

More significantly, the Appellate Body revisited the definition given to the word 'necessary' by these early panels. Thus, in *Korea Beef*, the Appellate Body held that 'necessary' can have a range of meanings from 'indispensible to' to 'making a contribution to' (Appellate Body Report 2001: paras 160–4). The Appellate Body concluded:

> [i]n sum, determination of whether a measure, which is not 'indispensible', may nevertheless be 'necessary' within the contemplation of Article XX(d), involves in every case a process of weighing and balancing a series of factors which prominently include the contribution made by the compliance measure to the enforcement of the law or regulation at issue, the importance of the common interests or values protected by that law or regulation, and the accompanying impact of the law or regulation on imports or exports. (Appellate Body Report 2001: para. 164.)

In the *EC – Asbestos* case, the Appellate Body confirmed that the more vital or important the common interests or values pursued, the easier it would be to accept as 'necessary' measures designed to achieve those ends. It then held that the public policy objective of preventing health risks from asbestos fibres is 'both vital and important in the highest degree' and that France 'could not reasonably be expected to employ *any* alternative measure if that measure would involve a continuation of the health risk posed by asbestos fibres' (Appellate Body Report 2001: paras 171–4).

In the *US – Gambling Services* decision under GATS XIV(a), the Appellate Body explained that the weighing and balancing is affected by the relative importance of the interests and values at stake (Appellate Body Report 2005: paras 306–7) and concluded:

> [a]n alternative measure may be found not to be 'reasonably available' ... where it is merely theoretical in nature, for instance, where the responding Member is not capable of taking it, or where the measure imposes an undue burden on that Member, such as prohibitive costs or substantial technical difficulties. Moreover, a 'reasonably available' alternative measure must be a measure that would preserve for the responding Member its right to achieve its desired level of protection with respect to the objective pursued under paragraph (a) of Article XIV. (Appellate Body Report 2005: para 308)

This approach thus permits members to determine their own domestic policy objectives, and then accords a margin of appreciation to the measures taken to achieve those objectives, with a sliding scale of deference reflecting the relative importance of the interest or values at stake.

The absence of general exception provisions in investment treaties

In contrast to the 'New Deal' of the WTO system, BITs are typically written as simple instruments of FDI liberalization. This reflects an important feature of their development. For the most part, the historical debates over the meaning of customary international law were never resolved through a compromise text. Instead, BITs – the preponderance of which were signed during the Washington Consensus years of the 1990s – reflected the views of capital-exporting states. The bilateral nature of the instruments, and the uneven nature of some of the negotiations, made it inherently less likely that the resulting texts would reflect the more subtle balance of the multilateral GATT.

The result, not to put too fine a point on it, was usually a short text which details investor rights and is rather silent on domestic regulatory autonomy. For instance, the 1990 UK–Argentina BIT, which concisely guarantees national treatment, MFN treatment and freedom from expropriation, does not permit any exceptions save for other trade or customs arrangements, specific bilateral financing agreements and taxation treaties and laws.

There are, of course, good reasons for this drafting style. Investment, unlike trade, involves the investor locating its physical business within the territory of another sovereign power. This is a manifest vulnerability, which many have argued requires manifest guarantees of protection to ensure fair treatment.

Alvarez and Khamsi have set out in great detail the history of the USA's BIT programme which, for the purposes of this chapter, serves as a general approximation of the history of BITs generally (Alvarez and Khamsi, 2009).[2] They point out that the USA's post-World War II Friendship, Commerce and Navigation (FCN) treaties 'explicitly included provisions reflecting U.S. views of what it believed were traditional customary norms protecting aliens' rights to contract sanctity and property'(Alvarez and Khamsi 2009: 409). The first US Model BIT made public in the early 1980s was based on an FCN template, incorporated improvements from European models and now included an investor-state arbitration mechanism.

The purpose of these instruments was not mixed or ambiguous:

> the United States was candid with its prospective BIT parties that concluding a U.S. BIT would not guarantee an increase in incoming FDI flows or necessarily produce tangible benefits such as higher employment. U.S. negotiators were quite clear that the U.S. BIT was not designed to promote economic development or employment as such but was intended to achieve one clear purpose: to protect foreign investment. (Alvarez and Khamsi 2009: 411–12)

The USA was explicit that it was promoting in its BITs its own view of the minimum standards required by customary international law. Accordingly, the US negotiators resisted including provisions which would have permitted derogation from the investor protections they contained. Alvarez and Khamsi thus claim:

> the negotiation of a BIT afforded [the US] an opportunity to secure, at least bilaterally … absolute guarantees. As U.S. BIT negotiators in this period have repeatedly indicated, the United States was not about to negotiate these away via treaty or to 'balance' investors' rights vis-à-vis the rights of sovereigns, as urged by advocates of a [New International Economic Order] or the concept of 'permanent sovereignty over natural resources'. (Alvarez and Khamsi 2009: 414)

Perhaps unsurprisingly, then, several tribunals, constituted under different treaties, have affirmed the fundamental investment protection objective of the relevant instrument (see, for example, *CMS Gas* v. *Argentina*, 2005; *Occidental Exploration* v. *Ecuador*, 2004; *MTD Equity* v. *Chile*, 2004: para 113; *Metaclad Corp.* v. *Mexico*, 2000; see also decisions cited at Brower 2009: n.67). Even when a tribunal disavows any intention to interpret a BIT for or against an investor, it is still left with the text. And the text itself is unashamedly pro-investor. See, for instance, the *Azurix* case:

> [t]he Tribunal does not consider that the BIT should be interpreted in favor or against the investor. The BIT is an international treaty and should be interpreted in accordance with the interpretation norms set forth by the Vienna Convention on the Law of the Treaties ('the Vienna Convention'), which is binding on the States parties to the BIT. The Tribunal observes that the BIT itself is an instrument agreed by the two State parties to encourage and protect investment. In the preamble of the BIT, the parties agreed that 'fair and equitable treatment of investment is desirable in order to maintain a stable framework for investment and maximum effective use of economic resources'. Therefore, the BIT itself is a document that requires certain treatment of investment which the parties have considered necessary to 'stimulate the flow of private capital'. The Tribunal in interpreting the BIT must be mindful of the objective the parties intended to pursue by concluding it. (*Azurix Corp.* v. *Argentina* 2006: para. 307)[3]

Investment treaty interpretation without general exception provisions

That is not to say that there is no way to balance investor rights against state regulation within existing BITs. Indeed, Newcombe and Paradell go so far as to argue that general exception provisions may be unnecessary because sufficient flexibility already exists within the substantive protections of BITs. This argument is not entirely far-fetched. There is certainly room for balanced interpretation of, for instance, 'like circumstances' in the national treatment guarantee; or fair and equitable treatment (Newcombe and Paradell 2009: 503–6). The critical question is whether the creative burden this places on tribunals is too great.

I suggest it is and that a general exception provision would lend a greater coherence and legitimacy to the interpretation process. A signal example of the difficulties for tribunals is the issue of defining indirect expropriation, particularly where the offending measure is a regulation intended to achieve a public objective. The *Santa Elena* case notoriously sought to tackle the question head-on:

> [e]xpropriatory environmental measures – no matter how laudable and beneficial to society as a whole – are, in this respect, similar to any other expropriatory measures that a state may take in order to implement its policies: where property is expropriated, even for environmental purposes, whether domestic or international, the state's obligation to pay compensation remains. (*Compañía del Desarrollo* v. *Costa Rica* 2000)[4]

In contrast, other tribunals have sought to deem legitimate regulation to be non-expropriatory, even if it has the effect of removing the value of the relevant investment (see, for example, *Methanex Corp.* v. *United States* 2005: Part IV, Chap. D, para. 15; *Technicas Medioambientales* v. *Mexico* 2003: para 121; *Marvin Feldman* v. *Mexico* 2002: paras 98–9). The reasoning process is now perilously close to incoherent. Thus, the *LG&E* Tribunal confirmed that expropriation in *any* of its modalities requires compensation (*LG&E Energy* v. *Argentina* 2006: para. 186) but then asserted nine paragraphs later:

> [w]ith respect to the power of the State to adopt its policies, it can generally be said that the State has the right to adopt measures having a social or general welfare purpose. In such a case, the measure must be accepted without any imposition of liability, except in cases where the State's action is obviously disproportionate to the need being addressed. (*LG&E Energy* v. *Argentina* 2006: para. 195)

This tentative carve-out is fuzzy indeed. Although there is some support for state police powers in customary international law (*LG&E Energy* v. *Argentina* 2006: paras 196–7), it is far from clear how and in what form this truly survived BIT codification. Take, for instance, Article 5 of the UK-Argentina BIT, which provides that '[i]nvestments of investors of the Contracting Party shall not be nationalised, expropriated or subject to measures tantamount to expropriation of nationalisation … except for a public purpose related to the internal needs of that Contracting Party on a non-discriminatory basis and against prompt, adequate and effective compensation'. A businessperson reading this text would quite reasonably assume that she would be guaranteed compensation where a governmental action destroyed the value of her business, even if that governmental action was publicly motivated, proportionate and non-discriminatory. To smuggle into the very definition of indirect expropriation an exception for police powers is arbitrator-fashioned jurisprudence.

The heavy burden placed upon investment treaty tribunals by incomplete BIT drafting has been exposed more starkly in the context of the *Argentina* cases arising out of Argentina's 2001/2002 financial crisis. I focus very briefly on five cases brought by US investors under the US–Argentina BIT: *CMS Gas* v. *Argentina* (2005), *Enron* v. *Argentina* (2007), *Sempra* v. *Argentina* (2007), *LG&E*

Energy v. *Argentina* (2006) (all gas sector investors) and *Continental Casualty* v. *Argentina* (2008) (a financial services investor).

The question in each case was whether the measures Argentina took to respond to this crisis – which included terminating the US dollar–peso convertibility policy and then converting US dollar deposits to pesos, freezing bank deposits, prohibiting the transfer of funds overseas and rescheduling interest and debt payments – breached Argentina's obligations under the BIT causing loss to the investor claimant.

Whilst Argentina contested whether its measures *prima facie* contravened any investment protection guarantees in the BIT, the debate centred on whether Argentina's conduct could be justified or excused on the basis of two mechanisms: the customary international law doctrine of necessity, encapsulated in Article 25 of the International Law Commission's Articles of State Responsibility; and Article XI of the US–Argentina BIT, which is a non-precluded measures exception for essential security interests. As the cases show, however, neither provision is well adapted to the modern debate over the intersection between investor rights and regulatory autonomy.

The findings of the five Tribunals can be briefly summarized as follows:

Case	*Breaches*	*Justification/excuse*	*Damages*	*Annulment*
CMS	FET Umbrella clause	No	US$133m	Application filed; not annulled[a]
Enron	FET Umbrella clause	No	US$106m	Award annulled[b]
Sempra	FET Umbrella clause	No	US$128m	Award annulled[c]
LG&E	FET Discriminatory and arbitrary treatment Umbrella clause	State of necessity existed between December 2001 and April 2003, leading to no liability under Article XI for measures taken during this period	US$57m	Application filed; pending but suspended on 12 June 2009 as a result of parties' agreement
Continental Casualty	FET, with respect to specific losses only	State of necessity existed leading to no liability under Article XI	US$2.8m	Application filed for partial annulment; pending

Notes

a Some negative comments were, however, made by the *ad hoc* Annulment Committee (*CMS* Annulment Decision 2007: paras 101–36).

b *Enron* Annulment Decision 2010.

c *Sempra* Annulment Decision 2010.

It is interesting to compare excerpts from the tribunals' respective reasoning on the necessity/non-precluded measures issue.

The *LG&E* Tribunal held:

> [c]laimants contend that the necessity defense should not be applied here because the measures implemented by Argentina were not the only means available to respond to the crisis. The Tribunal rejects this assertion. Article XI refers to situations in which a State has no choice but to act. A State may have several responses at its disposal to maintain public order or protect its essential security interests. In this sense, it is recognized that Argentina's suspension of the calculation of tariffs in U.S. dollars and the PPI adjustment of tariffs was a legitimate way of protecting its social and economic system. (*LG&E Energy* v. *Argentina* 2006: para. 239)

The *CMS* Tribunal held:

> [t]he Treaty in this case is clearly designed to protect investments at a time of economic difficulties or other circumstances leading to the adoption of adverse measures by the Government. The question is, however, how grave these economic difficulties might be. A severe crisis cannot necessarily be equated with a situation of total collapse. And in the absence of such profoundly serious conditions it is plainly clear that the Treaty will prevail over any plea of necessity … As stated above, the Tribunal is convinced that the Argentine crisis was severe but did not result in total economic and social collapse. When the Argentine crisis is compared to other contemporary crises affecting countries in different regions of the world it may be noted that such other crises have not led to the derogation of international contractual or treaty obligations. Renegotiation, adaptation and postponement have occurred but the essence of international obligations has been kept intact. (*CMS Gas* v. *Argentina* 2005: paras 354–5)

The *CMS* Annulment Committee observed that the *CMS* Tribunal had made several legal errors in its consideration of Article XI and customary international law, but that the high threshold for annulling an award had not been reached (*CMS* Annulment Decision 2007: paras 128–36).

The *Enron* Tribunal held:

> [t]he Tribunal has no doubt that there was a severe crisis and that in such context it was unlikely that business could have continued as usual. Yet, the argument that such a situation compromised the very existence of the State and its independence so as to qualify as involving an essential interest of the State is not convincing. Questions of public order and social unrest could be handled as in fact they were, just as questions of political stabilization were handled under the constitutional arrangements in force. … A rather sad world comparative experience in the handling of economic crises, shows that there are always many approaches to address and correct such critical events, and it is difficult to justify that none of them were available in the Argentine case. (*Enron* v. *Argentina* 2007: 306, 308 and 331)

An almost identical passage appears in the decision of the *Sempra* Tribunal (*Sempra* v. *Argentina* 2007: paras 348 and 350).

Both the *Enron* and *Sempra* awards were subsequently annulled within a month of each other; giving, for the first time, decisive effect to the essential criticism made by the *CMS* Annulment Committee.

The *Sempra* Annulment Committee held first that 'the Tribunal adopted Article 25 of the ILC Articles as the primary law to be applied, rather than Article XI of the BIT, and in so doing made a fundamental error in identifying and applying the applicable law'(*Sempra* Annulment Decision 2010: para 208). In other words, the Tribunal erred in applying Article 25 of the ILC Articles to the exclusion of Article XI and accordingly manifestly exceeded its powers by depriving Argentina of its entitlement to have its right of preclusion in Article XI subjected to legal scrutiny.

The *Enron* Annulment Committee then held that the approach taken by the Tribunal to the question of whether alternatives existed for Argentina was deficient in a number of respects, concluding that the Tribunal focused on an artificial and improper 'only way' test for proving necessity under Article 25 of the ILC Articles or non-preclusion under Article XI of the BIT. The Committee concluded that:

> in determining that the measures adopted were not the 'only way', the Tribunal did not in fact apply Article 25(1)(a) of the ILC Articles (or more precisely, customary international law as reflected in that provision), but instead applied an expert opinion on an economic issue. In all the circumstances, the Committee finds that this amounts to a failure to apply the applicable law, as ground of annulment under Article 52(1)(b) of the ICSID Convention. …
>
> The Committee has concluded above that the Tribunal's finding that the requirements of Article 25 of the ILC Articles are not satisfied in this case must be annulled. Because that finding formed the basis of the Tribunal's finding that Article XI of the BIT was inapplicable in this case, the Committee concludes that the latter finding of the Tribunal must also be annulled. (*Enron* Annulment Decision 2010: paras 378 and 405)

The *Enron* Annulment Committee did not, however, go further and define the correct legal tests, holding that this was an issue for reconsideration by a Tribunal, if either party were to request resubmission (*Enron* Annulment Decision, 2010: paras 405 and 408).

In *Continental Casualty*, (which is at the time of writing still awaiting consideration by an Annulment Committee), the Tribunal held:

> [s]ince the text of Art. XI derives from the parallel model clause of the U.S. FCN treaties and these treaties in turn reflect the formulation of Art. XX of GATT 1947, the Tribunal finds it more appropriate to refer to the GATT and WTO case law which has extensively dealt with the concept and requirements of necessity in the context of economic measures derogating to the obligations contained in GATT, rather than to refer to the requirement of necessity under customary international law. (*Continental Casualty* v. *Argentina* 2008: para. 192)

The Tribunal then went on to quote excerpts from the Appellate Body decisions in *Korea – Beef*, *EC – Asbestos* and *US – Gambling* (*Continental Casualty* v. *Argentina* 2008: paras 193–5). It concluded that the WTO weighing and balancing approach should be imported into its analysis in determining 'whether the Measures contributed materially to the realization of [Argentina's] legitimate aims under Art. XI of the BIT, namely the protection of the essential security interests of Argentina in the economic and social crisis it was facing' (*Continental Casualty* v. *Argentina* 2008: para. 196).

Given my professed admiration for the GATT/WTO approach to exceptions, one might suppose I would support the *Continental Casualty* approach. But, in fact, I share the misgivings of Alvarez and Khamsi, who submit that:

> Article XX of the GATT is grounded in a balancing test that is absent from the test of the U.S.–Argentina BIT's Article XI. Article XI suggests an on/off switch; either a measure is 'necessary' for the stipulated reasons or it is not. Nothing in it suggests the balancing test implied in the preamble of GATT's Article XX … or in the lengthy laundry list of exceptions contained in the rest of Article XX (which presumably extend beyond the usual customary law defences). (Alvarez and Khamsi 2009: 441)

In contrast, the Tribunal in *Enron* had concluded:

> [i]n examining this discussion, the Tribunal must first note that the object and purpose of the Treaty is, as a general proposition, to apply in situations of economic difficulty and hardship that require the protection of the international guaranteed rights of its beneficiaries. To this extent, any interpretation resulting in an escape route from the obligations defined cannot be easily reconciled with that object and purpose. Accordingly, a restrictive interpretation of any such alternative is mandatory. (*Enron* v. *Argentina* 2007: para. 331)

This seems harsh, and has been specifically criticized by Newcombe and Paradell (2009: 485). As noted above, it was also not the view taken by the *Enron* Annulment Committee. Yet, arguably, it does reflect the original intent of the parties to the BIT – or specifically, the US negotiators. In short, the problem is not so much the content of, or the inconsistency between, the five decisions, but with the lack of a firm textual basis grounding them. All of the tribunals appear to be trying to do too much with too little. First, recourse was swiftly had to Article 25 of the ILC Articles, which were applied by the *CMS*, *Sempra* and *Enron* Tribunals similarly to a statute, to the exclusion of the actual words in Article XI. Then the *Continental Casualty* Tribunal chose effectively to apply WTO case law, notwithstanding the different contexts of the two systems.

It is apparent from reading any of these decisions how unsettled is this area of interpretation.[5] Even after the *Enron* Annulment Decision, the contours of the non-precluded measures defence and Article 25 of the ILC Articles remain to be settled by future tribunals. Like Newcombe and Paradell, the respected authors of another textbook claim that 'general concepts [contained in BITs] do in fact contain within them considerable flexibility. This enables arbitrators to balance the public and the private interest, and to ensure that the treaty provisions retain their role as a safety net, leaving a considerable margin of appreciation for the exercise of state sovereignty' (McLachlan *et al.* 2007: 23).

This approach, however, leaves the key policy issues to arbitrator discretion. and it is far from clear that arbitrators are the most suitable policy-makers. As Professor Brower has written:

> [w]hen compared to the open and systematic application of interpretative principles favouring the protection of foreign investment, pursuit of the public interest through hints and veiled reference suggest that tribunals regard it as a tertiary consideration in resolving investment disputes. Furthermore, the subtextual motivations of individual tribunals provide no stable or rigorous framework for consideration of the public interest, even as a tertiary factor, in future investment disputes. (Brower 2009: 360–1)

In a system with *ad hoc* adjudicators and no right of appeal, stakeholders need to have confidence that these tribunals will pay close attention to the text and not be distracted by exogenous sources. But it is obviously difficult for arbitrators to do so if the text they must interpret is incomplete and limited. The present drafting of BITs cries out for judicial creativity.

Much as I value creativity, I prefer the more explicit approach already taken by some BITs and FTAs. Although most do not contain general exceptions clauses (see Newcombe and Paradell 2009: 500), some now do. For instance, Canada's BITs habitually include general exception provisions based on Article 10 of the 2003 Canadian Model Agreement. The same is true for the investment chapters of the New Zealand–China and the ASEAN–Australia–New Zealand FTA – the former of which expressly subjects the investment regulation to GATT Article XX and both of which include Annexes defining indirect appropriation (New Zealand–China FTA 2008: Art. 200; ASEAN–Australia–New Zealand FTA: Arts 1–5, Chap. 15). The 2004 US Model BIT does not include a broad general exception provision, but does contain expanded exception provisions in Articles 12, 13, 18 and 20, as well as a detailed Annex B defining indirect expropriation (US Model Bilateral Investment Treaty 2004).[6] The Norwegian Draft Model BIT had included such a provision also (Norwegian Model Bilateral Investment Treaty, issued for comment 2007: Art. 24 and n 6), but it has recently been withdrawn – as a result, sadly, of the failure to find stakeholder consensus on several drafting issues.

Implications and concluding thoughts

What has been largely absent in investment law is what is now a staple of trade law – the 'investment and' debate (though see Reinisch 2007: 203). There has been insufficient principled discussion of how international investment law connects with other values and objectives. One reason this is missing is the absence of a legal mechanism which provides a focus for detailed analysis. Accordingly, the reasoning in many BIT cases lacks the coherence and resonance of the leading Appellate Body decisions.

This section addresses – rather more shortly – what underlying philosophy should motivate the next generation of BIT text. I believe that there is a limit as to what can be done with many of the older generation of treaties. Certainly, there is room for a balancing process within some of the substantive investment rights provided and the existing non-precluded measures clauses. Equally certainly, some assistance can be gained from 'general concepts', customary international law and previous cases. But the scope for legitimate creativity is confined.

The BIT landscape is, however, changing faster than many participants might think. The text of today's Model BITs is important not only as a template for new agreements, but as an example of what might be renegotiated by individual states. Many existing BITs have limited lives – such as the UK–Argentina BIT, which may now be terminated by either party on twelve months' notice. A period of global financial retrenchment (including of global FDI) is a good time to reassess how these agreements might be written. It is also likely in the coming years that many BITs will be superseded, or at least augmented, by FTAs containing investment chapters. And it is possible that a wider form of MFN clause could allow *state parties* to benefit from more favourable exception clauses in other BITs.

At present, most BITs deliberately represent a laissez-faire liberalism, rather than the embedded liberalism of the WTO system. Some commentators, such as Vandevalde, are unhappy with this philosophical approach – but only because BITs do not go far enough in single-mindedly pursuing the goal of investment liberalization (Vandevalde 1998a: 636–40). Others, of course, take the opposite view. To turn again to Professor Ruggie, this time in his capacity as Special Representative of the UN Secretary-General for Business and Human Rights:

> [r]ecent experience suggests that some treaty guarantees and contract provisions may unduly constrain the host Government's ability to achieve its legitimate policy objectives, including its international human rights obligations. That is because under threat of binding international arbitration, a foreign investor may be able to insulate its business venture from new laws and regulations, or seek compensation from the Government for the cost of compliance. A Norwegian draft model agreement and commentary address such concerns about bilateral investment treaties [and] stresses the vulnerability of developing countries to agreements 'that tie up political freedom of action and the exercise of authority …'. (Report of the Special Representative of the Secretary-General 2009: paras 29–31)

The concept informing Ruggie's comments, and the now-defunct Norwegian draft, is really that of sustainable development. It would be a mistake to dismiss this out of hand. Defined in the 1987 Brundtland Report as 'development that meets the needs of the present without compromising the ability of future generations to meet their own needs' (Report of the Brundtland Commission 1987: Chap. 2, para. 1), explicated in the 1992 Rio Declaration on Environment and Development (Report of the UNCED 1992), affirmed in the 2002 Monterrey Consensus (Report of the International Conference on Financing for Development 2002) and further developed in the 2008 Doha Declaration on Financing for Development (Doha Declaration 2008), sustainable development has become a defining issue for the present wave of globalization. Although it has most closely been identified with environmental issues, it is a much broader idea. Indeed, through the human development theory constructed by Amartya Sen and others, development has been identified with the basic human desire for freedom. On this view, development is an increase of basic capabilities and wealth which facilitates the expansion of substantive freedoms (Sen 1999: 14, 19–20, 33, 225). Sustainable development occurs when, on numerous levels, this increase in substantive freedoms happens in an incremental and permanent way.

Many agree that 'the development dimension of IIAs remains to be more fully realised' (Muchlinski 2009: 48). Certainly, international investment is not a virtue in and of itself. Its value is as a means to an end; the question being, how to define that end? I suggest that, just as Ruggie's embedded liberalism has become the philosophical basis for WTO law, Sen's human development theory could be a lodestar for international investment law.

But even if one resists Sen's theory, one should not reject the concepts of clarity, predictability and longevity that are common-sense principles of good treaty drafting. There is a pressing need to better define the appropriate balance between investor and state interest in the international investment. That balance may be different from that for the international trade context. One need not go so far as to embrace IISD's Model Investment Agreement (IISD Model International Agreement on Investment for Sustainable Development 2006: Art. 25[7]), or even the Norwegian draft, to appreciate that some form of wording is better than none. While there may be a legitimate debate as to how best craft such a provision, the debate should be had.

Looking to the long term, Vandevalde has argued that the principal benefit of a BIT is 'stabilization' of the investment environment (Vandevalde 1998b: 522). But how really stable is a system which is textually one-sided and relies upon beneficent interpretation by *ad hoc* tribunals to redress the balance? In this regard, I have in mind Amy Chua's thesis that investment disputes are cyclical, and a privatization–nationalization dynamic is the inexorable consequence of domestic political forces (including ethnic rivalries) (Chua 1995). If so, it is not in the long-term interest of investors to override domestic political issues by investment rights – even if it may lead to short-term gain. If BITs do not adequately provide for the balancing of competing interests, the inevitable balancing process may take place with considerably less subtlety outside of the international investment system – for instance by countries such as Bolivia and Ecuador pulling out entirely.[8]

To conclude, public goods are part of the international political economy. Indeed, much of the contemporary debate is turning towards how to ensure provision of global public goods – such as a sustainable climate – in our interconnected, globalized world. BITs cannot address this larger problem, but they can seek to ensure that public, as well as private goods are adequately and expressly taken into account in what is an important, but still immature, form of international regulation of domestic state action.

Notes

1 In another article, Professor Alvarez has tentatively remarked that one might see in BITs some aspects of the contracts of adhesion: Alvarez and Khamsi 2009: 473.
2 It is believed, of course, that the first BIT was that concluded between the Federal Republic of Germany and Pakistan in 1959: see Lowenfeld 2008: 554–5.
3 See also a similar passage in *LG&E Energy* v. *Argentina* 2006: para. 124.
4 See also *Pope* v. *Talbot* v. *Canada* 2000: para. 99.
5 See, for example, Muchlinski 2009: 53: 'investment tribunals, dealing with investor-state litigation following the Argentine financial crisis, have not come to very clear or satisfactory conclusions on this crucial point regarding the effectiveness of IIAs'.
6 Note that the Energy Charter Treaty 1991: Art. 24 includes an exception but this does not extend to the treaty's provisions on expropriation; see also Japan-Singapore Economic Partnership Agreement 2002: Art. 83.
7 This provision is intended to affirm the inherent right to regulate, rather than be a mere general exception provision, allegedly on the basis that even the WTO approach is too restrictive. See Newcombe and Paradell 2009: 503n.89.
8 Perhaps in favour of the Venezuela-led Bolivarian Alternative for the Americas. See, for example, Alvaro 2009.

11 China's evolving international investment treaty policy towards liberalism

Chunbao Liu

Introduction

International investment agreements (IIAs)[1] are instruments of international law through which states make commitments to other states with respect to treatment they will accord to investors and investments from those other states. IIAs are often equipped with a dispute settlement mechanism that allows investors to bring claims directly against the host state before an international arbitration tribunal. The main reason for making IIAs is to reduce the space for unprincipled and arbitrary actions of the host state, thus promoting international investment. One of the most remarkable phenomena in international law during the past two decades has been the extraordinary increase in the number of IIAs. By the end of 2009, the total number of BITs in existence reached 2,750 (UNCTAD 2010a: 81). Some 474 regional trade agreements (RTAs) have been notified to the World Trade Organization (WTO), many of which address an expansive set of investment matters. Furthermore, the number of known investor-state arbitration cases filed under IIAs rose to 357. More than half of them were initiated in the last five years (UNCTAD 2010b: 1).

This chapter seeks to examine China's participation in and positions on IIAs. China is the second largest contracting party to BITs worldwide, surpassed only by Germany. In 1982 China signed its first BIT with Sweden. By the end of October 2010, it had concluded BITs with 130 countries, of which more than 100 had entered into force (MOFCOM 2010b). China has also concluded ten free trade agreements (FTAs). Its active participation in IIAs has raised the following questions: what are China's motivations; how are China's patterns of IIA practice explainable; what is the potential impact of China on international investment regimes?

I show in this chapter that China has gradually changed its attitudes towards protection of foreign investment by international law during the past three decades. Its traditional standpoint had been to support Calvo doctrine that the law applicable to foreign investment should be national law. However, in order to attract foreign investment, China started to conclude BITs soon after initiating the 'Reform and Opening-Up' policy in 1978. But early Chinese BITs were highly restrictive and characterized by a certain hesitance about important standards of protection. A new generation of BITs were launched in the late 1990s by accepting, most notably, a comprehensive investor-state dispute settlement mechanism. Despite some remaining limitations imposed by 'clauses with Chinese characteristics', in all major aspects recent Chinese IIAs guarantee protections similar to what can be considered standard international practice. These changes can be understood in the broad context of China's liberal-oriented domestic regulatory reform and its relation with international investment.

The rest of the chapter proceeds as follows. The section on China's changing attitudes towards international investment provides an overview of China's changing attitudes towards foreign direct investment (FDI) since 1978 for understanding the background against which China's IIA policies are developed. Next, the section headed 'Overview of China's participation in IIAs' presents a general survey of China's IIAs. This is followed by 'Evolution of key provisions in China's IIAs', which discusses in further detail the evolution of key provisions in China's IIAs. A final section brings the chapter to a close.

China's changing attitudes towards international investment

Since 1949 when the People's Republic of China was established, its policy on foreign investment has undergone dramatic changes. In line with Marxist ideology, Western capital was vigorously rejected in the first three decades. But attracting foreign investment became one of the key pillars of the open-door policy initiated in 1978. Now as summarized in the proposed twelfth Five-Year Plan (2011–15), China's investment policy has shifted from 'attracting FDI first' to 'paying equal attention to inward FDI and outward FDI'.

The first decade after the Communist Party took over China saw mass nationalization of foreign enterprises (Chew 1994; Thompson 1979). Before 1949, foreign investors controlled key sectors of the Chinese economy, such as railroads and mines (Feuerwerker 1976; Xu and Long 1996). The new communist government regarded foreign capital as an agent of imperialism that had weakened China, and committed itself to eliminate Western enterprises in China. The primary method adopted by the government was known as 'slow-motion nationalization'. Occasionally, the government took direct and physical control of foreign property in retaliation for what it considered hostile or unlawful actions taken by the investor's host country (Chew 1994: 627). As a result, the government effectively ended foreign investment in China by 1957, except for Sino-Soviet joint ventures. In the following two decades, China practised self-reliance and refused to accept foreign investments.

The new leadership headed by Deng Xiaoping made an unprecedented decision to open China to the outside world in 1978: 'It doesn't matter whether the cat is black or white, as long as it catches mice.' Unlike Chairman Mao, Deng Xiaoping took a pragmatic view of the future of China and socialism. The liberalization of FDI policy has been a dynamic, continuous process. In early 1980s, foreign invested enterprises (FIEs) were separated from the domestic economy – geographically and legally. Four Special Economic Zones were created in 1980 as 'experimental fields' where special policies could be adopted to attract foreign capital. The first Sino-foreign joint venture law was promulgated by the National

People's Congress in 1979. Following the promulgation of the initial law, Chinese legislators and administrators created a special legal framework which applied only to FIEs (Wang 1988). It provided some guidance for foreign investors on many important issues, including business organization, contracts, employment and taxation. In 1992 China decided to accept a 'market economy' as the goal of economic reform. A particular move relating to this new goal was that the government decided to gradually grant 'national treatment' to FIEs (Shan 2005: 10–13). Accordingly, a number of laws and regulations were unified to regulate both domestic and foreign enterprises. Accession into the WTO further liberalized China's investment regulatory regime (Qin 2007). The catalogue for the guidance of foreign investment industries, the official list of industries in which FDI is encouraged or restricted, has been revised four times since 1997. Each time greater market access was provided. After entry into the WTO in 2001, FDI in China experienced a dramatic increase until the global financial crisis of 2008. By the end of 2009, FDI stock in China had reached US$473.08 billion, accounting for up to 9.6 per cent of FDI stock in developing countries and 2.6 per cent of global FDI stock (UNCTAD 2010a). Recently, however, there has been a concern that China is now less welcoming of foreign investment (Chen 2010; Anderlini 2010). For instance, China reversed its earlier tax policy concerning FDI in 2008 (Li 2007). Under the old policy, foreign investors were provided with 'super-national treatment' and taxed at a lower rate than domestic investors. The tax incentives based on nationality have been removed in the new unified tax law. On 13 April 2010, the State Council published the 'Several Opinions of the State Council on Further Doing a Good Job in the Utilization of Foreign Investment', which clearly demonstrates that what concerns the Chinese government now is no longer to attract more FDI but how to attract FDI of higher quality.

While still receiving large amounts of FDI, China has recently also been perceived as an important capital exporter. The years following 2003 saw a sharp growth in annual outward FDI, from US$2.90 billion in 2003 to US$48.00 billion in 2009 (UNCTAD 2010a). China's outward FDI stock surged to US$229.60 billion by the end of 2009, accounting for 8.5 per cent of outward FDI (OFDI) stock from developing countries and 1.21 per cent of global outward FDI stock. Although Chinese FDI outflows are still subordinate to FDI inflows in absolute terms, China's role in global FDI has been redefined. The government perspective on OFDI has gone through two stages, from 'regulation' to 'encouragement' (Cai 2006; Luo *et al.* 2010). During the 1980s and the 1990s, OFDI projects were subject to a strict approval process. The first and foremost concern for the Chinese government was to attract foreign capital. OFDI policy would have been supplementary to trade policy. As a result, China's OFDI stayed at a relatively low level. With rapid economic growth and a huge trade surplus, the Chinese government started the 'Go Out' strategy in 1998 primarily by promoting OFDI. The process of approving application has therefore been simplified. The government has also taken a series of measures to provide administrative and financial support for Chinese OFDI. It can be expected that Chinese OFDI will continue to expand. This has led to a strong incentive for the Chinese government to adjust IIA policy to protect its own investments (Berger 2008; Shang 2005).

Overview of China's participation in IIAs

As a result of its bitter historical experience with 'unequal treaties' (Wang 2005) and the influence of Marxist ideology, China's attitude towards protection of foreign investment by international law was very sceptical before 1979. China joined the movement by developing countries to establish a 'New International Economic Order' and supported the Calvo doctrine, which essentially denied any protection of foreign investment under international law (Deng 1974). The launch of the open-door policy created the need for participation in international investment regimes. From the outset of its decision to attract FDI, the Chinese government has realized that lack of a credible legal framework was the major problem facing foreign investors (Xiao 1984; Yao 1980). It was also observed that signing IIAs would contribute to the objective of attracting FDI. China thus became a heavy IIA practitioner.

BITs

China's first BIT was signed with Sweden in 1982, soon after opening its door for foreign investment. In the subsequent two years, all of China's BITs were entered into with developed countries. From 1985 China stated to sign BITs with developing countries while continuing to enter into BITs with other developed countries. China formally signed the Convention on the Settlement of Investment Disputes between States and Nationals of Other States (ICSID Convention) on 9 February 1990 and ratified the Convention on 7 January 1993. More than half of China's BITs were signed in the 1990s. The obligations contained in early Chinese BITs were weak. Yet they had a signalling function addressed to the international community, demonstrating that China had undertaken a major policy change in relation to foreign investment.

China launched a new generation of BITs in the late 1990s, by accepting, most notably, national treatment and a comprehensive investor-state dispute settlement mechanism (A. Chen 2006; Schill 2007). The current China Model BIT as the base for negotiations was formulated in around 1997 (Gallagher and Shan 2009: 433–7). Closely following this new prototype, China has entered into about 40 BITs. Most of them were signed with African and South American countries. China also revised a dozen of its existing BITs, the majority of which were renegotiated with capital-exporting countries.[2] These BITs often went slightly beyond the Model BIT in favour of investors. Revisions to the current Model BIT are under discussion and reportedly will conclude with a new Model BIT text to be released by the government in the near future.

It is worth noting that some of China's important investment partners are absent from the expansive BIT network, including Brazil, Canada and the USA.[3] China has not yet concluded a BIT with Brazil, probably because of the country's general reluctance to sign and ratify BITs. Negotiations with the USA on a BIT started as early as 1983 but failed through wide divergence between the two parties over a range of issues (Cai 2009: 457). After lengthy discussions, China and the USA announced the reopening of BIT negotiations on 18 June 2008. Negotiations between China and Canada started in 1994 and resumed in September 2004. Given the significant difference between China's Model BIT and those of Canada and the USA, it will be interesting to see how the negotiations will produce a BIT acceptable to all parties.

According to UNCTAD, thus far 81 countries have had the experience of being a respondent country before ICSID or an *ad hoc* tribunal (2010b:1). Despite signing such a large number of BITs and the huge volume of FDI coming into and out of China, no investor-state arbitration case has been brought against China. The only published tribunal decision interpreting a Chinese BIT is the recently released decision in *Tza Yap Shum* v. *Peru.* On 29 September 2006, Mr Tza Yap Shum, a Chinese national and resident in Hong Kong, filed a claim against Peru with the ICSID under the 1994 China–Peru BIT. The rare use of investor-state arbitration is in sharp contrast with China's experience with the WTO dispute settlement mechanism. Although it acceded to the WTO only in 2001, it has to date been complaint in 7 cases, respondent in 20 cases and third party in 71 cases.[4]

FTAs

The primary economic rationale for dealing with investment in RTAs is that trade and investment are no longer seen merely as substitutes but as complements in the global era. Deeper economic integration requires lowering barriers both to trade and to investment (Taylor 1998; UNCTAD 2006a: 2–11). In addition, linking negotiations on trade and investment has the advantage of increasing the variability of exchange and thus the possibility of concluding an agreement (Leebron 2002). Finally, RTAs provide a larger textual capacity than BITs to balance private and public interests (Falsafi 2008).

Since China completed its WTO accession negotiations with major economies, negotiating FTAs has been adopted as an important part of its open-door policy. By the end of June 2010, China had concluded ten FTAs: ASEAN countries (2002), Hong Kong (2003), Macao (2003), Chile (2005), Pakistan (2006), New Zealand (2008), Singapore (2008), Peru (2009), Costa Rica (2010) and Taiwan (2010).[5] It has also been in the process of negotiating FTAs with the Gulf Cooperation Council, Australia, Iceland, Norway and Southern Africa Customs Union (MOFCOM, 2010a). China's FTAs generally consists of three pillars: trade in goods, trade in services and investment. As a new arrival, China often took a piecemeal approach to FTA negotiations. It would start with an agreement on trade in goods and then expand to trade in services and investment only after the commitments on goods had been substantially implemented. Examples include the ASEAN FTA, CEPAs, the Chile FTA and the Pakistan FTA. However, more recently negotiated FTAs, such as the New Zealand FTA, the Singapore FTA, the Peru FTA and the Costa Rica FTA, are 'single undertakings', addressing all elements in one comprehensive agreement.

China's FTAs often divide investment rules between the service chapter/agreement and the investment chapter/agreement. All of them have included or are negotiating a GATS-style service chapter/agreement. The commitments scheduled for 'commercial presence' are essentially liberalization provisions for services investment. Service chapters/agreements provide schedules of commitments in a higher number of sectors and sub-sectors compared with those made under the GATS. In contrast to the relatively consistent approach to the service chapter/agreement, the approach of China's FTAs to the investment chapter/agreement varies substantially. Like NAFTA Chapter XI, the Pakistan FTA, the New Zealand FTA and the Peru FTA contain a BIT-like investment chapter in a comprehensive agreement. There are also FTAs incorporating an independent investment agreement. For example, China and ASEAN countries signed the Framework Agreement on Comprehensive Economic Cooperation as a roadmap for establishing an FTA in 2002. According to the objectives set out in the Framework Agreement, the parties concluded an Investment Agreement in August 2009. This agreement is also incorporated, *mutatis mutandis*, into and forms an integral part of the Singapore FTA (Art. 84). Similarly China and Costa reaffirmed their commitments under an up-to-date BIT in their FTA (Art. 89). An investment agreement under the Chile FTA is in the process of negotiation. Finally, although Hong Kong and Macao are important FDI partners with the mainland, the CEPAs do not contain a BIT-like investment chapter. One possible explanation is that the CEPAs are essentially unilateral concessions made by the mainland, and thus the special administrative governments lack leverage to barter for an investment chapter.

Investments between China and its FTA partners, except for Hong Kong, Macao and Taiwan, have already been subject to BITs. A majority of them were entered into in the last century and fall into China's old-generation BITs.[6] Presumably the main reason behind China's acceptance of a BIT-like investment chapter/agreement in FTAs is to update investment rules with its investment partners. In all major aspects, investment chapters/agreements in China's FTAs seem to provide similar protection standards to investors and their investments as the new generation BITs. However, the FTAs do occasionally introduce new elements which cannot be found in BITs. For example, the Pakistan FTA provides a framework for the establishment of 'China–Pakistan Investment Zones', where investors are entitled to a package of incentives granted by the government of Pakistan. In addition, the interaction between investment chapters and other parts of an FTA might make them differ from BITs. For instance, the FTAs often contain a general chapter on exceptions applicable to the entire agreement, thus providing greater regulatory flexibility to the host country than regular BITs.[7] To date the most detailed and comprehensive investment rules among all Chinese IIAs are found in Chapter 11 of the New Zealand FTA.

WTO

Under the current WTO framework, investment provisions are limited in scope and fragmented in structure (Gugler and Chaisse 2008). The Agreement on Trade-Related Investment Measures (TRIMs) and the General Agreement on Trade in Services (GATS) are the main instruments which directly deal with foreign investment. The main aim of the TRIMs is to prohibit the use of performance requirements. However, it does little more than elaborate and clarify certain aspects of the GATT provisions concerning national treatment and prohibition on quantitative restrictions. In addition to the TRIMs, GATS applies to the supply of trade in services through 'commercial presence', which is in essence an investment activity. Unlike BITs, which focus on protection of investment and investors, GATS is designed with the main purpose of liberalization. It is a framework agreement which takes a 'bottom-up' approach to market access. Commitments on services investment need to be scheduled by the individual WTO members. In the 2001 Doha Declaration, the WTO members recognized the need for 'a multilateral framework to secure transparent, stable and predictable conditions for long-term cross-border investment' (WTO 2001: para. 20). However, in the lead-up to the Cancun Conference, a wide range of developing countries expressed their opposition to starting negotiations on investment in the setting of the WTO. As a result, investment was dropped from the Doha Round agenda at the Cancun Conference.[8]

China entered into the WTO at the Doha Ministerial Conference in 2001, the same Conference that launched the Doha Round negotiations. Although China has been active in the negotiations, it has maintained 'a pragmatic, leadership-avoiding and low-profile approach' (Huang 2008). A key negotiation strategy of China is to take a middle-position and keep flexibility (Lim and Wang 2009). On investment, it basically adopted a defensive position. The proponents of an investment agreement have been seeking new rights for investors without parallel disciplines on their behaviours. In November 2002, China joined a group of the WTO members who urged the Working Group on Investment and Trade to discuss investors' and home countries' obligations in a balanced manner.[9] The USA proposed that the agreement must have a broad, open-ended definition that included portfolio investment.[10] In response to the US proposal, China argued that the definition should be limited to FDI and exclude portfolio investment.[11] With respect to transparency, China supported a section on transparency included in the possible agreement.[12] But China also supported exceptions to the principle of transparency and the need to provide technical and capacity-building assistance to developing countries for implementing provisions on transparency.

Evolution of key provisions in China's IIAs

China's IIAs are often similar in structure. A typical BIT starts with a preamble stating the purposes and objectives of the agreement. The first article deals with the scope of application by providing definitions of 'investment' and 'investor'. The following five or six articles address substantive obligations of the contracting parties, including treatment of investment, expropriation and transfer. Then two articles respectively stipulate procedures for settlement of disputes between contracting parties and between investors and one contracting party. The last articles are miscellaneous provisions concerning application of the treaty. One trend can be observed is that recent IIAs often include a protocol or an annexe.

Scope of application

The scope of application of an investment treaty is mainly established through definitions of 'investment' and 'investor'. Covered investments must be invested in the territory of a contracting party by investors of another party.

With the single exception of the 2008 Mexico BIT (Art. 1), all the Chinese IIAs adopt a broad asset-based definition by defining an investment as 'every kind of asset'. This broad definition is supplemented by an illustrative list of particular assets covered by the IIA. One generally applied qualification to the definition of investment is 'in accordance with laws and regulations' of the host country. The reason for such qualification is that China wishes to preserve its regulatory control over foreign investment and confer protection only on investments that conform to domestic laws (Gallagher and Shan 2009: 55–7). Notably, the qualification does not appear in some recent Chinese IIAs (see Germany BIT 2003: Art. 1; New Zealand FTA 2008: Art. 135). This omission may prevent the state parties from claiming that an investment is made fraudulently and therefore is not qualified for protection.

Investors include natural persons and legal entities. To qualify as a covered investor, it must be a national of the home country. The nationality of natural persons generally is determined by the domestic law of the home country. In most of China's IIAs, the nationality of legal entities is defined by a combination of two criteria. A qualified legal entity must be established in accordance with the laws of one contracting party and be seated in the territory of that contracting party. However, many recent BITs stipulate that legal entities having the nationality of a third country but owned or controlled by nationals of another contracting party shall be treated as nationals of the latter (see Germany BIT 2003; Seychelles BIT 2007; and New Zealand FTA 2008). This development has the effect of extending benefits to considerable investors based in Hong Kong who are owned or controlled by nationals of an IIA-partner country.

An important limit exists, however, with respect to the temporal applicability of Chinese IIAs. Following European model BITs, the scope of Chinese IIAs is limited to post-establishment measures. In China, foreign-invested enterprises must be set up with approval from the government, while domestic enterprises can be set up by registration only. It had been expected that the ASEAN Agreement would make a breakthrough on this point, because one objective of the agreement set up in the Framework Agreement is to 'progressively liberalize the investment regime' (Art. 5). During the negotiations, although ASEAN countries demanded pre-establishment national treatment, China was not willing to discuss concessions on market access (H. Chen 2006). As a result, the parties simply agreed on a post-establishment national treatment qualified by a 'grandfather' clause (ASEAN Agreement 2009: Art. 4). After the Lisbon Treaty the European Community is authorized to negotiate more ambitious IIAs, addressing both investment protection and liberalization issues (de Mestral 2010). It remains to be seen whether the negotiations of the China–US BIT, the China–Canada BIT and the potential China-EU BIT will result in a market access component.

National treatment

The national treatment (NT) clause is not a common feature in Chinese IIAs. The old-generation BITs generally do not contain a national treatment provision at all, with a few exceptions where the NT is only a 'best effort' obligation (see UK BIT 1985: Art. 3(3); Japan BIT 1988: Art. 3(2)). One reason for China's initial reluctance to accept national treatment was to protect domestic industry. At the beginning of the opening up of its economy, Chinese industries were too weak to withstand international competition (Gallagher and Shan 2009: 165). As domestic industries gradually developed in the past three decades, China felt more conformable to accept national treatment qualified with exceptions. Another approach to explaining the evolution of China's policy on national treatment links it to the regulatory structure of the Chinese economy (Gallagher and Shan 2009: 166). There was no 'uniform national standard' under a central planned economy. Enterprises were divided into several categories, including state-owned enterprises, collectively owned enterprises, privately owned enterprises and foreign-invested enterprises. The treatment granted to an enterprise depended on the nature of its ownership.

Starting in the late 1990s, China has increasingly accepted a post-establishment national treatment clause. The change of national treatment policy was a response to China's decision to abandon the planned economy and move towards a market economy in the 1990s. However, as a 'full market economy' has not yet been established, the new-generation BITs and FTAs still contain substantial restrictions to full national treatment. For example, Article 48(2) of the Pakistan FTA stipulates:

> *Without prejudice to its laws and regulations*, each Party shall accord to investments and activities associated with such investments by the investors of the other Party treatment not less favourable than that accorded to the investments and associated activities by its own investors. [emphasis added]

Such a clause makes the NT obligation contingent on the domestic legislation of the host country and allows the host country to discriminate against foreign investors by changing old or enacting new laws in favour of domestic investors. It simply prevents discriminatory measures which are not imposed by formal laws or regulations.

In some renegotiated European BITs and some FTAs, the reservation 'without prejudice to its laws and regulations' has been replaced by a 'grandfather' clause. A typical example of such a 'grandfather' clause can be found in Article 130 of the Peru FTA:

> 1 Article 129 (National Treatment) does not apply to:
>
> (a) any existing non-conforming measures maintained within its territory;
> (b) the continuation of any non-conforming measure referred to in subparagraph (a); or
> (c) an amendment to any non-conforming measure referred to in subparagraph (a) to the extent that the amendment does not increase the non-conformity of the measure, as existed immediately before the amendment, with those obligations.
>
> 2 The Parties will endeavour to progressively remove the non-conforming measures.

The scope of the exceptions granted by the grandfather clause is clearly narrower than the one established by 'without prejudice to its laws and regulations'. The grandfather clause allows the preservation of non-conforming measures but prohibits the introduction of new discriminations. This development reflects the ongoing 'national treatment movement' of China's domestic regulatory reform.

Surprisingly neither of the two qualifications appears in the NT provision of the Seychelles BIT (Art. 5). The BIT was concluded in 2007 and has not yet come into force. It remains unclear why China accepted the unconditional NT obligation only in this BIT. Since all Chinese IIAs include a most-favoured-nation treatment (MFN) clause, it may be possible to argue that the broad NT obligation of the Seychelles BIT can be invoked by non-Seychelles investors as well, once the BIT enters into force.

Most-favoured-nation treatment

Nearly all Chinese IIAs contain an MFN clause. In principle, on the basis of an MFN clause a foreign investor is able to invoke preferential treatment that the host country grants to investors of a third country. Therefore, the ever-evolving Chinese IIA practice will have repercussions on its existing and more restrictive old-generation BITs.

The MFN clause in most Chinese BITs applies only to the post-establishment stage. However, some recent IIAs extend MFN to admission of investment. For example, the New Zealand FTA provides that investors, investments and associated activities from the other contracting party shall receive MFN treatment with respect to 'admission, expansion, management, conduct, operation, maintenance, use, enjoyment and disposal' (Art. 139(1)). A similar approach has been taken by some recent BITs and other FTAs (see Finland BIT 2004: Art. 3(2); Peru FTA 2009: Art. 131(1); ASEAN Agreement 2009: Art. 5(1)).

In the old-generation BITs, China's consent to investor-state arbitration was limited to disputes concerning the amount of compensation for expropriation. The question, therefore, arises whether the investor can rely on an MFN clause to bring disputes relating to the violation of other substantive rights. The tribunal in *Tza Yap Shum* v. *Peru* declined such a request by the claimant Mr Tza (paras 216–22). Article 8(3) of the Peru BIT explicitly provides that any disputes concerning other matters rather than expropriation may be submitted to arbitration only in accordance with a separate agreement by the parties. In the tribunal's view, this specific language of Article 8(3) overrode any more general application of the MFN clause. For greater certainty, some FTAs expressly state that the MFN clause does not encompass a dispute settlement mechanism (see New Zealand FTA 2008: Art. 139(2); Peru FTA 2009: Art. 131; ASEAN Agreement 2009: Art. 5(4)).

Fair and equitable treatment

Unlike national treatment and MFN treatment, which are contingent on treatment accorded to a reference group, Fair and Equitable Treatment (FET) is an absolute standard that does not depend on treatment given to other investors. However, the exact meaning of this standard is often the subject of controversy (Tudor 2008; Newcombe and Paradell 2009: 233–98). In particular, there is debate as to whether the standard is equivalent to the international minimum standard (IMS) under customary international law, or whether it constitutes a treaty-based obligation that should be interpreted independently in IIAs.

Although the FET standard is included in the majority of Chinese IIAs, there are important variations among IIA texts. This is another good example reflecting China's changing attitudes towards international law. When China started to sign BITs, the majority of Chinese scholars denied the existence of IMS. It was regarded as 'essentially an imperialist and colonialist theory' and inconsistent with principles of modern international law (Yao 1980: 12–13). Because of the fear that FET would be interpreted as an 'abstract and all-inclusive international minimum standard', China has tried as far as possible to avoid any reference to international law as a criterion for the determination of the FET standard (Xu 2008: 121–31).

Some IIAs refer to international law in their FET clause in a very cautious manner. For example, the 2007 Costa Rica BIT grants the FET standard 'in accordance with universally accepted principles of international law' (Art. 3(1)). In the same vein, the New Zealand FTA makes reference to 'commonly accepted rules of international law' (Art. 143(1)). Therefore, the applicable law for interpreting the FET standard remains unclear. It has been anticipated that the interpretation of 'accepted' would be another subject of controversy in case of any dispute (Gallagher and Shan 2009: 131).

More recently China has started to accept international law without restriction to what has been accepted by the parties. For example, the 2008 Mexico BIT adopts the style of the 2004 US Model BIT, grants treatment 'in accordance with international law' and specifies that this includes FET (Art. 5). Similarly, the 2009 Peru FTA grants the FET 'in accordance with customary international law' (Art. 132). In response to the expansive view of earlier jurisprudence, the two IIAs also clarify that FET does not require treatment in addition to IMS under customary international law.

The ASEAN Agreement is unique in providing a definition for the FET standard. It is exhaustively defined as 'the obligation of each Party not to deny justice in any legal or administrative proceedings' (Art. 7(2)). Although no uniform interpretation of denial of justice has been established, it has been widely acknowledged that denial of justice is only one element of the IMS (Newcombe and Paradell 2009: 238). The ASEAN Agreement thus provides the possibility of interpreting the FET standard to be lower than the IMS as illustrated in jurisprudence.

Expropriation and compensation

Given China's history of expropriation of foreign property after the communist takeover, in the early 1980s Chinese leaders publicly promised that China would refrain from nationalizing or expropriating foreign investment unless such expropriation became necessary (Gu 1984). The officially announced expropriation policy was then translated into IIAs. Almost all Chinese IIAs include provisions that require the host country to pay compensation if it expropriates a foreign investment.

IIAs often cover both direct and indirect expropriation. The issue of what sorts of host country actions constitute indirect expropriation often triggers disputes (Levesque 2004; Fortier and Drymer 2004; Newcombe 2005). Concern at possible over-expansive interpretation of the notion has been reflected in Chinese IIAs. The New Zealand FTA introduces an annexe to provide detailed guidance to tribunals on the interpretation of expropriation (Annexe 13). An indirect expropriation could occur only if a state 'deprives the investor in substance of the use of investor's property'. Moreover, the state's deprivation of the investor's property must be either severe or for an indefinite period; and disproportionate to the public purpose. In particular, the Annexe reaffirms the state's right to regulate for legitimate public purposes, such as public health, safety and the environment. Except in rare circumstances, such measures should not be considered as indirect expropriation. The Peru FTA takes a similar approach in clarifying indirect expropriation (Annexe 9).

Usually there are four requirements for a lawful expropriation stated in IIAs, namely for the public interests, under domestic legal procedure, non-discriminatory and against compensation. The New Zealand FTA adds an extra condition that the expropriation is 'not contrary to any undertaking which the Party may have given' (Art. 145(1)). This umbrella-type clause essentially provides a possibility of overriding the host country's right to expropriate by investment contract. Where the host country expropriates contrary to a contractual commitment, it may put beyond doubt that the expropriation will be in breach of the treaty.

China has always paid particular attention to the issue of the standard of compensation for expropriation. The old-generation BITs often provide a relatively low level of compensation. For example, the 1985 Thailand BIT simply provides that the compensation should be equivalent to the 'appropriate value of the expropriated investment' (Art. 5(1)). The 1989 Pakistan BIT allows the damages to be calculated under the laws and regulations of the host country (Art. 4(2)). Although the Hull Formula, which requires 'adequate, prompt and effective compensation', has never been used in its precise terms, the new-generation BITs spell out the meaning of the formula in different, yet roughly equivalent ways (see Nigeria BIT 2001: Art. 4(2); Mexico BIT 2008: Art. 7(2); Switzerland BIT 2009: Art. 6). The new-generation IIAs usually require the compensation to be 'equivalent to the fair market value'. Such value shall be determined in accordance with 'generally recognized principles of valuation'. In addition, interest shall be paid 'at a normal commercial rate' from the date of expropriation until the date of payment. The compensation shall also be made without delay, be effectively realizable and freely transferable.

Transfer

Most IIAs include transfer provisions dealing with the investor's right to repatriate funds relating to investment. Standard IIAs provide that transfers of investment-related funds may be made without delay, in a convertible currency and at the prevailing market exchange rate (Newcombe and Paradell 2009: 405). China traditionally implements strict foreign exchange and currency control polices (Liew and Wu 2007). Thus it has always attempted to reserve broad space for the host country to regulate cross-board capital flow in IIAs. A typical example can be found in Article 7 of the 2002 Trinidad and Tobago BIT, which provides that:

> Each Contracting Party shall, *subject to its laws and regulations*, grant to the investors of the other Contracting Party the unrestricted transfer of their investments and returns held in its territory, including … [emphasis added]
> Transfer shall be made in a freely convertible currency at the prevailing market rate of exchange in the territory of the Contracting accepting the investment and on the date of transfer.

The Trinidad and Tobago BIT subjects the guarantee on transfer to the 'domestic laws and regulations' of the host country. This restriction would substantially reduce the level of protection as the host country may change its legislation at any time. In addition, unlike a standard transfer provision which requires relevant payment to be transferred 'without delay', the Trinidad and Tobago BIT is silent on the speed with which a transfer must take place.

Transfer rules nevertheless have been further liberalized in some recent IIAs. For example, in the 2009 Switzerland BIT the local law requirement is replaced by merely subjecting transfer of funds to 'relevant formalities stipulated by the applicable Chinese laws and regulations relating to exchange control' (Ad. Article 5). To ensure such formalities will not be used as a means of avoiding the host country's obligations on transfer, relevant formalities are required to be completed within two months. Furthermore, if such formalities cease to exist in Chinese law, transfer shall be made without restriction. This approach can also be found in some other renegotiated European BITs and FTAs (Germany BIT 2003: Ad. Art. 6; New Zealand FTA 2008: Art. 142(3)). Since 1979 China's foreign exchange regime has undergone rapid changes towards liberalism. The new IIA transfer provisions give rise to a lock-in effect of the liberal-oriented domestic reform.

Investor-state dispute settlement

The ability of an investor to initiate a claim directly against the host country is perhaps the most important element in investment protection. Initially China was very hesitant to consent to investor-state arbitration under BITs. Its first BIT signed with Sweden in 1982 does not contain an investor-state dispute settlement mechanism at all. Before the ratification of the ICSID Convention in 1993, China accepted investor-state dispute settlement by an *ad hoc* tribunal in some BITs (see Australia BIT 1988: Art. 13; Bulgaria BIT 1989: Art. 9; Mongolia BIT 1991: Art. 8). Yet the jurisdiction of a tribunal was limited to disputes 'involving the amount of compensation for expropriation'. Even after entry into the ICSID, China consistently insisted on limited consent to investor-state arbitration.[13] *Tza*

Yap Shum v. *Peru* raised the question of whether the words 'involving the amount of compensation for expropriation' include not only the mere determination of the amount but also any other issues inherent to an expropriation (paras 130–86). Primarily basing its determination of the question on the text of the treaty, the tribunal concluded that the word 'involving' is not 'limiting' and should be read to include the amount, not simply the amount itself.

It was not until the late 1990s that China started to give consent to international arbitration for 'any dispute between an investor of one Contracting Party and the other Contracting Party'. The first BIT with an expansive investor-state dispute resolution provision was signed with Barbados on 20 July 1998 (Art. 9). Such a provision can now be found in more than 50 Chinese IIAs. According to Gallagher and Shan, the Barbados BIT became the first was a pure coincidence (2009: 40–1). The breakthrough was actually achieved during the BIT talks with Canada in 1997, where China's State Council had approved some key changes of negotiation policies, including investor-state dispute settlement.[14]

One remaining restriction to investor-state arbitration with 'Chinese characteristics' is the requirement to exhaust domestic administrative review procedure. The disputing party is allowed to 'require the investor concerned to go through the domestic administrative review procedures specified by the laws and regulations' of the state before the submission to the ICSID or an *ad hoc* tribunal (see Germany BIT 2003: Ad. Art. 9; Mexico BIT 2008: Appendix C; New Zealand FTA 2008: Art. 153). To ensure the host country will not abuse administrative review procedure, some renegotiated European BITs and FTAs stipulate that the maximum time allowed for such procedure is three months.[15] The purpose behind the local administrative remedy is to give the administrative agency a chance to be aware of and resolve the problem before the investor resorts to international arbitration. It does not involve court proceedings and is thus different from exhaustion of local remedies. In fact, most new-generation BITs contain a 'fork in the road' clause requiring the claiming party to choose either a local court or ICSID arbitration; once the investor has chosen a particular forum it is final (see Tunisia BIT 2004: Art. 9; Russia BIT 2006: Art. 9(3); Pakistan FTA 2006: Art. 53). Some recent IIAs allow the investor to withdraw a dispute from a domestic court before a final judgment has been reached in the case and submit it to international arbitration (see New Zealand FTA 2008: Art. 153(3); Switzerland BIT 2009: Art. 11(4)). This approach has the advantage of encouraging investors to submit their disputes before a domestic court.

In addition, recent IIAs are more likely to incorporate detailed rules on arbitration procedures which prevail over the normal procedures of the ICSID. The most elaborate provision is exemplified by the New Zealand FTA. For example, it directly responds to concerns about transparency in investment arbitration (VanDuzer 2007). In accordance with Article 48(5) of the ICSID Convention, the Centre shall not publish the arbitral award without the consent of the parties. However, an award which is not open to the public may affect the interests of various groups beyond the parties. Accordingly, the New Zealand FTA authorizes the state party, at its discretion, to make all tribunal documents public without consent of the disputing investor (Art. 157). It nevertheless does not go so far as the US Model BIT, which imposes on the disputing state an obligation to make the documents public (Art. 29). Another example refers to interpretation of the agreement. The FTA allows the disputing party to request a joint interpretation of the parties of any provision of the treaty concerned in a dispute and the joint decision is binding on the tribunal. This reflects the parties' concern at the trend of increasingly expansive interpretations of treaty language by international arbitrators.

Concluding remarks

The proceeding survey shows that China has slowly changed its attitudes towards protection of investment by international law. China started to enter into investment treaties shortly after adopting the open-door policy in 1978 as a signal to foreign investors that their investments were protected and promoted. However, early Chinese BITs were highly restrictive and provided limited protection for foreign investment. Significant development took place in the late 1990s. China accepted post-establishment national treatment and generally raised the level of other substantive protection standards. More importantly, China changed its practice of limiting investor-state arbitration to disputes concerning the amount of compensation for expropriation and consented to arbitration on all disputes. Despite some remaining limitations, in all major aspects recent Chinese IIAs guarantee protections similar to what can be considered standard international practice. All these suggest that China is proving 'a system maintainer' rather than 'a system reformer'.

What drives China to move towards a liberal approach to investment treaties? While there can be no single answer to this question, three factors can be emphasized. First, China's domestic legal framework relating to foreign investment has experienced dramatic changes since the early 1990s, particularly on the eve of entry into the WTO. Domestic reform increased China's ability to accept more liberal investment treaties. Second, competition for foreign investment was greatly intensified in the 1990s as more countries shifted to a neoliberal investment policy. Thus, the Chinese authorities felt an urge to improve the investment regime in order to further attract FDI, in particular 'high-quality investments'. Third, China is no longer a passive recipient of foreign investment but has become a significant capital exporter as well. The government saw the need to enter into treaties so that its increasing outgoing investments could be protected.

What are the possibilities of future development in China's IIA practice? With the entry into force of the new-generation IIAs and a growing public understanding of the new instruments, it is expected that China will be increasingly engaged in investor-state arbitration cases. And an expanding legal profession in China will enhance the Chinese government's and investors' capacity to handle IIA legal affairs. However, only when such changes take place can China be expected to have a more significant impact on international investment regimes.

Notes

1 'IIA's used through this chapter refer to bilateral investment agreements (BITs) and bilateral and regional trade agreements that include investment provisions.
2 Nigeria (2001), Sweden (2004), Germany (2003), France (2007), Belgium-Luxembourg (2005), Finland (2004), The Netherlands (2001), Switzerland (2009), Portugal (2005), Spain (2005) , Korea (2007), Cuba (2007).
3 The top ten FDI sources in China are Hong Kong, Taiwan, Japan, Singapore, the USA, Korea, the UK, Germany, Macao and Canada. The important destinations of Chinese OFDI include Hong Kong, Cayman Islands, Virgin Islands, Australia, Singapore, the USA, Luxemburg, South Africa, Russia and Macao (MOFCOM 2009).
4 WTO, Chronological List of Disputes Cases. Online. Available HTTP: <http://www.wto.org/english/tratop_e/dispu_e/dispu_status_e.htm> (accessed 5 February 2011).
5 Because of the principle of 'one country, two systems', the preferential agreement between the Chinese mainland and special administrative regions is officially named the 'Closer Economic Partnership Agreement' (CEPA). Similarly the arrangement between the mainland and Taiwan signed on 29 June 2010 is called the 'Economic Cooperation Framework Agreement' (ECFA).
6 Thailand BIT (1985), Singapore BIT (1985), Malaysia BIT (1988), New Zealand BIT (1988), Pakistan BIT (1989), the Philippines (1992), Vietnam (1992), Laos (1993), Indonesia (1994), Chile (1994), Peru (1994), Cambodia (1996), Brunei (2000), Myanmar BIT (2001).
7 The interpretation of general exception clauses has not been addressed in IIA jurisprudence. It is also possible to view them as 'codifying the qualifications to the scope of IIA obligations recognized in the existing jurisprudence' or 'providing even less regulatory flexibility to host states' (Newcombe and Paradell 2009: 503–6).
8 Doha Work Programme: Decision Adopted by the General Council on 1 August 2004, WT/L/579, 2 August 2004.
9 *Communication from China, Cuba, India, Kenya, Pakistan and Zimbabwe*, WT/WGTI/W/152, 19 November 2002.
10 *Communication from the United States*, WT/WGTI/W142, 16 September 2002.
11 *Communication from China*, WT/WGTI/W/159, 15 April 2003.
12 *Communication from China*, WT/WGTI/W/160, 15 April 2003.
13 The Chinese government filed a notification to ICSID in accordance with ICSID Convention Article 25(4) at the time of ratification, stating that it would consider submitting to the jurisdiction of the ICSID only over 'compensation resulting from expropriation and nationalization'.
14 The making of a BIT in China is primarily undertaken by the Ministry of Commerce (MOFCOM). It must seek approval from the State Council, or the cabinet, on the initiation of negotiating a new BIT, any 'major changes' of negotiation polices or formal signature of a BIT. Once approval is obtained from the State Council, there is no need for ratification by the National People's Congress or the legislature (see Gallagher and Shan 2009: 33–4).
15 In accordance with the Administrative Review Law of China, the time limit for administrative review is normally 60 days, with a maximum of 90 days. This is probably the reason for China's insistence on three months as the maximum administrative review time in its BITs. Administrative Review Law of the People's Republic of China (adopted by the Standing Committee of the National's People's Congress on 29 April 1999, effective on 1 October 1999), Art. 31.

List of public documents

International agreements and model agreements

Agreement between the Government of Canada and the Government of the United States of America Amending the Softwood Lumber Agreement between the Government of Canada and the Government of the United States of America, done 12 September 2006, signed on 12 October 2006.

Agreement between the Office of the United States Trade Representative, the United States Department of Commerce and Secretaría de Economía of Mexico on Trade in Cement, 14 March 2006, reprinted in 71 FR 13082.

Agreement on Implementation of Article VI of the General Agreement on Tariffs and Trade, done 12 April 1979, entered into force 1 January 1980. 31 U.S.T.S. 4919; T.I.A.S. 9650; 1186 U.N.T.S. 2.

Amendments to the ICSID Rules and Regulations, done 5 April 2006, entered into force 10 April 2006. Online. Available HTTP: <http://icsid.worldbank.org/ICSID/FrontServlet?requestType=CasesRH&actionVal=OpenPage&PageType=AnnouncementsFrame&FromPage=NewsReleases&pageName=Archive_%20Announcement26> (accessed 22 July 2010).

ASEAN–Australia–NZ Free Trade Agreement, signed 27 February 2009, entered into force 1 January 2010. Online. Available HTTP: <http://www.asean.fta.govt.nz.> (accessed 29 November 2010).

ASEAN Comprehensive Investment Agreement, 26 February 2009. Online. Available HTTP: <http://www.aseansec.org/22218.htm> (accessed 22 July 2010).

ASEAN–US Trade and Investment Framework Agreement, signed 25 August 2006. Online. Available HTTP: <http://www.ustr.gov/sites/default/files/uploads/agreements/tifa/asset_upload_file932_9760.pdf> (accessed 22 July 2010).

Australia–US Free Trade Agreement, signed 18 May 2004, entered into force 1 January 2005. Online. Available HTTP: <http://www.dfat.gov.au/fta/ausfta/final-text/Final_text_ausfta.pdf>.

Canada–Peru Free Trade Agreement, signed 29 May 2008, entered into force 1 August 2009. Online. Available HTTP: <http://www.international.gc.ca/trade-agreements-accords-commerciaux/agr-acc/peru-perou/peru-toc-perou-tdm.aspx?lang=eng> (accessed 22 July 2010).

Canadian Model Agreement for the Promotion and Protection of Investment, 2003. Online. Available HTTP: <http://www.international.gc.ca/trade-agreements-accords-commerciaux/assets/pdfs/2004-FIPA-model-en.pdf> (accessed 22 July 2010).

Convention on the Settlement of Investment Disputes between States and Nationals of Other States, done 18 March 1965, entered into force 14 October 1966, 575 U.N.T.S. 159, 4 *I.L.M.* 532.

Draft Norwegian Model Bilateral Investment Treaty, issued for comment 19 December 2007. Online. Available HTTP: <http://www.asil.org/ilib080421.cfm> (accessed 29 November 2010).

EC–Russia Agreement on Partnership and Cooperation, signed 24 June 1994, entered into force 1 December 1997. Online. Available HTTP: <http://ec.europa.eu/world/agreements/downloadFile.do?fullText=yes&treatyTransId=643> (accessed 22 July 2010).

Energy Charter Treaty, signed 17 December 1994, entered into force 16 April 1998. Online. Available HTTP: <http://www.encharter.org/fileadmin/user_upload/document/EN.pdf> (accessed 29 November 2010).

EU–CARIFORUM Economic Partnership Agreement, signed 15 October 2008, OJ L289/1/3, 30 October 2008.

EU–Chile Association Agreement, signed 18 November 2002, entered into force 1 March 2005, [2002] OJ L352/1. Online. Available HTTP: <http://eur-lex.europa.eu/LexUriServ/lexUriserv.do?uri=OJ:L:2002*352:0001:0002:EN:PDF>.

European Convention, Draft Articles on External Action in the Constitutional Treaty, 23 April 2003, CONV 685/03. Online. Available HTTP: <http://register.consilium.europa.eu/pdf/en/03/cv00/cv00685.en03.pdf>.

Exchange of Diplomatic Letters between Undersecretary Villalobos and Ambassador Crowder, 27 July 2006. Online. Available HTTP: <http://www.ustraderep.gov/assets/Trade_Agreements/Regional/NAFTA/asset_upload_file694_10810.pdf> (accessed 29 November 2010).

General Agreement on Tariffs and Trade, done 30 October 1947, provisionally applied 1 January 1948, 61 Stat. A-11, T.I.A.S. 1700, 55 U.N.T.S. 194.

IISD Model International Agreement on Investment for Sustainable Development, 2nd edn, April 2006. Online. Available HTTP: <http://www.iisd.org/pdf/2005/investment_model_int_handbook.pdf> (accessed 29 November 2010).

India–Singapore Comprehensive Economic Cooperation Agreement, signed 29 June 2005, entered into force 1 August 2005. Online. Available HTTP: <http://commerce.nic.in/ceca/toc.htm> (accessed 22 July 2010).

Investment Agreement for the COMESA Common Investment Area, adopted May 2007. Online. Available HTTP: <http://programmes.comesa.int//attachments/104_Investment%20agreement%20for%20the%20CCIA%20FINAL%20_English_.pdf> (accessed 22 July 2010).

Japan–ASEAN Comprehensive Economic Partnership Agreement, signed 26 March to 14 April 2008, entered into force 1 December 2008. Online. Available HTTP: <http://www.mofa.go.jp/policy/economy/fta/asean/agreement.pdf> (accessed 22 July 2010).

Japan–Singapore Economic Partnership Agreement, signed 13 January 2002, entered into force 30 November 2002. Online. Available HTTP: <www.mofa.go.jp/region/asia-paci/singapore/jsepa.html> (accessed 29 November 2010).

New Zealand–China Free Trade Agreement, signed 7 April 2008, entered into force 1 October 2008. Online. Available HTTP: <http://www.chinafta.govt.nz/1-The-agreement/2-Text-of-the-agreement/index.php> (accessed 22 July 2010).

North American Free Trade Agreement, signed 17 December 1992, entered into force 1 January 1994. 32 I.L.M. 670 (1993).

OECD Draft Convention on the Protection of Foreign Property, adopted 12 October 1967. Online. Available HTTP: <http://www.oecd.org/dataoecd/35/4/39286571.pdf> (accessed 22 July 2010).

Softwood Lumber Agreement between the Government of Canada and the Government of the United States of America, 29 May 1996. Online. Available HTTP: <http://www.international.gc.ca/controls-controles/assets/pdfs/softwood/treaty-e.pdf> (accessed 5 February 2011).

Treaty of Lisbon amending the Treaty on European Union and the Treaty establishing the European Community, signed 13 December 2007, entered into force on 1 December 2009.

UK–Argentina Bilateral Investment Treaty, signed 11 December 1990, entered into force 19 February 1993. Online. Available HTTP: <http://www.unctad.org/sections/dite/iia/docs/bits/uk_argentina.pdf> (accessed 29 November 2010).

United States Model Bilateral Investment Treaty, November 2004. Online. Available HTTP: <http://www.state.gov/documents/organization/117601.pdf> (accessed 22 July 2010).

United States–Uruguay Bilateral Investment Treaty, signed 4 November 2005, entered into force 1 November 2006. Online. Available HTTP: <http://tcc.export.gov/Trade_Agreements/All_Trade_Agreements/Uruguay_BIT.asp> (accessed 22 July 2010).

Cases and judgments

WTO dispute settlement cases

Appellate Body reports

European Communities – Regime for the Importation, Sale and Distribution of Bananas (Bananas III), WT/DS27/AB/R, adopted 25 September 1997.

United States – Import Prohibition of Certain Shrimp and Shrimp Products, WT/DS58/AB/R, adopted 6 November 1998.

Turkey – Restrictions on Imports of Textile and Clothing Products, WT/DS34/AB/R, adopted 22 October 1999.

United States – Antidumping Act of 1916, WT/DS136, 162/AB/R, adopted 26 September 2000.

Korea (Republic of) – Measures Affecting Imports of Fresh, Chilled and Frozen Beef, WT/DS161,169/AB/R, adopted 10 January 2001.

European Communities – Measures Affecting Asbestos and Products Containing Asbestos, WT/DS135/AB/R, adopted 5 April 2001.

United States – Definitive Safeguard Measures on Imports of Circular Welded Carbon Quality Line Pipe from Korea, WT/DS202/R, adopted 29 October 2001.

Mexico – Anti-Dumping Investigation of High Fructose Corn Syrup (HFCS) from the United States (Recourse to Article 21.5 of the DSU by the United States), WT/DS132/AB/RW, adopted 21 November 2001.

United States – Measures Affecting the Cross-Border Supply of Gambling and Betting Services, WT/DS285/AB/R, adopted 20 April 2005.

Mexico – Tax Measures on Soft Drinks and Other Beverages, WT/DS308/AB/R, adopted 24 March 2006.

WTO panel reports

Mexico – Anti-Dumping Investigation of High-Fructose Corn Syrup (HFCS) from the United States, WT/DS132/R, adopted 24 February 2000.

Mexico – Tax Measures on Soft Drinks and Other Beverages, WT/DS308/R, circulated 7 October 2005, adopted 24 March 2006.

Other WTO documents in dispute settlement cases

United States –Anti-Dumping Measures on Cement from Mexico, Request for Consultations by Mexico, WT/DS281/1, 11 February 2003.

Mexico – Tax Measures on Soft Drinks and Other Beverages, Agreement under Article 21.3(b) of the DSUWT/DS308/15, 5 June 2006.

United States – Final Dumping Determination on Softwood Lumber from Canada, Notification of Mutually Agreed Solution, WT/DS264/29, 16 November 2006.

United States – Anti-Dumping Measures on Cement from Mexico – Lapse of Authority for the Establishment of the Panel – Note by the Secretariat, WT/DS281/7, 23 March 2007.

GATT panel reports

United States – Section 337 of the Tariff Act of 1930, GATT Doc L/6439, adopted 7 November 1989, *BISD 36S*/345.

United States – Restrictions on Imports of Tuna, GATT Doc DS21/R, 3 September 1991 (not adopted).

United States – Anti-Dumping Duties on Gray Portland Cement and Cement Clinker from Mexico, ADP/82, 7 September 1992 (not adopted).

Awards of international arbitration

Awards of the NAFTA Chapter 19 binational arbitration panel

United States – Gray Portland Cement and Clinker from Mexico, USA-95-1904-02, 13 September 1996.

United States – Gray Portland Cement and Clinker from Mexico, USA-97-1904-02, 4 December 1998.

Mexico – Review of the Final Determination of the Antidumping Investigation on Imports of High Fructose Corn Syrup Originating from the United States of America, MEX-USA-98-1904-01, 20 February 1998.

Awards of other international arbitration

London Court of International Arbitration (LCIA) (2008) *Award on Liability*, Case No. 7941 (*United States* v. *Canada*), 3 March 2008. Online. Available HTTP: <http://www.ustr.gov/sites/default/files/award_on_export_measures.pdf> (accessed 5 February 2011).

London Court of International Arbitration (LCIA) (2009a) *Award on Remedies*, Case No. 7941 (*United States* v. *Canada*), 23 February 2009. Online. Available HTTP: <http://www.international.gc.ca/controls-controles/assets/pdfs/sofwood/USAvCanada09219AwardonRemedies.pdf> (accessed 5 February 2011).

London Court of International Arbitration (LCIA) (2009b) *Award on Canada's Claim of Cure*, Case No. 91312 (*Canada* v. *United States*), 21 September 2009. Online. Available HTTP: <http://www.ustr.gov/webfm_send/1379> (accessed 5 February 2011).

Awards in investment arbitrations

Azurix Corporation v. *The Argentine Republic*, ICSID Case No. ARB/01/12, Award, 14 July 2006.

CMS Gas Transmission Company v. *The Argentine Republic*, ICSID Case No. ARB/01/8 Decision of the Ad Hoc Committee, 25 September 2007.

CMS Gas Transmission Company v. *The Argentine Republic*, ICSID Case No. ARB/01/8, Award, 12 May 2005.

Compañía del Desarrollo de Santa Elena, S.A. v. *Republic of Costa Rica*, ICSID Case No. ARB/96/1, Award, 17 February 2000.

Continental Casualty Company v. *The Argentine Republic*, ICSID Case No. ARB/03/9, Award, 5 September 2008.

Enron Corporation & Anor v. *The Argentine Republic*, ICSID Case No. ARB/01/3, Award, 22 May 2007.

Enron Creditors Recovery Corporation Ponderosa Assets, L.P. v. *The Argentine Republic*, ICSID Case No. ARB/01/3, Annulment Proceeding, Decision of the ad hoc Committee, 30 July 2010.

LG&E Energy Corp. & Ors v. *The Argentine Republic*, ICSID Case No. ARB/02/1, Decision on Liability, 3 October 2006.

Maffezini v. *The Kingdom of Spain*, ICSID Case No. ARB/97/7, Decision on Jurisdiction, 25 January 2000, Award of the Tribunal of 13 November 2000, Rectification of Award, 31 January 2001.

Marvin Feldman v. *Mexico*, ICSID Case No. ARB(AF)/99/1, Award, 16 December 2002.

Metalclad Corporation v. *United Mexican States*, ICSID Case No. ARB(AF)/97/1, Award, 30 August 2000.

Methanex Corp. v. *United States*, UNCITRAL/NAFTA Arbitration, Award, 5 August 2005.

MTD Equity Sdn Bhd and MTD Chile S.A. v. *Republic of Chile*, ICSID Case No. ARB/01/7, Award, 25 May 2004.

Occidental Exploration and Production Company v. *The Republic of Ecuador*, LCIA Case No. UN 3467, Final Award, 1 July 2004.

Plama Consortium Limited v. *Bulgaria*, ICSID Case No. ARB/03/24, Decision on Jurisdiction, 8 February 2005.

Pope & Talbot Inc. v. *Government of Canada*, UNCITRAL/NAFTA Arbitration, Interim Award, 26 June 2000.

Salini v. *Jordan*, ICSID Case No. ARB/02/13, Decision on Jurisdiction, 9 November 2004.

Sempra Energy International v. *The Argentine Republic*, ICSID Case No. ARB/02/16, Award, 28 September 2007.

Sempra Energy International v. *The Argentine Republic*, ICSID Case No. ARB/02/16, Annulment Proceeding, Decision on Annulment, 29 June 2010.

Siemens v. *Argentina*, ICSID Case No. ARB/02/8, Decision on Jurisdiction, 3 August 2004.

Technicas Medioambientales Tecmed S.A. v. *The United Mexican States*, ICSID Case No. ARB(AF)/00/2, Award, 29 May 2003.

Tza Yap Shum v. *The Republic of Peru*, ICSID Case No. ARB/07/6, Decision on Jurisprudence and Competence, 19 June 2009.

Judgments of the European Court of Justice (ECJ)

ECJ, 22/70, *AETR* [1971] ECR 263.

ECJ, 4/73, *Nold* [1974] ECR 491.

ECJ, Opinion 1/75 [1975] ECR 1355.

ECJ, Opinion 1/94 [1994] ECR I, 5267.

ECJ, C-306/93, *SMW Winzersekt* [1994] ECR I, 5555.

ECJ, C-84/95, *Bosphorus* [1996] ECR I, 3953.

ECJ, C-466/08, *Commission* v. *United Kingdom*, Opinion of AG Tizzano [2002] ECR I, 9427.

ECJ, C-463/00, *Commission* v. *Kingdom of Spain* [2003] ECR I, 4581.
ECJ, Joined Cases C-37/02 and C-38/02, *Di Lenardo and Dilexport* [2004] ECR I, 0000.
ECJ, C-347/03, *Regione autonoma Friuli-Venezia Giulia and ERSA* [2005] ECR I, 3785.
ECJ, C-266/03, *Commission* v. *Luxembourg* [2005] ECR I, 4805.
ECJ, C-433/03, *Commission* v. *Germany* [2005] ECR I, 6985.
ECJ, C-459/03, *Commission* v. *Ireland* [2006] ECR I, 4635.
ECJ, C-446/04, *Test Claimants in the FII Group Litigation* [2006] ECR I, 11753.
ECJ, C-157/05, *Holböck* [2007] ECR I, 4051.
ECJ, C-112/05, *Commission* v. *Germany* [2007] ECR I, 8995.
ECJ, C-101/05, *Skatteverket* v. *A* [2007] ECR I, 11531.
ECJ, C-492/04, *Lasertec* [2007] ECR I, 3775.
ECJ, C-249/06, *Commission* v. *Sweden*, not yet in the official reports.
ECJ, C-205/06, *Commission* v. *Austria*, not yet in the official reports.
ECJ, C-118/07, *Commission* v. *Finland*, not yet in the official reports.
ECJ, Joined Cases C-402/05 P and C-415/05 P, *Kadi and Al Barakaat*, not yet in the official reports.

Judgments of domestic courts

Bundesverfassungsgericht (German Constitutional Court), 2 BvE 2/08, *Organstreit*.
United States Court of Appeals (USCA) D.C. Circuit *Coalition for Fair Lumber Imports Executive Committee* v. *United States*, No. 05-1366, 12 December 2006.
United States Court of International Trade (USCIT) *CEMEX, S.A.* v. *United States*, 790 F. Supp. 290 (Ct. Int'l Trade 1992) *aff'd*, 989 F.2d 1202 (Fed. Cir. 1993).
United States Court of International Trade (USCIT) *Tembec, Inc.* v. *United States*, 2006 Ct. Intl. Trade LEXIS 107 (CIT, 21 July 2006).

Decisions of domestic administrative organs

Mexican Ministry of Commerce and Industrial Development (SECOFI) (1998) *Resolución final de la investigación antidumping sobre las importaciones de jarabe de maíz de alta fructosa, mercancía clasificada en las fracciones arancelarias 1702.40.99 y 1702.60.01 de la Tarifa de la Ley del Impuesto General de Importación, originarias de los Estados Unidos de América, independientemente del país de procedencia*, 23 January 1998. Online. Available HTTP: <http://www.sice.oas.org/dispute/nafta/spanish/MU98191b.asp> (accessed 29 November 2010).
United States Department of Commerce (USDOC) (1990) *Gray Portland Cement and Clinker from Mexico*, 55 Fed. Reg. 35433, 20 August 1990.
United States Department of Commerce (USDOC) (2002) *Notice of Final Affirmative Countervailing Duty Determination and Final Negative Critical Circumstances Determination: Certain Softwood Lumber Products from Canada*, 67 Fed. Reg. 15545, 2 April 2002.
United States Department of Commerce (USDOC) (2009) *Rules: Mexican Cement Import Licensing System*, 74 FR 22094, 12 May 2009. Online. Available HTTP: <http://ia.ita.doc.gov/cement-agreement/index.html> (accessed 29 November 2010).

Other documents of international organizations

United Nations documents

United Nations (2008) *Follow-Up International Conference on Financing for Development to Review the Implementation of the Monterrey Consensus*, Doha, Qatar, 29 November–2 December 2008, A/CONF.212/L.1/Rev.1.

United Nations (2009) Report of the Special Representative of the Secretary-General, *Business and Human Rights*, 23 April 2009, A/HRC/11/13.

United Nations (2002) *Report of the International Conference on Financing for Development*, Monterrey, Mexico, 18–22 March 2002, A/CONF.198/11, E.02.II.A.7.

United Nations Conference on Environment and Development (UNCED) (1992) 'Rio Declaration on Environment and Development', Annexe 1 of *Report of the UNCED*, done at Rio de Janeiro, 3–14 June 1992, A/CONF.151/26.

WTO documents

Chronological List of Disputes Cases, Online. Available HTTP: <http://www.wto.org/english/tratop_e/dispu_e/dispu_by_country_e.htm> (accessed 4 October 2010).

Communication from China, Cuba, India, Kenya, Pakistan and Zimbabwe, WT/WGTI/W/152, 19 November 2002. Online. Available HTTP: <http://www.wto.org/english/thewto_e/minist_e/min01_e/min01_proposals_e.htm> (accessed 2 May 2010).

Communication from the United States, WT/WGTI/W142, 16 September 2002. Online. Available HTTP: <http://www.wto.org/english/thewto_e/minist_e/min01_e/min01_proposals_e.htm> (accessed 2 May 2010).

Communication from China, WT/WGTI/W/159, 15 April 2003. Online. Available HTTP: <http://www.wto.org/english/thewto_e/minist_e/min01_e/min01_proposals_e.htm> (accessed 2 May 2010).

Communication from China, WT/WGTI/W/160, 15 April 2003. Online. Available HTTP: <http://www.wto.org/english/thewto_e/minist_e/min01_e/min01_proposals_e.htm> (accessed 2 May 2010).

Doha Work Programme: Decision adopted by the General Council on 1 August 2004, WT/L/579, 2 August 2004. Online. Available HTTP: <https://www.ige.ch/e/jurinfo/documents/j10407e.pdf> (accessed 2 May 2010).

Documents of the European Union

Council and Commission Decision 98/181/EC, ECSC, EURATOM of 23 September 1997 on the conclusion by the European Communities of the Energy Charter Treaty and the Energy Charter Protocol on Energy Efficiency and Related Environmental Aspects, [1998] OJ L 69/1.

Council Directive 88/361/EEC of 24 June 1988 for the Implementation of Article 67 of the Treaty, [1988] OJ L 178/5.

European Commission, *Report on the Operation of the Treaty on European Union*, SEC(95)731.

European Commission Opinion in Accordance with Article 48 EU, COM(2000).

European Commission Proposal for a Regulation of the European Parliament and of the Council Establishing Transitional Arrangements for Bilateral Investment Agreements between Member States and Third Countries, COM(2010)344 Final.

European Commission Communication from the Commission to the Council, the European Parliament, the European Economic and Social Committee and the Committee of the Regions – Towards a Comprehensive European International Investment Policy, COM(2010)343 Final.

Bibliography

Adlung, R. and Molinuevo, M. (2008) 'Bilateralism in Services Trade: Is There Fire behind the (BIT-) Smoke?', *Journal of International Economic Law*, 11(2): 365–409.

Advisory Committee on International Economic Policy (ACIEP) (2009) Report of the Subcommittee on Investment of the Advisory Committee on International Economic Policy Regarding the Model Bilateral Investment Treaty, Washington, D.C: US Department of State. Online. Available HTTP: <http://www.state.gov/e/eeb/rls/othr/2009/131098.htm> (accessed 19 August 2010).

Ahmad, T. M. A. T and Shamsudin, M. N. (eds) (2008) *Market Liberalization and its Relationship with Market Structure, Conduct and Performance of the Food Processing Industry in ASEAN Economies*, Kuala Lumpur: APEC Secretariat. Online. Available HTTP: <http://www.iadb.org/intal/intalcdi/PE/2009/03350.pdf> (accessed 22 July 2010).

Ahn, K. A. (2004) 'East Asian Economic Integration and Currency Unions: Interests and Roles of China-Japan-Korea', *Journal of Social Paradigm Studies*, 23(11): 81–108.

Akatsu, K. (ed.) (2008) *Opportunities and Challenges for Foreign Investment in the APEC Region: Case Studies*, Tokyo: APEC Secretariat. Online. Available HTTP: <http://www.apec.org/apec/publications/all_publications/human_resources_development.html> (accessed 22 July 2010).

Alvarez, J. (2009) 'The Evolving BIT', *Transnational Dispute Management*, 3 June. Online. Available HTTP: <www.transnational-dispute-management.com> (accessed 29 November 2010).

Alvarez, J. and Khamsi, K. (2009) 'The Argentine Crisis and Foreign Investors', in Sauvant, K. P. (ed.) *Yearbook on International Investment Law and Policy 2008–2009*, New York: Oxford University Press.

Alvaro, M. (2009) 'Ecuador Will Become a Member of ALBA on June 24, 2009', *Dow Jones*. Online. Available HTTP: <http://www.easybourse.com/bourse-actualite/marches/ecuador-will-become-member-of-alba-on-june-24-688651> (accessed 29 November 2010).

Anderlini, J. (2010) 'Foreign Companies "Losing Out" in China', *Financial Times*, 2 September.

APEC (1994) The Non-Binding Investment Principles. Online. Available HTTP: <http://www.apec.org/apec/apec_groups/committee_on_trade/investment_experts.html> (accessed 22 July 2010).

—— (1997) The Menu of Options for Investment Liberalization and Business Facilitation to Strengthen the APEC Economies. Online. Available HTTP: <http://www.apec.org/apec/apec_groups/committee_on_trade/investment_experts.MedialibDownload.v1.html?url=/etc/medialib/apec_media_library/downloads/committees/cti/pubs/2003.Par.0031.File.v1.1> (accessed 22 July 2010).

APEC (2003) Investment Transparency Standards. Online. Available HTTP: <http://www.apec.org/apec/leaders__declarations/2003_leadersstmtimplapectranspstd.html> (accessed 22 July 2010).

—— (2008a) Joint Statement, 17 November 2008. Online. Available HTTP: <http://www.apec.org/etc/medialib/apec_media_library/downloads/news_uploads/2008/aelm/amm.Par.0004.File.tmp/08_amm_jms.pdf> (accessed 22 July 2010).

—— (2008b) 2008 Leaders' Declaration, 23 November 2008. Online. Available HTTP: <http://www.apec.org/apec/leaders__declarations/2008.html> (accessed 22 July 2010).

—— (2009) 'About APEC'. Online. Available HTTP: <http://www.apec.org/apec/about_apec.html> (accessed 22 July 2010).

Arner, D. (2009) 'The Global Credit Crisis of 2008: Causes and Consequences', *International Lawyer*, 43: 91–136.

Arner, D. and Buckley, R. P. (2010) 'Redesigning the Architecture of the Global Financial System', *Melbourne Journal of International Law*, 11(2): 1–55.

Arner, D., Lejot, P. and Wang, W. (2009) *Assessing East Asian Financial Cooperation and Integration*, AIIFL Working Paper No. 5, Hong Kong: Asian Institute of International Financial Law.

Arner, D., Lejot, P. and Wang, W. (2010) 'Assessing East Asian Financial Cooperation and Integration', *Singapore Yearbook of International Law*, 12: 1–42, Singapore: Asian Society of International Law

Arner, D. and Taylor, M. (2009) 'The Global Credit Crisis and the Financial Stability Board: Hardening the Soft Law of International Financial Regulation?', *University of New South Wales Law Journal*, 32: 488–513.

ASEAN (2007) ASEAN Economic Community Blueprint, signed at the Thirteenth ASEAN Summit in Singapore, November 2007.

—— (2009) Basic ASEAN Indicators (as of June 2009). Online. Available HTTP: <http://www.aseansec.org/13100.htm> (accessed 4 February 2011).

—— (2010) 'ASEAN–China Free Trade Area: Not a Zero-Sum Game' (press release, 7 January), Jakarta: ASEAN Secretariat. Online. Available HTTP: <http://www.aseansec.org/24161.htm> (accessed 10 February 2010).

ASEAN+3 (2000) Joint Ministerial Statement of the ASEAN+3 Finance Ministers' Meeting, May 2000. Online. Available HTTP: <http://www.aseansec.org/635.htm> (accessed 28 November 2010).

—— (2005) Joint Ministerial Statement of the Eighth ASEAN+3 Finance Ministers' Meeting, May. 2005. Online. Available HTTP: <http://www.aseansec.org/17448.htm> (accessed 9 February 2011).

—— (2008) Joint Ministerial Statement of the Eleventh ASEAN+3 Ministers' Meeting, May 2008. Online. Available HTTP: <http://www.aseansec.org/21502.htm> (accessed 28 November 2010).

—— (2009) Report from the Finance Ministers of the ASEAN+3 to Heads of States/Governments, February 2009. Online. Available HTTP: <http://www.aseansec.org/22158.htm> (accessed 4 February 2011).

Asian Development Bank (2002) 'Study on Monetary and Financial Cooperation in East Asia', *ADB Summary Report*, Manila: Asian Development Bank

—— (2007) *The Long-Term Strategic Framework of the Asian Development Bank 2008–2020*, December 2007. Online. Available HTTP: <http:www.adb.org/Documents/Policies/LTSF-W-Paper/LTSF-W-Paper.pdf> (accessed 28 November 2010).

—— (2008a) *Emerging Asian Regionalism*. Online. Available HTTP: <http://aric.adb.org/emergingasianregionalism/> (accessed 29 November 2010).

—— (2008b) *Key Indicators for Asia and the Pacific 2008*, Manila: Asian Development Bank.

Bagehot, G. (1873) *Lombard Street: A Description of the Money Market*, London: H. S. King.

Baldwin, R. E. (2006) 'Multilateralizing Regionalism: Spaghetti Bowls as Building Blocks on the Path to Global Free Trade', *World Economy*, 29(11): 1451–518.

Beck, T., Coyle, D., Dewatripont, M., Freixas, X. and Seabright, P. (2010) *Bailing Out the Banks: Reconciling Stability and Competition. An Analysis of State-Supported Schemes for Financial Institutions*, London: Centre for Economic Policy Research. Online. Available HTTP: <http://www.cepr.org/pubs/other/Bailing_out_the_banks.pdf> (accessed 27 July 2010).

Beeson, M. and Islam, I. (2005) 'Neoliberalism and East Asia: Resisting the Washington Consensus', *Journal of Development Studies*, 41(2): 97–219.

Bello, W. (1994) *Dark Victory: The United States, Structural Adjustment and Global Poverty*, London: Pluto Press.

Berger, A. (2008) *China and the Global Governance of Foreign Direct Investment: The Emerging Bilateral Investment Treaty Approach*, German Development Institute, Discussion Paper. Online. Available HTTP: <http://www.die-gdi.de/CMS-Homepage/openwebcms3.nsf/(ynDK_contentByKey)/ANES-7FXHY6/$FILE/DP%2010.2008.pdf> (accessed 7 April 2010).

Bergsten, C. F. (1997) *Open Regionalism*, IIE Working Paper No.97, Washington, D.C.: Institute for International Economics.

—— (2007) 'Toward a Free Trade Area of the Asia Pacific', paper presented at a joint conference of the Japan Economic Foundation and Peterson Institute for International Economics on New Asia-Pacific Trade Initiatives, Washington, D.C., November 2007.

Bernstein, E. M. (1995), 'The Making and the Remaking of the Bretton Woods Institutions', in Kirshner, Orin (ed.) *The Bretton Woods-GATT System: Retrospect and Prospect after Fifty Years*, New York: M. E. Sharpe.

Bhagwati, J. (1996) 'U.S. Trade Policy: The Infatuation with Free Trade Areas', in Bhagwati, J. and Krueger, A. O. (eds) *The Dangerous Drift to Preferential Trade Agreements*, Washington, D.C.: American Enterprise Institute.

—— (2008) *Termites in the Trading System: How Preferential Agreements Undermine Free Trade*, New York: Oxford University Press.

Bieda, K. (1970) *The Structure and Operation of the Japanese Economy*, Sydney and New York: Wiley.

Bird, G. and Rajan, R. (2006) 'The Political Economy of Sequencing: Monetary versus Trade Regionalism', *North American Journal of Economics and Finance*, 17: 335–41.

Borchard, E. M. (1915) *Diplomatic Protection of Citizens Abroad or the Law of International Claims*, New York: Banks Law.

Bordo, M. D. (1993) 'The Bretton Woods International System: A Historical Overview', in Bordo, Michael D. and Eichengreen, Barry (eds) *A Retrospective on the Bretton Woods System: Lessons for International Monetary Reform*, Chicago: University of Chicago Press.

Bos, E. R., Jamison, Dean T., Feachem, Richard G., Makgoba, Malegapuru W., Baingana, Florence K., Hofman, Karen J. and Rogo, Khama O. (eds) (2006) *Disease and Mortality in Sub-Saharan Africa*, 2nd edn, Washington, D.C.: World Bank.

Bowman, G., Covelli, N., Gantz, D. and Uhm, I. H. (2010) *Trade Remedies in North America*, Alphen aan den Rijn: Kluwer Law International.

Brower, C., II (2009) 'Obstacles and Pathways to Consideration of the Public Interest in Investment Treaty Disputes', in Sauvant, K. P. (ed.) *Yearbook on International Investment Law and Policy 2008–2009*, New York: Oxford University Press.

Brundtland Commission (1987) *Our Common Future*, Oxford: Oxford University Press.

Buckley, R. P. (2000) 'An Oft-Ignored Perspective on the Asian Economic Crisis: The Role of Creditors and Investors', *Banking and Finance Law Review*, 15: 431–54.

—— (2003) 'Do Cry for the Argentines: An Analysis of Their Crisis', *Banking and Finance Law Review*, 17: 373–93.

—— (2004) 'Turning Loans into Bonds: Lessons for East Asia from the Latin American Brady Plan', *Journal of Restructuring Finance*, 1: 185–200.

—— (2009) 'IMF Policies and Health in Sub-Saharan Africa', in Kay, A. and Williams, O. (eds) *Global Health Governance: Crisis, Institutions and Political Economy*, London: Palgrave Macmillan.

Buckley, R. P. and Fitzgerald, S. (2004) 'An Assessment of Malaysia's Response to the IMF during the Asian Economic Crisis', *Singapore Journal of Legal Studies*, July 2004: 96–116.

Burgstaller, M. (2010) 'European Law Challenges to Investment Arbitration', in Waibel, M., Kaushal, A., Chung, L. and Balchin, C. (eds) *The Backlash against Investment Arbitration*, Alphen aan den Rijn: Kluwer Law International.

—— (forthcoming) 'The Future of Bilateral Investment Treaties of EU Member States', *European Yearbook of International Economic Law*, special issue.

Burke-White, W. and Von Staden, A. (2008) 'Investment Protection in Extraordinary Times: The Interpretation and Application of Non-Precluded Measures Provisions in Bilateral Investment Treaties', *Virginia Journal of International Law*, 48(2): 307–410.

Busch, M. L. (2007) 'Overlapping Institutions, Forum Shopping, and Dispute Settlement in International Trade', *International Organization*, 61: 735–61.

Busch, M. L. and Reinhardt, E. (2000) 'Bargaining in the Shadow of the Law: Early Settlement in GATT/WTO Disputes', *Fordham International Law Journal*, 24 (1 and 2): 158–72.

Cai, Congyan (2006) 'Outward Foreign Direct Investment Protection and the Effectiveness of Chinese BIT Practice', *Journal of World Investment & Trade*, 7: 621–52.

—— (2009) 'China–US BIT Negotiations and the Future of Investment Treaty Regime: A Grand Bilateral Bargain with Multilateral Implications', *Journal of International Economic Law*, 12: 457–506.

Carmody, C. (2006) 'International Decisions: Softwood Lumber Dispute (2001–2006)', *American Journal of International Law*, 100(3): 664–74.

Castaneda, J. G. (1993) *Utopia Unarmed*, New York: Alfred A. Knopf.

Ceyssens, J. (2005) 'Towards a Common Foreign Investment Policy? Foreign Investment in the European Constitution', *Legal Issues of Economic Integration*, 32: 259–91.

Chatterjee, S. (1999) 'Regionalism, Open Regionalism, the APEC and the WTO: An Economic Perspective from New Zealand', Department of Applied and International Economics, Massey University. Online. Available HTTP: <http://economics-finance.massey.ac.nz/publications/discuss/dp99-03.pdf> (accessed 10 August 2010).

Chen, A. (2006) 'Should the Four Great Safeguards in Sino-Foreign BITs Be Hastily Dismantled? Comments on Provisions Concerning Dispute Settlement in Model U.S. and Canadian BITs', *Journal of World Investment & Trade*, 7: 899–33.

Chen, D. (2010) 'Thriving China Is Ever More Open for Business', *Financial Times*, 25 July.

Chen, H. (2006) 'China-ASEAN Investment Agreement Negotiations: The Substantive Issues', *Journal of World Investment & Trade*, 7: 143–63.

Chew, P. K. (1994) 'Political Risk and U.S. Investments in China: Chimera of Protection and Predictability?', *Virginia Journal of International Law*, 34, 615–83.

Cho, B.-H. (2006) 'Financial Globalization and Financial Cooperation in East Asia', *Journal of Korea Development Economics Association*, 12(1): 117–45.

Cho, J.-R. (2008) 'Japan's Position about the Discussion on East Asian Economic Integration', *Journal of International Area Studies*, 10(2): 279–305.

Cho, S. (2001) 'Breaking the Barrier between Regionalism and Multilateralism: A New Perspective on Trade Regionalism', *Harvard International Law Journal*, 42: 419–65.

—— (2006) 'Defragmenting World Trade', *Northwestern Journal of International Law and Business*, 27: 39–88.

Choi, S. P. (2006) 'Die Unabhängigkeit einer Asiatischen Zentralbank', unpublished dissertation, Würzburg University.

—— (2007) 'Die verfassungsrechtliche Grundlage der makroökonomische Politik der EU', *European Constitution Studies*, 1(1): 133–54.

Chua, A. (1995) 'The Privatization–Nationalization Cycle: The Link between Markets and Ethnicity in Developing Countries', *Columbia Law Review*, 95: 223–303.

CIA (2009) *The World Factbook*. Online. Available HTTP: <https://www.cia.gov/library/publications/the-world-factbook/> (accessed 10 February 2010).

Claessens, S. (2009) 'The Financial Crisis and Financial Nationalism', paper presented at Joint World Bank–CEPR conference, Brussels, 26–27 May. Online. Available HTTP: <http://www.cepr.org/meets/ltm/2407/Claessens.pdf> (accessed 27 July 2010).

Coase, R. (1974) 'The Lighthouse in Economics', *Journal of Law and Economics*, 17(2): 357–75.

Commission on Global Governance (1995) *Our Global Neighbourhood: The Report of the Commission on Global Governance*, Oxford: Oxford University Press.

Cone, S. M. (2005) 'The Promotion of Free-Trade Areas Viewed in Terms of Most-Favored-Nation Treatment and "Imperial Preference"', *Michigan Journal of International Law*, 26: 563–85.

Cooper, W. H. (2006) *Free Trade Agreements: Impact on U.S. Trade and implications for U.S. Trade Policy*, Congressional Research Service Report for Congress, Library of Congress, updated 1 August 2006, Washington, D.C.: Congressional Research Service, The Library of Congress. Online. Available HTTP: <http://fpc.state.gov/documents/organization/70293.pdf>.

Cottier, T. (2005) 'The Erosion of Non-Discrimination: Stern Warning without True Remedies', *Journal of International Economic Law*, 8: 595–607.

Cowen, D. and Salgado, R. (2006) 'Globalization of Production and Financial Integration in Asia', in Cowen, D., Salgado, R., Shah, H., Teo, L. and Zanello, A. (eds) *Financial Integration in Asia: Recent Developments and Next Steps*, IMF Working Paper No. 06/196, Washington, D.C.: IMF.

Craig, P. and de Burca, G. (2008) *EU Law*, Oxford: Oxford University Press.

Cutler, A. C. (2003) *Private Power and Global Authority: Transnational Merchant Law in Global Political Economy*, Cambridge: Cambridge University Press.

Dam, K. W. (1970) *The GATT: Law and International Economic Organization*, Chicago: University of Chicago Press.

D'Amato, A. (2005) 'International Law as an Autopoietic System', in Wolfrum, R. and Röben, V. (eds) *Developments of International Law in Treaty Making*, Berlin: Springer.

Dekle, R. (2005) 'The Chinese Economy: Perspectives from the Japanese Manga', *Harvard Asia Pacific Review*, 8(2): 47–50.

de Larosière J. *et al.* (2009) *The High-Level Group on Financial Supervision in the EU: Report*, Brussels: European Commission.

Dell, S. (1981) *On Being Grandmotherly: The Evolution of IMF Conditionality*, Essays in International Finance, No. 144, Princeton, NJ: International Finance Section, Department of Economics, Princeton University.

De Meester, B. (2010) 'The Global Financial Crisis and Government Support for Banks: What Role for the GATS', *Journal of International Economic Law*, 13(1): 27–63.

de Mestral, A. (2010) 'The Lisbon Treaty and the Expansion of EU Competence over Foreign Direct Investment and the Implication for Investor-State Arbitration', in Sauvant, K. P. (ed.) *Yearbook on International Investment Law and Policy 2009–2010*, New York: Oxford University Press.

Deng, X. (1974) 'Speech Delivered at the Sixth Special Session of the UN General Assembly', *People's Daily*, 11 April.

Dent, C. M. (2006) *New Free Trade Agreements in the Asia-Pacific*, Basingstoke and New York: Palgrave MacMillan.

—— (2007) 'Full Circle? Ideas and Ordeals of Creating a Free Trade Area of the Asia-Pacific', *Pacific Review*, 20: 447–74.

Desai, M. (2003) 'Public Goods: A Historical Perspective', in Paul, I., Concaicao, P., le Goulven, K. and Mendoza, R. (eds) *Providing Global Public Goods: Managing Globalization*, New York: Oxford University Press.

De Villepin, D. (2003) 'Fiche Amendement: Proposition d'amendement à l'Article III-211'. Online. Available HTTP: <http://european-convention.eu.int/Docs/Treaty/pdf/866/Art%20III%20211%20de%20Villepin%20FR.pdf> (accessed 22 August 2010).

Dolzer, R. and Schreuer, C. (2008) *Principles of International Investment Law*, Oxford: Oxford University Press.

Dosi, G., Imoli, M. and Stiglitz, J. E. (2009) 'Preface', in Dosi, G., Imoli, M. and Stiglitz, J. E., *Industrial Policy and Development: The Political Economy of Capabilities Accumulation*, Oxford: Oxford University Press.

Drabek, Z. and Payne, W. (2001), *The Impact of Transparency on Foreign Direct Investment*, World Trade Organization Economic Research and Analysis Division Staff Working Paper ERAD-99-02. Online. Available HTTP <http://www.wto.org/english/res_e/reser_e/erad-99-02.doc> (accessed 22 August 2010).

Easterly, W. (2002) 'How Did Heavily Indebted Poor Countries Become Heavily Indebted? Reviewing Two Decades of Debt Relief', *World Development*, 30(10): 1677–96.

Economist Intelligence Unit (1993) *World Outlook 1993*, London: Economist Intelligence Unit.

—— (1995) *World Outlook 1995*, London: Economist Intelligence Unit.

Eeckhout, P. (2004) *External Relations of the European Union*, Oxford: Oxford University Press.

Eichengreen, B. and Bayoumi, T. (1999) 'On Regional Monetary Arrangements for ASEAN', paper presented at an international conference on exchange rate regimes in emerging market economies, 17–18 December, Tokyo, Japan.

Eminent Persons Group (2007) *Towards a New Asian Development Bank in a New Asia: Report of the Eminent Persons Group to the President of the Asian Development Bank*, Manila: Asian Development Bank.

European Commission (2008) Communication on the Application of State Aid Rules to Measures Taken in Relation to Financial Institutions in the Context of the Current Global Financial Crisis ('Banking Communication'), OJ C 270, 25.10.2008, 8.

—— (2009a) Communication on the Recapitalization of Financial Institutions in the Current Financial Crisis: Limitation of Aid to the Minimum Necessary and Safeguards against Undue Distortions of Competition, OJ C 10, 15.1.2009, 3.

—— (2009b) Communication on the Treatment of Impaired Assets in the Community Banking Sector, OJ C 72, 26.3.2009, 1.

—— (2009c) Special Edition on State Aid Interventions in the Current Financial and Economic Crisis, Report, COM(2009) 164 Final.

—— (2009d) Commission Communication on the Return to Viability and the Assessment of Restructuring Measures in the Financial Sector in the Current Crisis under the State Aid Rules, OJ C 195, 19.8.2009, 9.

—— (2010a) Bank Resolution Funds, COM(2010) 254 Final, 26.5.2010. Online. Available HTTP: <http://ec.europa.eu/internal_market/bank/docs/crisis-management/funds/com2010_254_en.pdf> (accessed 27 July 2010).

—— (2010b) State Aid Scoreboard, Report on State aid granted by the EU Member States, Autumn 2010 update, 1 December 2010, COM(2010)701 final.

EWI (1998) Konvergenzbericht (nach Artikel 10pj EGV a.F. = Article 121 of EGV des Vertags zur Grüdung der europäischen Gemeinschaft vorgeschriebener Bericht).

Falsafi, A. (2008) 'Regional Trade and Investment Agreements: Liberalizing Investments in a Preferential Climate', *Syracuse Journal of International Law and Commerce*, 36: 43–85.

Feuerwerker, A. (1976) *The Foreign Establishment in China in the Early Twentieth Century*, Michigan: University of Michigan Center for Chinese Studies.

Financial Services Authority (UK) (2009) *The Turner Review: A Regulatory Response to the Global Banking Crisis*, London: Financial Services Authority.

Financial Stability Board (FSB) (2009) *Progress since the Pittsburgh Summit in Implementing the G-20 Recommendations for Strengthening Financial Stability.* Online. Available HTTP: <http://www.fsa.go.jp/inter/fsf/20091112/01/pdf> (accessed 7 December 2010).

—— (2010) *Framework for Strengthening Adherence to International Standard.* Online. Available HTTP: <http://www.financialstabilityboard.org/publications/r_100109a.pdf> (accessed 7 December 2010).

Financial Stability Forum (FSF) (2009a) 'Financial Stability Forum Decides to Broaden its Membership', FSF Press Release, March. Online. Available HTTP: <http://www.financialstabilityboard.org/press/pr_090312b.pdf> (accessed 28 November 2010).

—— (2009b) *FSF Principles for Sound Compensation Practices*, April. Online. Available HTTP: <http://www.financialstabilityboard.org/publications/r_0904b.pdf?frames=0> (accessed 28 November 2010).

Financial Times (2005), 'Argentina Sets a Dangerous Precedent: The IMF Should Set Tough Conditions for Further Lending', March 7, p. 20.

Fischer, J. (2003) 'Amendment Form: Suggestion for Amendment of Article: 23'. Online. Available HTTP: <http://european-convention.eu.int/Docs/Treaty/pdf/866/Art24Fischer.pdf> (accessed 22 August 2010).

Fischer-Lescano, A. and Teubner, G. (2004) 'Regime-Collisions: The Vain Search for Legal Unity in the Fragmentation of Global Law', *Michigan Journal of International Law*, 25(4): 999–1046.

Fortier L. Y. and Drymer, S. L. (2004) 'Indirect Expropriation in the Law of International Investment: I Know It When I See It, or Caveat Investor', *ICSID Review*, 19: 293–327.

France, A. (1894) *Le Lys Rouge* (trans. W. Stephens as *The Red Lily*, London: John Lane at the Bodley Head, 1908).

Franck, S. (2009) 'Development and Outcomes of Investment Treaty Arbitration', *Harvard International Law Journal*, 50(2): 435–89.

Fukasaku, K., Kawai, M., Plummer, M. G. and Trzeciak-Duval, A. (2004) *Policy Coherence Towards East Asia*, Policy Brief No. 26, OECD Development Centre. Online. Available HTTP: <http://www.oecd.org/dataoecd/15/41/34982822.pdf> (accessed 7 December 2010).

Fukushima, K. (2004) 'Challenges for Currency Cooperation in East Asia', *Asia-Pacific Review*, 11(1): 20–45.

G20 (2008a) Washington Declaration: Summit on Financial Markets and the World Economy, 15 November 2009. Online. Available HTTP: <http://www.pittsburghsummit.gov/resources/125136.htm> (accessed 28 November 2010).

—— (2008b) Washington Action Plan to Implement Principles for Reform, November 2008. Online. Available HTTP: <http://www.pittsuburghsummit.gov/resources/125137.htm> (accessed 28 November 2010).

—— (2009a) Global plan for Recovery and Reform: The Communiqué from the London Summit, 2 April. Online. Available HTTP: <http://www.londonsummit.gov.uk/en/summit-aims/summit-communique> (accessed 28 November 2010).

—— (2009b) Declaration on Delivering Resources through the International Financial Institutions, April. Online. Available HTTP: <http://www.londonsummit.gov.uk/resources/en/PDF/annex-ifi> (accessed 28 November 2010).

—— (2009c) Leaders' Statement: The Pittsburgh Summit, 24–25 September. Online. Available HTTP: <http://www.pittsburghsummit.gov/mediacenter/129639.htm> (accessed 7 December 2010).

—— (2010) The G20 Toronto Summit Declaration, 27 June. Online. Available HTTP: <http://www.g20.utoronto.ca/2010/g20_declaration_en.pdf> (accessed 28 November 2010).

Galbraith, J. K. and Liu, J. (2000) *Sustainable Development and the Open Door Policy in China*, UTIP Working Paper No. 16, Austin, TX: University of Texas Inequality Project. Online. Available HTTP: <http://utip.gov.utexas/edu/papers/utip_16.pdf> (accessed 29 November 2010).

Gallagher, N. and Shan, W. (2009) *Chinese Investment Treaties: Policies and Practices*, New York: Oxford University Press.

Garnaut, J. (2008) 'China Pours Billions into Social Policy', *Sydney Morning Herald*, 6 March, p. 9.

George, S. (1990) *A Fate Worse Than Debt*, New York: Grove Weidenfeld.

Ghosh, J. (2005) 'China and India: The Big Differences'. Online. Available HTTP: <http://www.networkideas.org/news/aug2005/news25_China_India.htm> (accessed 29 November 2010).

Green, D. (1995) *Silent Revolution – The Rise of Market Economics in Latin America*, London: Cassell.

Grimes, W. W. (2006) 'East Asian Financial Regionalism and U.S. National Interests', E-Notes. Online. Available HTTP: <http://www.fpri.org/enotes/200604.asia.grimes.eastasianfinancialregionalism.html> (accessed 7 December 2010).

Group of 30 (2009) *Financial Reform: A Framework for Financial Stability*, Washington, D.C.: Group of 30.

Gu, M. (1984) 'Investment Environment Seen as Favourable', *Beijing Review*, 16 July.

Gugler P. and Chaisse J. (2008) 'Foreign Investment Issues and WTO Law: Dealing with Fragmentation While Waiting for a Multilateral Framework', in Chaisse, J. and Balmelli, T. (eds) *Essays on the Future of the World Trade Organization*, vol. 1, *Policies and Legal Issues*, Geneva: Edis.

Gugler, P. and Tomsik, V. (2006) *A Comparison of the Provisions Affecting Investment in the Existing WTO Obligations*, NCCR Trade Regulation Working Paper 2006/15, Berne: Swiss National Centre of Competence in Research.

Hain, P. (2003) 'Amendment Form: Suggestion for Amendment of Article: Part II, Title B, Article 23'. Online. Available HTTP: <http://european-convention.eu.int/Docs/Treaty/pdf/866/Art23Hain.pdf> (accessed 22 August 2010).

Hajnal, P. I. (1999) *The G7/G8 System: Evolution, Role and Documentation*, Farnham: Ashgate.

Herring, R. J. and Chatusripitak, N. (2000) *The Case of the Missing Market: The Bond Market and Why It Matters for Financial Development*, ADB Institute Working Paper, Manila: Asian Development Bank. Online. Available HTTP: <http://fic.wharton.upenn.edu/fic/papers/01/0108.pdf> (accessed 7 December 2010).

Hakenes, H. and Schnabel, I. (2004) *Banks without Parachutes – Competitive Effects of Government Bail-Out Policies*, MPI Collective Goods Research Paper No. 2004/12, Bonn: Max Planck Institute for Research on Collective Goods.

Hornbeck, J. F. (2004) 'Argentina's Sovereign Debt Restructuring', CRS Report for Congress, RL 32637, 19 October, Washington, D.C.: Congressional Research Service, The Library of Congress. Online. Available HTTP: <http://fpc.state.gov/documents/organization/39301.pdf> (accessed 29 November 2010).

Houde, M. F. and Yannaca-Small, K. (2004) *Relationships between International Investment Agreements*, Working Paper on International Investment No. 2004/1, Paris: OECD.

Huang, Z. (2008) 'Doha Round and China's Multilateral Diplomacy', *International Review*, 18: 18–29.

Hufbauer, G. and Schott, J. (2007) 'Multilateralizing Regionalism: Fitting Asia-Pacific Agreements into the WTO System', paper presented at conference on multilateralizing regionalism, Geneva, 10–12 September.

Hüpkes, E. (2009) 'Special Bank Resolution and Shareholders' Rights: Balancing Competing Interests', *Journal of Financial Regulation and Compliance*, 17(3): 277–301.

IMF (1993) *Balance of Payments Manual*, 5th edn, Washington, D.C.: IMF.

—— (2003) Proposals for a Sovereign Debt Restructuring Mechanism. Online. Available HTTP: <http://www.imf.org/external/np/exr/facts/sdrm.htm> (accessed 28 November 2010).

—— (2009) *World Economic Outlook 2009*, Washington, D.C.: IMF.

International Law Commission, Study Group (2006) *Report on Fragmentation of International Law: Difficulties Arising from the Diversification and Expansion of International Law*, 13 April, A/CN.4/L.682, Geneva: United Nations.

Janoski, T., Alford, R., Hicks, A. and Schwartz, M. (eds) (2005) *The Handbook of Political Sociology: States, Civil Societies and Globalization*, Cambridge: Cambridge University Press.

Jenks, C. W. (1953) 'The Conflict of Law-Making Treaties', *British Year Book of International Law*, 30: 401–53.

Jin, C.-S. (2005) 'Japan's Foreign Economic Policy: Return to Asia?', *New Asia*, 12(3): 49–71.

Jo, Y. (2005) *Significance and Prospect of East Asian Financial Cooperation*, Policy Studies Series, 2004-1, Seoul: Institute of Foreign Affairs and National Security.

Kaplan, E. and Rodrik, D. (2003) *Did the Malaysian Capital Controls Work?*, National Bureau of Economic Research Working Paper No. 8142, Cambridge, MA: National Bureau of Economic Research. Online. Available HTTP: <http://papers.nber.org/papers/W8142> (accessed 29 November 2010).

Karl, J. (2004) 'The Competence for Foreign Direct Investment – New Powers for the European Union', *Journal of World Investment & Trade*, 5: 413–48.

Kester, Anne Y. (2001) *International Reserves and Foreign Currency Liquidity: Guidelines for a Data Template*, Washington, D.C.: IMF.

Kiguel, M. (2002) 'Structural Reforms in Argentina: Success or Failure?', *Comparative Economic Studies*, 44(2): 83–102.

Kim, W.-H. (2002) 'Reappraisal on the Governance of IMF', *Global Economic Review*, 5(3): 90–4.

Kim, W.-S. (1991) 'The Effect of IMF Programs in Economic Stabilization', *Journal of the Korean Political Science Association*, 25(1): 495–519.

Kim, Y.-M. (2007) 'The Construction of East Asia Community and Comprehensive Agreement by Japan. Comprehensive Economic Partnership in East Asia (CEPEA) Strategy', *Asian Studies*, 10(2): 1654–88.

Kim, Y.-S. (2002) 'Rationale for an Asian Monetary Fund', *Journal of the Korean Economy*, 3(2): 345–67.

Kirton, J. (2010) 'The G-20 Finance Ministers: Network Governance', in Alexandroff, A. S. and Cooper, A. F. (eds) *Rising States, Rising Institutions*, Baltimore: Brookings Institution Press.

Koenig, C. (2008) '"Instant State Aid Law in a Financial Crisis, State of Emergency or Turmoil', *European State Aid Law Quarterly*, 4: 627–29.

Kohlscheen, E. and Taylor, M. P. (2008) 'International Liquidity Swaps: Is the Chiang Mai Initiative Pooling Reserves Efficiently?', *International Journal of Finance & Economics*, 13: 323–32.

Krajewski, M. (2005) 'External Trade Law and the Constitution Treaty: Towards a Federal and More Democratic Common Commercial Policy?', *Common Market Law Review*, 42: 91–128.

Krasner, S. (1982) 'Structural Causes and Regime Consequences: Regimes as Intervening Variables', *International Organization*, 36: 185–205.

Krueger, A. O. (2002) 'A New Approach to Sovereign Debt Restructuring', International Monetary Fund, April. Online. Available HTTP: <http://www.imf.org/external/np/speeches/2001/122001.htm> (accessed 17 February 2011).

—— (2005) 'China and the Global Economic Recovery', keynote address to the American Enterprise Institute seminar, Washington, D.C., 10 January. Online. Available HTTP: <http://www.imf.org/external/np/speeches/2005/011005.htm> (accessed 29 November 2010).

Kwak, K. and Marceau, G. (2006) 'Overlaps and Conflicts of Jurisdiction between the WTO and RTAs', in Bartels, L. and Ortino, F. (eds) *Regional Trade Agreements and the WTO Legal System*, Oxford: Oxford University Press.

Lang, A. (2006) 'Reconstructing Embedded Liberalism: John Gerard Ruggie and Constructivist Approaches to the Study of the International Trade Regime', *Journal of International Economic Law*, 9: 81–116.

Lastra, R. M. (2002) 'IMF Conditionality', in Norton, Joseph J. and Andenas, Mads (eds) *International Monetary and Financial Law upon Entering the New Millennium: A Tribute to Sir Joseph and Ruth Gold*, London: British Institute of International and Comparative Law.

—— (2006) *Legal Foundations of International Monetary Stability*, Oxford: Oxford University Press.

Lawrence, R. Z. (2007) 'Regionalism and the WTO: Should the Rules be Changed?', in Freund, C. (ed.) *The WTO and Reciprocal Preferential Trading Arrangements*, Cheltenham: Edward Elgar.

Lee, C. H. (2004) 'To Thine Own Self Be True: IMF Conditionality and Erosion of Economic Sovereignty in the Asian Financial Crisis', *University of Pennsylvania Journal of International Economic Law*, 24(4): 875–904.

Lee, D. (2008), 'Improvement Plan for the Problems in the Lending System of the IMF', *Weekly Financial Brief* [Korea Institute of Finance], 18(3): 10–11.

Lee, J.-W., Park, Y.-C. and Shin, K.-H. (2002) 'A Currency Union in East Asia (Background Paper for Asian Development Bank)', in *Study on Monetary and Financial Cooperation in East Asia*, Manila: Asian Development Bank. Online. Available HTTP: <http://www.apfc.nccu.edu.tw/asiandollarfolder/A%20Currency%20Union%20in%20East%20Asia.pdf> (accessed 7 December 2010).

Leebron, D. W. (2002) 'Linkages', *American Journal of International Law*, 96: 5–27.

Lejot, P. (2011) 'Institutional Completeness in the Chiang Mai Initiatives', in Buckley, R. P., Hu, R. W. and Arner, D. (eds) *East Asian Economic Integration: Law, Trade and Finance*, Cheltenham: Edward Elgar.

Levesque, C. (2004) 'Distinguishing Expropriation and Regulation under NAFTA Chapter 11: Making Explicit the Link to Property', in Kennedy, K. (ed.) *The First Decade of NAFTA: The Future of Free Trade in North America*, New York: Transnational Publishers.

Lewis, M. K. (2005) 'The Free Trade Agreement Paradox', *New Zealand Universities Law Review*, 21: 554–74.

—— (2008) 'The Prisoners' Dilemma and Free Trade Agreements: An Application of Game Theory to Trade Liberalization Strategy', in Buckley, R. P., Lo, V. I. and Boulle, L. (eds) *Challenges to Multilateral Trade: The Impact of Bilateral, Preferential and Regional Agreements*, Leiden: Kluwer.

Li, H. (2005) 'The Chinese Path of Economic Reform and its Implications', *Asian Affairs: An American Review*, 31(4): 195–211.

Li, J. (2007) 'Fundamental Enterprise Income Tax Reform in China: Motivations and Major Changes', *Bulletin for International Fiscal Documentation*, 61: 519–28.

Liew, L. H. and Wu, H. Y. (2007) *The Making of China's Exchange Rate Policy: From Plan to WTO Entry*, Cheltenham: Edward Elgar.

Lim, C. L. and Wang, J. (2009) 'China and the Doha Development Agenda', working paper prepared for presentation at the World Trade Organization Forum, Geneva, 28 September. Online. Available HTTP: <http://www.nsi-ins.ca/english/pdf/China%20at%20Doha.pdf> (accessed 2 May 2010).

Limão, N. (2006) 'Preferential Trade Agreements as Stumbling Blocks for Multilateral Trade Liberalization: Evidence for the United States', *American Economic Review*, 96(3): 896–914.

Lipsey, P. (2003) 'Japan's Asian Monetary Fund Proposal', *Stanford Journal of East Asian Affairs*, 3: 93–104.

Liu, Q., Arner, D. and Lejot, P. (forthcoming) *Finance in Asia: Institutions, Markets and Regulation*, Abingdon: Routledge.

Lowenfeld, A. (2008) *International Economic Law*, 2nd edn, New York: Oxford University Press.

Luo, Y., Xue, Q. and Han, B. (2010) 'How Emerging Market Governments Promote Outward FDI: Experience from China', *Journal of World Business*, 45: 68–79.

Lustig, N. (1998) *Mexico: The Remaking of an Economy*, Washington, D.C.: Brookings Institution Press.

—— (2000) *Social Protection for Equity and Growth*, Washington, D.C.: Inter-American Development Bank.

McLachlan, C., Shore, L. and Weiniger, M. (2007) *International Investment Arbitration: Substantive Principles*, Oxford: Oxford University Press.

McLean, J. (2009) 'Will ASEAN's New Charter Bring Greater Cooperation?', *Development Asia*, 3, April 2009. Online. Available HTTP: <http://development.asia/issue03/cover-03.asp>.

Madhur, S. (2002) *Costs and Benefits of a Common Currency for ASEAN*, ERD Working Paper Series No. 12, Manila: Asian Development Bank.

Mann, H., Moltke, K., Peterson, L. E. and Cosbey, A. (2005) *IISD Model International Agreement on Investment for Sustainable Development: Negotiator's Handbook*, 2nd edn, Winnipeg: International Institute for Sustainable Development.

Manzini, P. (2001) 'The Priority of Pre-Existing Treaties of EC Member States within the Framework of International Law', *European Journal of International Law*, 12: 781–92.

Marsden, P. and Kokkoris, I. (2010) The Role of Competition and State Aid Policy in Financial and Monetary Law, *Journal of International Economic Law*, 13(3): 875–92

Mavroidis, P. (2006) 'If I Don't Do It, Somebody Else Will (Or Won't): Testing the Compliance of Preferential Trade Agreements with the Multilateral Rules', *Journal of World Trade*, 40: 187–214.

Mencken, H. L. (1917), 'The Divine Afflatus', *New York Evening Mail*, 16 November.

Mercurio, B. and Leung, C. S. N. (2009) 'Is China a "Currency Manipulator"? The Legitimacy of China's Exchange Regime under the Current International Legal Framework', *International Lawyer*, 14: 1257–300.

Meyer, L. H. (1999) *Lessons from the Asian Crisis: A Central Banker's Perspective*, Levy Economics Institute Working Paper No. 276. Annandale-on-Hudson, NY: Bard College

Mingers, J. (1995) *Self-Producing Systems: Implications and Applications of Autopoiesis*, New York: Plenum Press.

Ministry of Commerce of China (MOFCOM) (2009) *2009 Statistical Bulletin of China's Outward Foreign Direct Investment*. Online. Available HTTP: <http://fec.mofcom.gov.cn/article/tjzl/jwtz/201009/960978_1.html> (accessed 6 February 2011).

—— (2010a) 'China FTA Network'. Online. Available HTTP: <http://fta.mofcom.gov.cn/english/index.shtml> (accessed 10 September 2010).

—— (2010b) 'BITs Have Been Concluded with 130 Countries', *Xinhua*, 1 November. Online. Available HTTP: <http://news.xinhuanet.com/fortune/2010-11/01/c_12724364.htm> (accessed 1 November 2010).

Mosley, P., Harrigan, J. and Toye J. (eds) (1991) *Aid and Power: The World Bank and Policy-Based Lending*, London: Routledge.

Muchlinski, P. (2000) 'The Rise and Fall of the Multilateral Agreement on Investment: Where Now?', *International Lawyer*, 34: 1033–53.

—— (2008) 'Policy Issues', in Muchlinski, P., Ortino, F. and Schreuer, C. (eds) *The Oxford Handbook of International Investment Law*, Oxford: Oxford University Press.

—— (2009) 'Trends in International Investment Agreements: Balancing Investor Rights and the Right to Regulate. The Issue of National Security', in Sauvant, K. P. (ed.) *Yearbook on International Investment Law and Policy 2008–2009*, New York: Oxford University Press.

Mundell, R. A. (1961) 'Optimum Currency Areas', *American Economic Review*, 51(4): 657–65.

Musgrave, R. and Musgrave, P. (2003) 'Prologue', in Paul, I., Concaicao, P., le Goulven, K. and Mendoza, R. (eds) *Providing Global Public Goods: Managing Globalization*, New York: Oxford University Press.

Nakagawa, J. (2007) 'No More Negotiated Deals? Settlement of Trade and Investment Disputes in East Asia', *Journal of International Economic Law*, 10: 837–67.

—— (2009) 'Competitive Regionalism through Bilateral and Regional Rule-Making: Standard Setting and Locking-in', in Solís, M., Stallings, B. and Katada, S. (eds) *Competitive Regionalism: FTA Diffusion in the Pacific Rim*, Basingstoke: Palgrave Macmillan.

—— (forthcoming a) 'Reconstructing Global Monetary/Financial Governance: Beyond the Bretton Woods System', *Japanese Yearbook of International Law*, 53.

—— (forthcoming b), *International Harmonization of Economic Regulation*, Oxford: Oxford University Press.

Nakagawa, J., Suzuki, Y., Ogawa, T., Yamashita, K., Sakuma, S., Kawai, K. and Araki, I. (2005) 'Zadankai: Henkakuki no kokusaitsūshōhō to Nihon' (Roundtable: international trade law in times of transition and Japan), *Hōritsu Jihō* (Law Journal), 77(6): 4–26 (in Japanese).

The Nation (2002) ‘Chaos in Argentina’, 21 January, p. 3.

Newcombe, A. (2005) ‘The Boundaries of Regulatory Expropriation in International Law’, *ICSID Review*, 20: 1–57.

Newcombe, A. and Paradell L. (2009) *Law and Practice of Investment Treaties: Standards of Treatment*, Austin, TX: Wolters Kluwer.

Obstfeld, M. and Rogoff, K. (1995) ‘Exchange Rate Dynamics Redux’, *Journal of Political Economy*, 103: 626–60.

Obstfeld, M., Shambaugh, J. C. and Taylor, A. M. (2005) ‘The Trilemma in History: Tradeoffs among Exchange Rates, Monetary Policies, and Capital Mobility’, *Review of Economic Statistics*, 87(3): 423–38.

OECD (1998) Multilateral Agreement on Investment Documentation from the Negotiations. Online. Available HTTP: <http://www.oecd.org/daf/mai/intro.htm> (accessed 22 July 2010).

—— (1999) *Benchmark Definition of Foreign Direct Investment*, 3rd edn, Paris: OECD.

—— (2008) *International Investment Law: Understanding Concepts and Tracking Innovations*, Paris: OECD.

—— (2009) Competition and the Financial Crisis, February. Online. Available HTTP: <http://www.oecd.org/dataoecd/52/24/42538399.pdf> (accessed 27 July 2010).

OECD Global Forum on Taxation (2009) *A Progress Report on the Jurisdictions Surveyed by the OECD Global Forum in Implementing the Internationally Agreed Tax Standard*, Paris: OECD.

OECD, WTO and UNCTAD (2010) Report on G20 Trade and Investment Measures. Online. Available HTTP: <http://www.wto.org/english/news_e/news10_e/summary_oecd_unctad_june10_e.pdf> (accessed 27 July 2010).

Oh, Y.-H. and Oh, S.-W. (2009) ‘The Significance and Suggestion from the Multi-Lateralization of the CMI’, *World Economy Update* [KIEP], 9(15): 1–5.

Palacio, A. (2003) ‘Fiche Amendement: Proposition d’amendement à l’Article: 23: Chapitre 2, Titre B, Partie II’. Online. Available HTTP <http://european-convention.eu.int/Docs/Treaty/pdf/866/Art23Palacio%20FR.pdf> (accessed 22 August 2010).

Palley, T. I. (1999) ‘Toward a New International Economic Order: Goodbye Washington Consensus, Hello Washington Alternative’. Online. Available HTTP: <http://www.thomaspalley.com/docs/articles/economic_development/new_intl_economic_order.pdf> (accessed 29 November 2010).

Park, Joeng-Pil (2006) ‘Management of ABF and Policy Issues on EMEAP’, *Foreign Exchange & International Finance*, 115–49.

Passell, P. (1998) ‘Critics: The I.M.F. Is Misguided. Skeptics: Too Much Rot in Asia’, *New York Times*, 15 January, D2, col. 1.

Paulsson, J. (1987) ‘Third World Participation in International Investment Arbitration’, *ICSID Review Foreign Investment Law Journal*, 2: 19–65.

Pauwelyn, J. (2006) ‘Adding Sweeteners to Softwood Lumber: The WTO-NAFTA “Spaghetti Bowl” Is Cooking’, *Journal of International Economic Law*, 9(1): 197–206.

—— (2007) ‘Legal Avenues to “Multilateralizing Regionalism”: Beyond Article XXIV’, paper presented at the conference on multilateralizing regionalism, September.

Perez, O. (2006) ‘Multiple Regimes, Issue Linkage and International Cooperation: Exploring the Role of the WTO’, *University of Pennsylvania Journal of International Economic Law*, 26(4): 735–78.

Petrovic, A. and Tutsch, R. (2009) *National Rescue Measures in Response to the Current Financial Crisis*, European Central Bank Legal Working Paper Series No. 8, Frankfurt: European Central Bank. Online. Available HTTP: <http://www.ecb.eu/pub/pdf/scplps/ecblwp8.pdf> (accessed 27 July 2010).

Picker, C. B. (2005) 'Regional Trade Agreements v. the WTO: A Proposal for Reform of Article XXIV to Counter this Institutional Threat', *University of Pennsylvania Journal of International Economic Law*, 26: 267–319.

Prasad, E. (2004) 'Growth and Stability in China: Prospects and Challenges', paper presented at *Harvard China Review* annual conference, Cambridge, MA, 17 April. Online. Available HTTP: <http://www.imf.org/external/np/speeches/2004/041704.htm> (accessed 29 November 2010).

Qin, J. Y. (2007) 'Trade, Investment and Beyond: The Impact of WTO Accession on China's Legal System', *China Quarterly*, 191: 720–41.

Qureshi, A. H. (2007), *International Economic Law*, 2nd edn, Oxford: Oxford University Press.

Rana, P. B. (2002) *Monetary and Financial Cooperation in East Asia: The Chiang Mai Initiative and Beyond*, ERD Working Paper Series No.6, Manila: Asian Development Bank.

Reinisch, A. (2007) '"Investment and ..." – the Broader Picture of Investment Law', in Reinisch, A. and Knahr, C. (eds) *International Investment Law in Context*, Vienna: Eleven.

Rich, S. (2010) 'Chinese Currency Float Lifts Aussie Dollar', *The Australian*, 22 June.

Roessler, F. (2000) 'Are the Judicial Organs Overburdened?', paper presented at conference in honor of Raymond Vernon, Kennedy School of Law, Harvard University, June 2000.

Sachs, L. E. and Sauvant, K. P. (2009) 'BITs, DTTs, and FDI Flows: An Overview', in Sauvant, K. P. and Sachs, L. E. (eds) *The Effect of Treaties on Foreign Direct Investment: Bilateral Investment Treaties, Double Taxation Treaties, and Investment Flows*, New York: Oxford University Press.

Sakakibara, E. (2003) 'Financial Cooperation in East Asia and Korea', Speech Paper of KITA distinguished lecture forum.

Samuelson, P. (1954) 'The Pure Theory of Public Expenditure', *Review of Economics and Statistics*, 36(4): 387–9.

Schaefer, M. (2007) 'Ensuring that Regional Trade Agreements Complement the WTO System: US Unilateralism a Supplement to WTO Initiatives?', *Journal of International Economic Law*, 10: 585–603.

Schill, S. W. (2007) 'Tearing Down the Great Wall: The New Generation Investment Treaties of the People's Republic of China', *Cardozo Journal of International and Comparative Law*, 15:73–118.

Schreuer, C. (2009) *The ICSID Convention – A Commentary*, 2nd edn, Cambridge: Cambridge University Press.

Schwarcz, S. (2008) 'Systemic Risk', *Georgetown Law Journal*, 97(1): 193–249.

Schwebel, S. (2006) 'The United States 2004 Model Bilateral Investment Treaty: An Exercise in the Regressive Development of International Law', *Transnational Dispute Management*, 3(2). Online. Available HTTP: <www.transnational-dispute-management.com> (accessed 29 November 2010).

Scott, H. S. (2003) 'A Bankruptcy Procedure for Sovereign Debtors?', *International Lawyer*, 37: 103–36.

Seager, A. (2010) 'China Becomes World's Third Largest Economy', *Guardian*, 14 January.

Seck, S. (2008) 'Home State Responsibility and Local Communities: The Case of Global Mining', *Yale Human Rights and Development Law Journal*, 11: 177–206.

Sen, A. (1999) *Development as Freedom*, New York: Anchor Books.

Shan, W. (2005) *The Legal Framework of EU–China Investment Relations: A Critical Appraisal*, Oxford: Hart Publishing.

Shang, M. (2005) 'Touzi Baohu Xieding Duihaiwaitouzide Falv Baozhang' (Roles of investment protection treaty in protecting overseas investment), *Touzi Beijing* (Invest Beijing), 8: 30–2 (in Chinese).

Simpson, M. T. (2007) 'Chopping Away at Chapter 11: The Softwood Lumber Agreement's Effect on the NAFTA Investor-State Dispute Resolution Mechanism', *American University International Law Review*, 22(3): 479–515.

Smith, A. (1776) *An Enquiry into the Nature and Causes of the Wealth of Nations*, London: W. Strahan and T. Cadell.

Sohn, B.-H. (2004) 'Ideal East Asian Regionalism in the Tri-Polar Trading System', *Journal of International Trade and Industry Studies*, 9(2): 21–38.

Sohn, I.-J. (2007) *East Asia's Counterweight Strategy: Asian Financial Cooperation and Evolving International Monetary Order*, G-24 Discussion Paper Series, No. 44, New York and Geneva: UNCTAD.

Solís, M. and Katada, S. (2009) 'Explaining FTA Proliferation: A Policy Diffusion Framework', in Solís, M., Stallings, B. and Katada, S. (eds) *Competitive Regionalism: FTA Diffusion in the Pacific Rim*, Basingstoke: Palgrave Macmillan.

Solís, M., Stallings, B. and Katada, S. (eds) (2009) *Competitive Regionalism: FTA Diffusion in the Pacific Rim*, Basingstoke: Palgrave Macmillan.

Stiglitz, J. (2002) *Die Schatten der Globalisierung*, Berlin: Siedler.

Sun, J. (2004) 'The Asian Bond Market: Background, Progress and East Asia', *Regional Development Studies*, 36(12): 1–26.

Taylor, C. O. (1998) 'Linkage and Rule-Making: Observations on Trade and Investment, and Trade and Labor', *University of Pennsylvania Journal of International Law*, 19: 639–96.

Teubner, G. (1993) *Law as an Autopoietic System*, Oxford: Blackwell.

—— (1997a) '*Altera pars Audiatur*: Law in the Collision of Discourses', in Rawlings, R. (ed.) *Law, Society and Economy*, Oxford: Oxford University Press.

—— (1997b) 'Global Bukowina: Legal Pluralism in the World Society', in Teubner, G. (ed.) *Global Law without a State*, Aldershot: Dartmouth Publishing.

—— (2006) 'Dealing with Paradoxes of Law: Derrida, Luhmann, Wiethölter', in Perez, O. and Teubner, G. (eds) *Paradoxes and Inconsistencies in the Law*, Oxford: Hart Publishing.

—— (2009) 'Hybrid Networks beyond Contract and Organisation', in Amstutz, M. and Teubner, G. (eds) *Networks: Legal Issues of Multilateral Co-operation*, Oxford: Hart Publishing.

Thompson, T. (1979) 'China's Nationalisation of Foreign Firms: The Politics of Hostage Capitalism 1947–1957', *Series in Contemporary Asian Studies*, 6: 1–80.

Tietje, C. (2009) *Die Außenwirtschaftsverfassung der EU nach dem Vertrag von Lissabon*, Beiträge zum Transnationalen Wirtschaftsrecht, 83, Halle: Institute of Economic Law, Martin Luther University Halle-Wittenberg.

Tudor, I. (2008) *The Fair and Equitable Treatment Standard in the International Law of Foreign Investment*, New York: Oxford University Press.

UNCTAD (2003) *World Investment Report 2003: FDI Policies for Development: National and International Perspectives*, New York and Geneva: United Nations.

—— (2006a) *Investment Provisions in Economic Integration Agreements*, New York: United Nations.

—— (2006b) *World Investment Report 2007: Transnational Corporations, Extractive Industries and Development*, New York and Geneva: United Nations.

—— (2007a) *World Investment Prospects Survey 2007–2009*, New York and Geneva: United Nations.

UNCTAD (2007b) *World Investment Report 2008*, New York and Geneva: United Nations.

—— (2008a) *Recent Developments in International Investment Agreements (2007–June 2008)*, IIA Monitor No. 2 (2008), New York and Geneva: United Nations.

—— (2008b) *Identifying Core Elements in Investment Agreements in the APEC Region*, New York and Geneva: United Nations.

—— (2008c) *International Investment Rule-Making: Stocktaking, Challenges and the Way Forward*, New York and Geneva: United Nations.

—— (2008d) *Investment Promotion Provisions in International Investment Agreements*, New York and Geneva: United Nations.

—— (2009a) *Latest Developments in Investor-State Dispute Settlement (2007–June 2008)*, IIA Monitor No. 1 (2009), New York and Geneva: United Nations.

—— (2009b) *Recent Developments in International Investment Agreements (2008–June 2009)*, IIA Monitor No. 3 (2009), New York and Geneva: United Nations.

—— (2010a) *World Investment Report 2010: Investing in a Low-Carbon Economy*, New York and Geneva: United Nations.

—— (2010b) *Latest Developments in Investor-State Dispute Settlement*, New York and Geneva: United Nations. Online. Available HTTP: <http://www.unctad.org/en/docs/webdiaeia20103_en.pdf> (accessed 20 August 2010).

Vacek-Aranda, A. (2006) 'Sugar Wars: Dispute Settlement under NAFTA and the WTO as Seen through the Lens of the HFCS Case, and Its Effects on U.S.–Mexican Relations', *Texas Hispanic Journal of Law and Policy*, 12: 121–60.

Van Aaken, A. and Kurtz, J. (2009) *The Global Financial Crisis: Will State Emergency Measures Trigger International Investment Disputes?*, Columbia FDI Perspectives No. 3, 23 March, New York: Vale Columbia Center on Sustainable International Investment, Columbia University. Online. Available HTTP: <http://www.vcc.columbia.edu/documents/Perspective3-vanAakenandKurtz-FINAL.pdf> (accessed 13 December 2010).

—— (2010) 'Prudence or Discrimination? Emergency Measures, the Global Financial Crisis and International Economic Law', *Journal of International Economic Law*, 12(4): 859–94.

Vandevalde, K. (1998a) 'The Political Economy of a Bilateral Investment Treaty', *American Journal of International Law*, 92: 621–41.

—— (1998b) 'Investment Liberalization and Economic Development: The Role of Bilateral Investment Treaties', *Columbia Journal of Transnational Law*, 36: 501–22.

—— (2009) 'A Comparison of the 2004 and 1994 U.S. Model BITs: Rebalancing Investor and Host Country Interests', in Sauvant, K. P. (ed.) *Yearbook on International Investment Law and Policy 2008–2009*, New York: Oxford University Press.

VanDuzer, J. A. (2007) 'Enhancing the Procedural Legitimacy of Investor-State Arbitration through Transparency and Amicus Curiae Participation', *McGill Law Journal*, 52: 681–723.

VanDuzer, J. A., Simons, P. and Mayeda, G. (2008) 'Modeling International Investment Agreements for Economic Development', in Qalo, V. (ed.) *Bilateralism and Development: Emerging Trade Patterns*, London: Cameron May.

Van Harten, G. (2007) *Investment Treaty Arbitration and Public Law*, New York: Oxford University Press.

Van Harten, G. and Loughlin, M. (2006) 'Investment Treaty Arbitration as a Species of Global Administrative Law', *European Journal of International Law*, 17: 121–50.

Vis-Dunbar, D. (2009a) 'United States Reviews Its Model Bilateral Investment Treaty', *Investment Treaty News*, 5 June. Online. Available HTTP: <http://www.investmenttreatynews.org/cms/news/archive/2009/06/05/united-states-reviews-its-model-bilateral-investment-treaty.aspx> (accessed 22 July 2010).

—— (2009b) 'Norway Shelves Its Draft Model Bilateral Investment Treaty', *Investment Treaty News*, 8 June. Online. Available HTTP: <www.investmenttreatynews.org> (accessed 29 November 2010).

Wang, D. (2005) *China's Unequal Treaties: Narrating National History*, Lanham: Lexington Books.

Wang, G. (1988) *China's Investment Laws: New Directions*, Singapore: Butterworths.

—— (2009) 'China's Practice in International Investment Law: From Participation to Leadership in the World Economy', *Yale Journal of International Law*, 34: 575–87.

Weber, R. H. (2009) 'State Interventions and Competition Distortion in Financial Markets', *Schweizerische Zeitschrift für Wirtschafts- und Finanzmarktrecht*, 6: 428–38.

Weber, R. H. and Arner, D. (2007) 'Toward a New Design for International Financial Regulation', *University of Pennsylvania Journal of International Law*, 29: 391–453.

Weber, R. H. and Grosz, M., (2009) 'Governments' Interventions into the Real Economy under WTO Law Revisited: New Tendencies of Governmental Support of the Automobile Industry', *Journal of World Trade*, 43(5): 969–1013.

Weber, R. H. and Gruenewald, S. (2009) 'Finanzkrise und Wirtschaftspolitik: Herausforderungen für das Europäische Wettbewerbsrecht', *Zeitschrift für Europarecht*, 11(3): 58–67.

Weber, R. H. and Gruenewald, S. (2010) 'Overcoming Special Resolution Regimes for Financial Institutions', *Butterworths Journal of International Banking and Financial Law*, 25(4): 233–36.

Wielpütz, D. (2010) 'Wenn der Staat bürgt – Finanzmarktkrise und Europäisches Beihilfenrecht', *Europäisches Wirtschafts- und Steuerrecht*, 21(1–2): 14–19.

World Bank (2009), *Education at a Glance: China.* (Last updated July 2009.) Online. Available HTTP: <http://siteresources.worldgbank.org/EXTEDSTATS/Resources/3232763-1171296190619/3445877-1172014191219/CHN/pdf> (accessed 29 November 2010).

—— (1996) Singapore Ministerial Declaration, WT/Min(96)/DEC/1, 13 December.

—— (2001) Doha Ministerial Declaration, WT/MIN(01)/DEC/1, 20 November.

WTO Consultative Board (2005) Report to the Director-General Supachai Panitchpakdi, 'The Future of the WTO: Addressing Institutional Challenges in the New Millennium', Geneva: WTO.

WTO Negotiating Group on Rules (2006) Report by the Chairman to the Trade Negotiations Committee, 13 July 2006, TN/RL/18.

Xiao, Y. (1984) 'Jinji Kaifang Zhencede Falv Tixian' (The legal embodiment of open economic policy), *People's Daily*, 10 October (in Chinese).

Xu, C. (2008) 'Gongpingyu Gongzheng Daiyu Biaozhun: Guoji Touzifa Zhongde "Diwangtiaokuan"?' (Fair and equitable treatment: an 'empire clause' in international investment law?), *Xiandai Faxue* (Modern Law Science), 5: 121–31 (in Chinese).

Xu, Y. and L, W. (1996) 'Jindai Zhongguode Waiguo Zaihuatouzi' (Foreign investment in modern China), *Caizheng Yanjiu* (Public Finance Research), 8: 51–8 (in Chinese).

Yamamoto, Y. (2008) *Kokusai rejīmu to gabanansu* (International regime and governance), Tokyo: Yūhikaku.

Yao, M. (1980) 'Guoji Touzide Fade Baohu' (Legal protection of international investment), *Faxue Pinglun* (Law Review), S1: 1–22 (in Chinese).

Yokoi-Arai, M. (2006) 'Legal and Political Effects of Financial and Monetary Regional Integration in Asia', *Law and Business Review of the Americas*, 12(1): 47–69.

Yun, D.-R. (2005) 'Chiang Mai Initiative: Present Status and Improvement', *KIEP World Economy*, 8(9): 54–63.

Zimmer, D. and Blaschczok, M. (2010) 'Die Banken-Beihilfenkontrolle der Europäischen Kommission: Wettbewerbsschutz oder Marktdesign?', *Wirtschaft und Wettbewerb*, 60(2): 142–57.

Index